The Computer
in Psychology

The Computer
in Psychology

Edited by

Michael J. Apter
George Westby
*Department of Psychology,
University College, Cardiff*

JOHN WILEY & SONS
LONDON   NEW YORK   SYDNEY   TORONTO

Library of Congress catalog card number 72-5711

ISBN 0 471 03260 3

Made and Printed in Great Britain by
The Garden City Press Limited
Letchworth, Hertfordshire
SG6 1JS

To the memory of
Professor W. Ross Ashby whose help was at all times
generously given

Foreword

Science, at about the time of World War II, underwent a great change by extending to forms of knowledge previously excluded.

Before that time science was not only analytic, concerned essentially with taking everything to pieces, but it insisted, in practice if not in theory, that no piece should be more complex than could be handled by the individual, the one-man scientist. The triumphs achieved by this method cannot be denied: the chemists found atoms, the physicists found the laws of inverse square and energy, and the biologists found the gene and the basic laws of its combination.

Yet all was not well. Some systems, notably the biological and especially those involving the brain, could be analysed into parts only at the cost of losing sight of the whole. The fact was that science before World War II, having identified the components, could not in general put the pieces together again. It knew, for instance, practically all the chemical constituents of *Amoeba*, but was quite unable to trace their interactions in all their complexity to give the *Amoeba*'s actual behaviour. The natural deducer of consequences, i.e. the mathematician, could handle only a few variables simultaneously, very few if the functions were realistic or a few more if the functions were linear (and an inferior representation of the actual facts).

All the sciences that wanted to deal with complex dynamic systems were similarly handicapped. The degree of complexity that could be handled by one man, equipped with pencil and paper, was inadequate for many important questions in ecological systems, social systems, economics, physiological systems, and especially in the various branches of psychology.

Then came the 1940s when these limitations were suddenly removed, not totally but to a degree of several orders of magnitude. The big computer arrived, together with information theory and the discoveries of how to handle the difficult questions of feedback and non-linear dynamics. Though it might be argued that the change was only quantitative, in that each new facility had been detectable previously, yet the change was so great in degree as to call for a thorough revision of the methods and rules of 'classic' science, some of which had degenerated to thoughtless dogmas. In the 1930s of course R. A. Fisher had demolished the earlier dogma that allowed variation of only one factor at a time, but there are doubtless yet others on their way to being recognized as obsolete.

We are today largely in the throes of finding out to what degrees, and in what ways, psychology must be re-formulated if it is to take advantage of the great opportunities offered by the powers of the computer. We need not regard these powers as being opposed to the earlier established branches of psychology: there is no reason why these powers should in any way lessen what was available before; if we use them wisely they can provide purely an extension of our capacity to understand and control our environment.

At first the computer tended to be used merely as a way of doing just what was done before, but more quickly. Such a use is, in my opinion, quite wrong. It was like using a great astronomical telescope in order to read one's newspaper a mile away. The proper use of an astronomical telescope is to make it yield knowledge that is quite unavailable to the naked eye. Similarly, the big computer will, I suggest, show its real powers only when it is doing new things, perhaps some of those very things that 'classic' science either could not or would not do.

The search for quite new types of knowledge demands workers who have grown up with the big computer and who think naturally in ways truly appropriate to it. For the training of such workers in psychology a good text is needed, one that is technically expert in the details of the computer yet written throughout from the point of view of the psychologist (rather than the various other users). For these reasons I welcome this book, and hope that many workers will develop the lines that it explains so clearly.

W. ROSS ASHBY

Preface

The authors of this book, all members of the department of psychology at University College Cardiff in the University of Wales, felt there was a special need for such a text. The growing use of computers for teaching and research in psychology has been one of the most striking features of this discipline during the last decade. At one time the psychologist who used a computer was regarded by his colleagues with something approaching awe; today the use of computers is rapidly becoming as commonplace among psychologists as the use of statistics has been since R. A. Fisher introduced us to small sample techniques. The sight of a program in FORTRAN is now no more daunting than a formula for 't'. The ability to design research which will take full advantage of the increased opportunities opened up by the use of a computer is in the process of becoming a standard part of the intellectual equipment of all psychologists, as indeed it is of other social scientists.

The specific purpose of the book is twofold: to introduce the undergraduate and graduate student to the special and varied use of computers in psychology; and to chart its development in some representative areas of the subject. The book is therefore divided into two parts which differ not so much in subject-matter as in emphasis and orientation.

The first part consists of a general introduction to computers and computer programming and their general relevance to psychology. In the course of this, the three major uses of computers in studying behaviour are introduced:

(i)   in data processing;
(ii) in experimentation;
(iii) in the modelling of behaviour.

Although the first of these represents at the present time the major use of computers by psychologists, this is not dealt with in as much detail as the other two because its use in this respect is straightforward and generally well known. Many other books already deal with data processing and statistical analysis by computer and do so in a way directly relevant to psychology. Reference to some books of this kind is made at the end of Chapter 2. In contrast, the use of the computer in experimentation, especially in the on-line control of experiments, and in theorizing through

ix

the technique of simulation, are much newer and these uses have been dealt with comparatively little elsewhere. Also, their use in psychology raises problems which may be specific to this particular subject. The emphasis of the first part of this book, then, is on techniques which may be used, singly or together, in various areas of psychology.

The second part of the book is topic-oriented. It surveys the use to which techniques of the kind described in Part I, especially in experimentation and simulation, have in fact been put in a number of important areas of both pure and applied psychology. Part II therefore constitutes an introduction to the ever-growing literature of psychological research in which computers have played a central part and deals especially with current developments—particularly those which are regarded as having significance for the future. The areas of application dealt with are not exhaustive but give a good indication of the breadth of computer developments in psychology.

The term 'computer' today usually means 'digital computer' and it is used in this sense throughout the book unless otherwise stated. Analog computers also have a part to play in psychology, although at present it would be true to say that they are used considerably less than digital computers. Whether this will always be the case remains to be seen; but the area of digital computing in psychology is itself already so vast that it was thought more sensible in this introductory text to concentrate mainly on this form of computing.

At the end of each chapter in the book further reading is suggested on the subject-matter concerned for those students who wish to inquire further.

It should be said at the outset that the increasing use of computers in psychology does present some dangers. One of these is that computer problems can come to dominate psychological problems, either because of the refractoriness of the computer or, alternatively, because it is such a powerful piece of equipment that it is seductively attractive. A second danger is heuristic: experiments and theories may become unnecessarily complex and research in psychology may therefore become even less elegant than it often is at present. It has been said that there might have been no Copernican revolution if Copernicus or his predecessors had had access to a computer and were familiar with modern statistics. It would be a tragedy if the advent of the computer militated against the attainment of new insights into organismic behaviour. This book would not have been written without the belief that, despite such dangers, the computer can provide psychology with unparalleled opportunities for progress.

MICHAEL J. APTER
GEORGE WESTBY

Biographical Notes

M. J. APTER, B.Sc. (Bristol), Ph.D. (Bristol), A.B.Ps.S., is author of four books, the most recent of which is about *The Computer Simulation of Behaviour* (Hutchinson, 1970). *The New Technology of Education* (Macmillan, 1968) dealt, among other topics, with computer-assisted instruction. His first book *Cybernetics and Development* (Pergamon Press, 1966) described the results of his research into biological development using computer and other cybernetic modelling techniques. Before lecturing in psychology at Cardiff he worked for Educational and Scientific Developments Ltd. in Bristol. His research interests centre on teaching machines and on cybernetics.

G. BARRETT, B.Sc. (Wales), graduated with a psychology degree in 1968. His interest in computers stems from a grounding in mathematics, especially information theory. While at University College Cardiff, he worked on an information processing model of human time estimation and on computer-assisted instruction. He was at Cardiff during the writing of this book. He is now at the National Hospital, London, running computer-controlled experiments on evoked potentials.

S. J. DIMOND, B.Sc. (Bristol). Ph.D. (Bristol), M.A. (Dublin), carried out his original research into the problems of skilled behaviour. His research interests include the study of early learning and brain functions and he is particularly interested in the theoretical problems of animal behaviour. He has written a number of papers on these topics and has published two books: *The Social Behaviour of Animals* (Batsford, 1970) and *The Double Brain* (Churchill, 1972) which is a study of hemisphere function in animal and human behaviour.

G. HARRISON, B.Sc. (Exeter), Ph.D. (Sheffield), did his doctoral reach in the field of short-term memory at Sheffield and worked postdoctorally, on the possibilities of small computers, in the experimental laboratories of the department of psychology at Hull. He has recently developed an interest in psycholinguistics and computer techniques in this special research area. He has 'bedded in' Elliott 903 Computers in two psychology departments for a variety of experimental projects.

J. O. ROBINSON, B.Sc. (Hull), B.Sc. (London), M.Sc. (Hull), Ph.D. (London), F.B.Ps.S., worked for the Medical Research Council Neuropsychiatric Research Unit and, later, for the Social Psychiatry Research Unit on symptoms in psychiatric and psychosomatic disorder. He has experience of computer analysis of complex survey data and use of multivariate techniques. He is currently interested in the possibilities presented by automation of clinical techniques and also in the experimental psychology of perception. Publications include *The Psychology of Visual Illusion* (Hutchinson, 1972).

J. A. WILSON, B.Sc. (London), Ph.D. (Bristol), M.I.Mech.E., was trained in engineering, and then took a degree in Psychology. He worked in the Borehamwood Laboratories of Elliot Bros. 1949–58, much of this time on microwave instruments and systems, using *Nicholas*, the Elliott prototype computer, for a number of jobs. Later, at the National Physical Laboratory 1958–63 he was a Senior Scientific Officer in the Autonomics Division, which was concerned with control systems, machine translation of language, pattern recognition, experimental psychology and neurophysiology. Here he used the English Electric Deuce and the NPL ACE computers for simulation of control systems and networks, and for the treatment of experimental data. He also has some experience with analog computers on man-machine interaction.

G. WESTBY, M.A. (Oxon.), F.B.Ps.S., Head of the Department of Psychology at University College Cardiff studied Philosophy, Politics and Economics at the University of Oxford, returning after World War II to study Psychology at the Institute of Experimental Psychology. He was invited to the first chair of psychology in the University of Wales in 1961. He is a Past President of the British Psychological Society and of the Psychology Section of the British Association for the Advancement of Science. He has recently been specially interested in developments in psychology which have raised problems, both philosophical and social, connected with freedom and control in human behaviour (*vide: Behaviour Theories and the Status of Psychology*, University of Wales Press, 1963).

Acknowledgements

We should like to thank Mrs. Pamela Tainsh, Miss Linda Cresswell and Mr. Russell Thomas for their helpful comments.

Our thanks are due to L. Uhr for permission to use, as Figure 6.12, an illustration based on Figure 3 in the article by L. Uhr and C. Vossler which appeared on p. 254 of *Computers and Thought* (Ed. E. A. Feigenbaum and J. Feldman) published by McGraw-Hill, New York, 1963. As used, the figure comes from Figure 16 of *The Computer Simulation of Behaviour* by M. J. Apter, published by Hutchinson University Library, London, 1970, to whom our thanks are also due for their permission.

We should also like to thank: Richard Stillman for permission to reproduce, as Figure 9.1, a figure which appeared in a paper in *The American Journal of Psychiatry*, **125**, pp. 8–11, (January supplement) 1969; Robert L. Spitzer for permission to reproduce as Figure 9.2 and Table 9.1, a figure and a table which also appeared in a paper in *The American Journal of Psychiatry*, **125**, pp. 12–21, (January supplement) 1969; The American Psychiatric Association for their permission as publishers of *The American Journal of Psychiatry* to reproduce both these figures and the table.

Our further thanks are due to: A. d'Agapayeff for permission to use in Chapter 3 a table originally published in *Science Journal*, **6**, 10, p. 94, 1970; R. N. Haber for permission to reproduce a short program in Chapter 3 which appeared in a paper in *Behavior Research Methods and Instrumentation*, **2**, 5, 1970, entitled 'On-line FORTRAN for the PDP-8' written with S. H. Barry and T. Uhlman; R. N. Shepard for permission to reproduce as Figure 6.3 a figure which appeared originally in a paper in *Science*, 171, 1971; P. Suppes for permission to base Figure 10.2 on a figure which appeared in *Computer Assisted Instruction: Stanford's 1965–1966 Arithmetic Program* by P. Suppes, M. Jerman and D. Brian, Academic Press, New York, 1968 (p. 25); J. R. Hartley for permission to reproduce as Figure 10.5 a flow-diagram which appeared in a paper in *The British Journal of Educational Psychology*, **41**, 1, p. 40, 1971, entitled 'Some learning models for arithmetic tasks and their use in computer based learning' written in conjunction with P. Woods; J. A. Swets for permission to reproduce in Chapter 10 an extract from a computer-assisted instruction dialogue which appeared in a paper in *Science*,

150, p. 574, 1965, entitled 'Computer-aided instruction' written in conjunction with W. Feurzeig.

The programs whose output is shown in Chapter 2 and Chapter 6 were run in the Computer Centre of University College Cardiff; it is a pleasure to acknowledge the unfailing helpfulness of the staff of that Centre.

Contents

Part 1
Introduction and Techniques

CHAPTER 1

An Introduction to Computers

John A. Wilson and Geoffrey Barrett

The development of calculating machines

If our bodies are mechanical, then calculation by machine has a venerable history; men have always used their fingers for counting. Nowadays we count on our fingers only when the numbers are small, but primitive peoples often used their fingers for all their counting and calculation. To do this they developed intricate systems of finger numerals, which by the variety of their symbolic positions were capable of representing large numbers (see: *Encyclopædia Britannica*, 'Finger Numerals').

Pebbles were also used—the Latin *calculi*. To represent large numbers the pebbles were used on grooved counting boards: a pebble in the first groove would represent *one*, in the second groove it would represent *ten* and so on, in a kind of positional notation. Then the pebbles were replaced by beads which were strung on wires and the result was a self-contained calculating instrument, the abacus.

But perhaps these are aids rather than machines. Pascal invented and made the first calculating machine in 1642, when he was a boy of eighteen. Each digit was pointed out on a dial by a rotating hand, like that of a clock; a four-digit number would require four dials, each with its hand. A number could be added into the machine by turning the hands; and here, perhaps, was the significant part of Pascal's invention, that a simple mechanism connected the hands to make the machine 'carry' automatically. The abacus holds the number, giving its operator an extra memory; but with the automatic carry, the machine is taking over from its operator some of the logic of the calculation.

Pascal was followed in 1671 by Leibniz, who invented a new kind of mechanism, the stepped pinion, in which 1, 2, 3, ..., teeth can be engaged. With this mechanism the number is first set on levers and then added in by turning a handle. This makes it possible to add or subtract the same number repeatedly, and this in turn allows multiplication and division, far more useful than mere addition and subtraction. Machines with this mechanism are still in common use.

3

Another kind of calculator even more commonly used is the slide-rule, which was invented in England just before Pascal's time. On a slide-rule numbers are represented by distances, as shown by graduation marks on the rule or the slide, whereas in the machine made by Leibniz numbers are represented by numbers of teeth in a gear. Distance can be measured; teeth can be counted. Therein lies the difference between the two kinds of computer which have been developed, analog computers and digital computers. An *analog* computer, like the slide-rule, works with continuous quantities which can be measured; it represents numbers in terms of distance, voltage, velocity, current flow and so on. To make the machine calculate, its parts are connected so that they represent the equation which is to be examined. The result might be, for example, a voltage which varies in accordance with the equation which has been set up. Instead of these continuous quantities which vary smoothly, the *digital* computer works with discrete items which can be counted separately or which can be handled by the rules of logic. It is made to calculate by the same sort of process which we use when we do arithmetic, going through a sequence of steps, in which numbers are added, multiplied, shifted from one place to another and so on.

Both kinds of computer have been developed rapidly in recent years, but the digital computer has turned out to be much more versatile. Analog computers are sometimes made for general use, but usually they are restricted to special purposes; because the interconnected parts which represent the different variables all work together in concert, analog computers are most useful in situations where many variables interact, as in calculations for electrical distribution networks. An example of greater interest to psychologists is the use of analog computers for training aircraft pilots: the equipment is designed to simulate the characteristic performance of a particular type of aircraft. Pilots can then be taught to fly that type of aircraft without ever having to leave the ground, by 'flying' the trainer. However, even in these uses analog computers are often aided by digital computers, or threatened by them. It is the general-purpose digital computer which is working such a revolution in our lives and in our ideas, and which is being used to such a great extent in psychology. For these reasons we shall leave aside the analog computers and concentrate on digital computers.

Three developments have led to the modern computer: an increase in storage capacity, so that numbers obtained during a calculation need not be written down but can be left in the computer until they are needed; the development of automatic machines, which could perform complicated calculations by following a pre-set program; and the development of electronic devices which could work at speeds which were inconceivable even thirty years ago.

A simple calculator need hold only two numbers: one which is the result of the calculation so far, and another which is to be added to or subtracted from the first. For simple addition and subtraction such a machine is quite adequate; we can simply set in each number to be added or subtracted until all have been dealt with, then read out the final value from the register which holds the results. But as our calculations become more complex, with several intermediate steps, we find that we must write down the results of these intermediate steps. The work becomes tedious and slow, and errors are likely.

These difficulties are overcome by providing extra registers to hold the intermediate results. Modern desk calculators are often equipped with two or three of these extra registers; some even are mini-computers with several hundred registers, but even a few extra registers can greatly increase the convenience and versatility of the machine. General-purpose computers go far beyond this, having many thousands of registers; each register stores one 'word', and the size of the computer store is specified in kilowords; one kiloword (k) is equal to 1,024 words. This figure is chosen rather than, say 1,000 because computers work with 'binary' numbers rather than decimal; they count in twos, not in tens. 1,024 is equal to ten twos multiplied together, i.e. 2^{10}. For convenience we can think of 'k' as being roughly 1,000, 2k as being roughly 2,000, and so on. The main store of a small laboratory computer might have a capacity of 4k; a computer used to provide computing services might have 96k, extendable to 240k or more. The main store capacities are usually extended by auxiliary stores, of magnetic discs or magnetic tape; these auxiliary stores are slower in use but cheaper to provide.

To carry out a calculation, we must go through a sequence of steps: to get $(A+B)^2/C$, we must add A to B, square the sum, divide by C, step by step. Frequently the same sequence of operations must be repeated again and again, each time working with new figures to get a new result. This is what we must do when we calculate tables of logarithms for example. Astronomical tables also require repetitive calculation, and in the early nineteenth century Charles Babbage set out to construct a machine, his *Difference Engine*, which would go through the sequence automatically. Labour would be saved, but Babbage's main purpose was to reduce the frequency of errors; a machine can be more reliable than a man. Apart from this special-purpose machine, he also set out to make a more versatile automatic machine, which could be programmed by punched cards to perform any desired sequence of operations. He was too ambitious; many of the gears and parts were made, and a part of the machine was assembled and run; but the cost of finishing the work was too great and the work was abandoned.

The idea of using cards punched with patterns of holes had been introduced by the Frenchman, Jacquard, in 1801 to control the patterns woven by silk-weaving looms. This use was entirely successful, allowing rapid production of a great variety of beautiful silks.

When Babbage had tried to use the punched cards for calculation, he had failed. The first successful application of this sort was by Hollerith, who built machines for processing the data from the American census of 1890. It will be noticed that Hollerith was using punched cards to represent data, whereas Jacquard had used them to represent instructions to the loom. These two uses will become clear as we go on; here we remark only that holes in cards can be used in both ways, just as symbols on paper can be made to give both information and instructions.

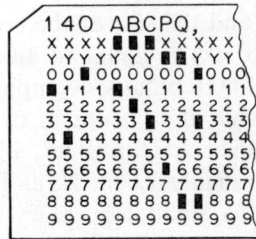

Figure 1.1—*Part of a Hollerith card, showing the punching for the characters:* 1 4 0 A B C P Q,

These Hollerith machines speeded up the work and produced a great saving of labour. Once the information obtained from the census was punched on to cards, calculations could be done by machine; moreover, the cards could be used again and again for different calculations. A stack of cards could be put into the machine and the machine could sort them, or print out lists of data with totals, or punch new cards which summarized the data from the original cards.

On the Hollerith cards, one digit of a number is represented by a hole in a particular place in a column; successive digits are punched on a card as in the first three columns of Figure 1.1.

The machine reads the card either by mechanical feelers which sense the presence of holes, or by light which can pass through the card and reach a photocell only if a hole is punched in that position on the card.

The card can also be punched to represent letters of the alphabet, so that it becomes possible to put names and other written information on to the card. Obviously this could be done by having colums with twenty-six possible places for holes, one for each letter of the alphabet. In practice, a more economical arrangement is used; columns are made twelve places high, and the character is represented by two (or sometimes three) holes punched in the same column. The codes for the letters A, B, C, P, Q and the comma are shown in Figure 1.1.

We can also use the card to indicate the classification of data. We divide the card into 'fields'; a number punched into one field represents age, in another field it represents income, and so on. In the simplest case the punching of a hole means that the card belongs to that class; we can record male or female, married or single, occupational group, each with a hole in the appropriate place on the card.

These punched-card machines were very successful but they have a number of limitations. For each task the machine must be set appropriately, a process which takes some time since it involves plugging wires into a connexion-board. This can be speeded up by having pre-plugged boards which can be interchanged, but even then only a few operations can be performed for each setting; and each time, the data cards must again be passed through the machine. This restricts the uses to simple calculations which are to be performed on masses of data.

Yet, if the right machine were to be used great versatility would be possible. This was shown by Alan Turing, an English mathematician (Turing, 1936). In 1936 he worked out on paper a design for a simple computer, which has come to be known as a Turing machine. This machine had, in the theory, a tape on which a sequence of symbols could be written. The machine could read the tape and perform operations on it (i.e. change one symbol). The choice of which operation was to be performed would depend on the internal state of the machine, and on the symbol which had last been read. In accordance with these the machine would go into a new state, erase the symbol from the tape and replace it by a new one, and finally move the tape by one step to right or left. By these processes (worked out only in theory but with no difficulty about putting them into practice) the hypothetical machine could perform a calculation: it could start with a sequence of symbols on the tape, and when it had finished its work there would be a different sequence of symbols on the tape.

The exact rules of operation could vary from machine to machine, but Turing proved that this did not matter. He showed that Universal Turing machines could be made, each of which could perform any calculation that could be performed by any other Turing machine. Thus Turing showed that his machine was a general-purpose computer; and in this sense any general-purpose computer is equivalent to any other. In practice, computers vary widely in convenience and in speed; but, in theory at least, any one of them, with a tape for storage if necessary, can perform any calculation which can be performed by any other.

During World War II these paper machines were developed into hardware; but instead of the gears and shafts of Babbage's difference engine, they used electromagnetic relays of the type which had come into use for automatic switching in telephone exchanges. The relay is an electrically operated switch which can be closed (on) or left open (off); these two positions can be used like the hole in the card to represent the presence or absence of a symbol. For position of the hole, we now have position of the switch in the network wiring. But because the relay can be switched electrically, one relay can be used to cause the next to switch. The symbols which were passive when punched in the card, become active when transferred to the relays. They count, they calculate or they perform logical operations, according to the present state of the relays and the wired connexions between them.

These computers were far more versatile than the punched-card machines. One of them, built by Professor Howard Aiken, could work through a complicated sequence of operations, controlled by a program punched on to paper tape; as the machine performed each operation, the tape was stepped on to give the instruction for the next.

The speed of calculation was greatly increased when, in the ENIAC calculator, the electromagnetic relays were replaced by electronic switches with no mechanical parts to be moved. This calculator was built by Eckert and Mauchly with a team at the University of Pennsylvania, to produce ballistic tables for the army artillery. At first the ENIAC was set up by hand; but during its construction it was suggested by Von Neumann that the program could be stored in the machine, in the same way that numbers were stored. A new machine was built, with a larger storage capacity, to store its own program. With the stored program the modern computer was achieved.

The stored program computer

A simple computer

The idea of a stored program is ingenious, simple and powerful. Let us get rid of any mystery which may be lurking here, by designing a simple machine.

Start with a store of a hundred registers, and number them 00, 01, 02, 03, 04, 05, 06, . . . , 98, 99. We start numbering from zero rather than one, so that we can keep to two digits. In each register we will store one number or instruction. It turns out, as the design proceeds, that we need seven digits to specify an instruction and seven digits will give fair accuracy of calculation, so we choose to use registers which are capable of holding seven digits.

These are decimal digits, counting by tens in the usual way. If we had wished, we could have chosen some other number system. In fact, computers work in the binary system with base two. The reason is that many of the components used in computers can most easily be made with two states rather than ten: a switch is on or off, a hole is present or absent, and so on. Since human operators find the binary system rather awkward, it is usual for a conversion to be made in the machine so that the user can work in octal (base eight) or even in decimal. For clarity of exposition, our machine will be designed to use the decimal system (we shall deal with the various number systems in Chapter 2).

Our machine must be able to add, subtract, multiply, divide; it must also be able to read in new data from the input, and display the result of its calculation at the output. To make the machine perform a calculation, it must be made to do these operations one after the other, going through the sequence until the calculation is complete. Consequently, a program will consist of a list of operations to be performed in the sequence which is to be followed.

In each of the registers we can store a number. Therefore, if we can represent the list of required operations as a list of numbers, we shall be able to store the list with successive operations in successive registers. The program will then be in the machine, and the machine can obey the program by obeying each register in turn.

To represent the operations as numbers we simply list them in some convenient order and give each item a number. The number is of course only another name for the operation, but it is a name which can be stored and which, as we shall see later, can cause the machine to perform the operation.

The list of operations is shown below; to the arithmetic and input-output operations mentioned above, we have added two operations which will be used to allow loops and branches in the program.

Operations
0 Read in from the input
1 Display for output
2 Add
3 Subtract
4 Multiply

5 Divide
6 Go To order specified
7 Test, and If the number tested is Negative, Go To the order specified.

Our operations are now represented as numbers, but this is not quite enough. It is no good being able to add if we add the wrong numbers, trying to find the price of cheese by adding the number of eggs to the length of the basket. We must not only perform the correct sequence of operations, but also make sure that we perform them on the appropriate data. This is done in our everyday arithmetic by giving names to the various items with which we must work—apples, price per apple, total cost, etc. In algebra we give more abstract names, usually letters of the alphabet: x,y,a,b,c. When we write a program we can use names like these, but we can also keep track of a number by remembering where we have put it. So we can number the registers of the computer and then use the number of each register as a name for it or as an address by which we can find it again. What all this amounts to is that with each operation we must store the address of the numbers to which that operation is to be applied, and the address in which the result is to be put. In this way the book-keeping of the calculation will be looked after.

One way to fulfil these requirements is to use an order which contains three addresses and an operation. Usually, the operation will work on the numbers in the first two addresses, and put the answer in the third. Thus if we write the order 15 16 2 17, we shall want the machine to add (operation 2) the numbers in registers 15 and 16, and put the sum in register 17. To divide the number in 22 by the number in 35, and put the quotient in 36, we write 22 35 5 36. Since these orders are written as numbers they can be stored in the machine just like any other number. We need only ensure that the registers are big enough to hold numbers with at least seven decimal digits. We have in fact done this.

We can now see what form the program will take. It will be a sequence of seven-digit numbers. These numbers will be put into the machine, and the machine will obey each one in turn. But how will it obey them? How can a number in the machine be translated into the operation which it represents? We can make the machine do this by making the order control the positions of a set of switches, the position of each switch being set according to the number given in the order.

The order has in it four numbers, so we use four switches. The first two numbers represent the addresses from which data must be taken; we use two switches, of 100 positions each, to connect the appropriate addresses to the processor. The third number represents an operation;

we use a switch of ten positions to connect into the processor the
mechanism which will perform the required operation. (We have as yet
no operation 8 or operation 9; they can be kept spare, to be used if
we need any operations other than those already specified.) The fourth
and last number represents the destination for the result; we use a
switch of 100 positions to pass the result to the proper address. The
arrangement of the machine and the switches is shown in Figure 1.2.

Now let us write a simple program for this machine. Suppose we wish
to have a table of the squares of the numbers 1, 2, 3, ..., . We can

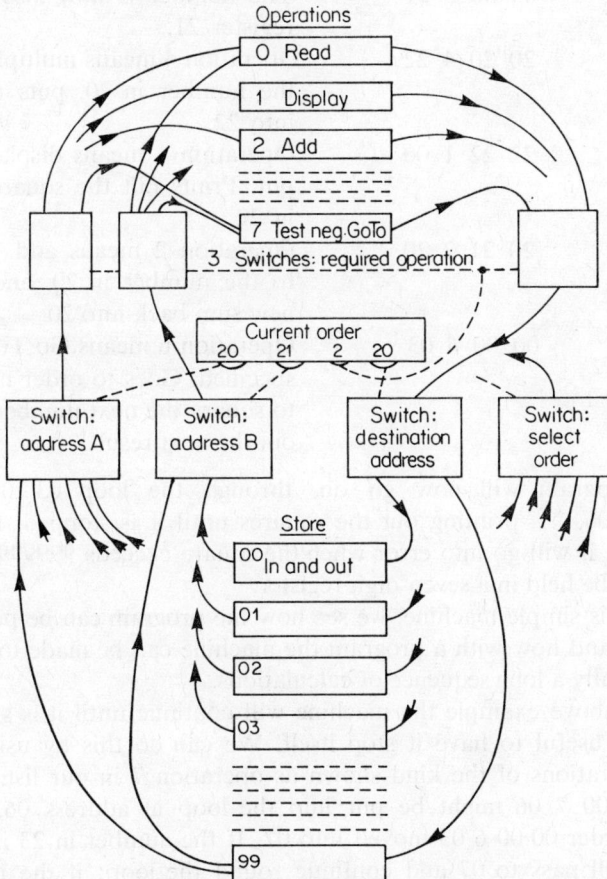

Figure 1.2—*The arrangement of the computer, showing the way in which
the switches control the flow of information between the parts of the
machine*

start with one, square it and print the answer; then add one to the one with which we started, square the sum and print the answer, and so on. The program to do this is as follows:

Register	Order	Meaning of the order
01	00 00 0 20	Operation 0 means Read in. In the input 00, we must put the number one; this order reads the number from the input into register 20 (leaving registers 00 to 19 available for program).
02	00 00 0 21	The number is now also read into register 21.
03	20 20 4 22	Operation 4 means multiply. Squares the number in 20, puts the square into 22.
04	22 22 1 00	Operation 1 means display for output. Prints out the square which is in 22.
05	20 21 2 20	Operation 2 means add. Adds one to the number in 20, and puts the new sum back into 20.
06	00 00 6 03	Operation 6 means Go To the order specified. Goes to order number 03, to square the next number and print out the next result.

The program will now go on, through the loop 03 04 05 06, 03 04 05 06, . . ., printing out the squares until it is stopped. If allowed to run on, it will go into error when the square exceeds 9999999 and can no longer be held in a seven-digit register.

With this simple machine, we see how the program can be put into the machine, and how with a program the machine can be made to carry out automatically a long sequence of calculations.

In the above example the machine will continue until it is stopped. It would be useful to have it stop itself. We can do this by using conditional operations of the kind shown as operation 7 in our list. Here the order 23 00 7 06 might be put into the loop at address 06, with the existing order 00 00 6 03 moved into 07. If the number in 23 is positive, control will pass to 07 and continue round the loop; if the number is negative, control will return to 06 and the machine will be stopped. We could use an order like this in our program by putting into the relevant register 23 the number of times which the loop must be traversed, say 20; then with an order in the loop we can count down, subtracting one for each time the loop is traversed, until the count goes negative and the conditional order takes the machine out of the loop. A register used in this way is known as a 'counter'.

A technique closely related to the conditional order is that in which an order is modified during a calculation. This is possible because orders are stored in the same way as numbers. If numbers can be added so too can orders, and any other operations which the machine can perform on numbers can also be used to modify orders.

The simplest example of this kind of alteration is the *change of address*. Suppose that we have in the machine a list of fifty numbers, stored in successive registers 20, 21, 22, 23, 24, . . ., 69, and that we want to add them, i.e. we want to find the total.

Without modification of orders, we could proceed as follows: we choose a free register in which to put the total, say register 19. We then write a program which will first set register 19 to zero; then add to it the contents of register 20, then of register 21, and so on. To add the contents of register 20 to the running total in 19 and put the result in 19, we would need an order thus: 19 20 2 19 (Operation 2 means *add*). Suppose that we have already put a zero into register 18. The program will be as shown in Table 1.1.

Table 1.1—*Example of program for finding Sum total of fifty numbers, stored in successive registers*

01	18 18 2 19	Sets the running total to zero.
02	19 20 2 19	
03	19 21 2 19	
04	19 22 2 19	
05	19 23 2 19	
06	19 24 2 19	Performs the summation.
..	.. ..	
..	.. ..	
51	19 69 2 19	

This program requires fifty-one orders, and we would not have room in the store to accommodate all these as well as the fifty numbers. However, most of the instructions are the same except for a change in the second address. If we were to add a modifier, 00 01 0 00, to any one of these orders, we would obtain the order next in sequence. Let us put this modifier into register 17 and write a program which will make use of it. The program must first set register 19 to zero, as before. It must then enter a loop; each time it traverses the loop it adds a number to the running total and then modifies the order so that on the next traverse it will add the next number. It then checks whether the modified address has gone beyond register 69. If it has, then the program must stop; if not, it must return to add the next number. The program will be as shown in Table 1.2.

Table 1.2

Register	Order	
01	18 18 2 19	Sets an initial value (zero) of the running total in 19.
→02	19 20 2 19	Adds the number in 20 to the running total in 19.
03	02 17 2 02	Modifies the order, so that on the next traverse of the loop it will add the next number.
04	02 16 3 15	} Subtract the criterion number from the modified
—05	15 00 7 02	} order, and test whether the summation is complete. If the test value is still negative, go back to add the next number; if no longer negative, go on to the next order which is a stop.
06	00 00 6 06	STOP (Go to the same order as before)
..	. . . . . .	
15	Blank at start	Number which is negative as long as the summation is not complete.
16	19 70 2 19	Criterion for completion. If the modified order is the same as this, then the summation is complete.
17	00 01 0 00	Modifier.
18	00 00 0 00	Zero, for pre-setting of total.
19	Blank at start	Running total
20		}
..	. . . . . .	} The numbers which are to be added.
69		}

With this technique of modifying orders great versatility is achieved. Not only can we change the address on which an order is to act, we can also change the operation. For example, we may use a modifier which when added to the order will change the operation from addition to multiplication. Or if the operation is a jump ('Go To the address specified') we can by changing the address cause the program to follow a different course. This kind of change is often used as a switch, to guide the calculation through a program which has many alternative routes.

The operating cycle of a computer

Let us now put aside the detailed operations to look at the overall plan of the computer and its operating cycle.

Figure 1.3 shows the organization of a simple computer. The machine is built around a store, into which numbers can be put and in which the program can also be stored. Calculations are performed by an arithmetic

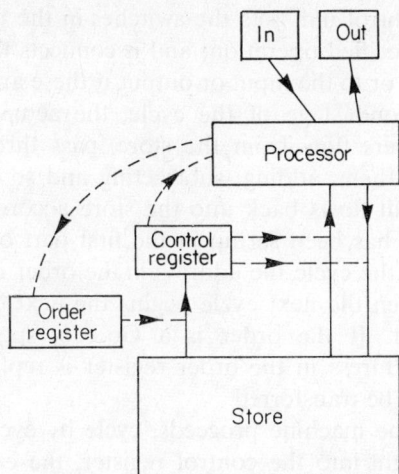

Figure 1.3—*The organization of a simple computer*

unit, or processor, which takes numbers from the store, performs arithmetic or logical operations on them and returns them to the store. We must have some kind of input device—a teletypewriter perhaps, by which information can be typed into the computer, or a card-reader by which the numbers on punched cards can be read in—and an output, perhaps again a teletypewriter or a card-punch, by which the computer can give out the results of its calculation.

The operation of this system is governed by a pair of units, each made up of some control switches and a register which is separate from the main store of the computer. The first of these separate registers, the *control register*, holds the order which is to govern the operation of the computer, and the second, the *order register,* holds the address of the next order which is to be put into *control*. These two units work together in a two-stage cycle, alternately picking up an order and carrying it out, as follows. Whatever the setting of the order register, it can be thought of as holding a number. Even if no number has been deliberately put into it, it will have been left at zero or at a number that had previously been in it; it will therefore be holding a number in the range 00 to 99. This number is interpreted by the machine as an address in the store, the address of the order which must next be obeyed. The switches are set correspondingly, and in the first stage of the cycle the order is taken from that address in the store and put into the control register. The order, now in the control register, specifies an operation; it also specifies the addresses of the numbers on which that operation is to be performed. The control unit sets the switches in the processor so that it will perform the specified operation; and it connects the processor to the specified addresses, or to the input or output if these are specified.

Then, in the second stage of the cycle, the actual operation is performed: the numbers flow from the store, pass through the processor which operates on them, adding, subtracting and so on, to produce the result; and the result flows back into the store according to the destination address which has been set up in the first part of the cycle. During this second part of the cycle the address in the order register is advanced by one, so that when the next cycle begins the next order will pass into the control register. If the order is a Go To, specifying transfer of control, then the address in the order register is replaced by the one to which control must be transferred.

In this fashion the machine proceeds, cycle by cycle. At each cycle a new order is brought into the control register, the calculation advances one step, and the results of the calculation to date are put into the store. If the order calls for input, the processor will read in whatever input is available; and if the order calls for output, the machine will print out its results or punch them on cards. If the order calls for transfer of control, the address in the order register is replaced by the new one. And if control is transferred to the same order which specifies that transfer, the address is never changed and the program stops.

Computer components, configurations and uses

Early computers were designed each as a single machine, organized around the central processor which was backed up by a store. All information passed through the processor and the processor itself, under program control, governed the flow of information from input through processor to store, from store through processor to output, and so on.

In recent years decentralization has taken place. The modern computer is no longer a single machine, but rather a group of machines which communicate with each other by wire; and the component machines are no longer slaves to the processor, but each may become master as the need arises. These modern components can be put together in the old centralized configuration but they can also be combined in other ways, by connecting several processors to the store, by using a separate processor to deal with a complicated input or output station, or in many other ways. The modular design, with interchangeable components which plug together, allows the installation to be designed to fit the anticipated use and to be modified as the pattern of use is changed.

Later in this section we shall look at some of the possible configura-

* *

tions and their uses. Before we do that, however, we must look at the components which are used to build up a computer or computer installation.

Storage devices

Stores are distinguished by their speed, their capacity and of course by their cost. (They were at one time also distinguished by their degrees of unreliability, but it would be fair to say that this has now become degrees of reliability.) If a store could be made which gave rapid access to its contents, had a large capacity and was also inexpensive, then we could simply use that by itself. In practice, however, the stores which are fastest in use are not those which have the largest capacity nor those which are cheapest; in consequence, it is usual for an installation to incorporate several types of store. The fastest types are used for the main store of the machine, the working store; the slower and cheaper types are used as backing store to give increased capacity.

The speed of the store can be measured in terms of access time. With the fastest stores access time is limited by the properties of the storage elements themselves, by the speed at which the elements can switch from one state to another. A more general limitation, however, is the relative difficulty of getting to the elements which must switch. With elements wired together in a network, any element can be reached at random by switching to the correct address; access time can be as short as the individual elements will allow. But when the elements are spread out, as for example by recording them on magnetic tape, then access is non-random, i.e. the elements must be covered in sequence until the required one is reached. Thus access time is extended, by the need to wait while the tape is wound to the section of the data which is needed.

One immediate-access store commonly used is the core store. This uses small magnetic 'cores' threaded onto wires in a frame. Each core is a ring the size of a split pea. The core can be magnetized in one direction or the other, to hold one element of information; the information can be extracted from it by sensing the direction of magnetization. Most modern computers use a core store for the main storage, with slower stores to extend the capacity. Using this arrangement, the machine can transfer information in blocks to and from the slower parts of the store, working all the time at high speed on the information which is in the core store.

The immediate-access store of a small machine might have a capacity of 1024 'words' of 16 binary digits each. A store of 1024 words is, as we have seen, a 1k store. A 'word' of 16 binary digits will store a five-decimal-digit number, not greater than 65,535 (i.e. $2^{16} - 1$); or it can

2—TCIP * *

store two alphanumeric characters, from a teletypewriter keyboard. A common size for the immediate-access store of a laboratory computer is 4k, and some large machines have capacities of 256k or more (e.g. Univac 1110). The access time for any number in such a store is of the order of microseconds, as compared to the milliseconds or even seconds of the slower types of store. (A microsecond is equal to a millionth of a second; a millisecond is a thousandth of a second.)

A very much slower store, which has also been used as the main store for small computers, is the magnetic drum. This is a rapidly rotating drum with a magnetic coating on its circumference. Writing and reading heads are placed against the surface, so that they can transfer information to and from any of a number of tracks on the drum. Access time is long, since the computer cannot read a word at random; once a word has gone past the heads the machine must wait for it to come round again, and even a fast-spinning drum is slow in comparison with the electronic processing circuits.

Like the drum, but with a much larger capacity, is the magnetic disc. A single disc could have a capacity of 256k, and a unit with a stack of 8 discs would have a capacity of over 2000k, with an average access time of under 20 milliseconds (PDP-11). One unit commercially available (Philips) has a capacity of thirty times this. Disc-packs are available, with 10 or 20 surfaces, which can be kept with data on them and loaded on to the computer when needed.

These are useful capacities and times, and the magnetic disc has become an important part of the modern computer. Many installations have 'disc-resident' systems, in which the user's programs and data are loaded on to the discs in batches, and in which libraries of commonly-used programs are kept on the discs. With such a system, too, output from the computer would be put on to the discs to be printed out later while the computer is busy on other work.

The cheapest of the large-capacity stores use magnetic tape, and these are employed particularly when large quantities of information are to be preserved. A pocket-sized reel of tape can hold 128k words, and larger reels are frequently used. Information is stored on the tape in blocks of perhaps 256 words. Short sections of tape can be read rapidly without having to accelerate the heavy reels, by having loops of slack tape. To run from end to end of the reel is a long operation, but this may not be a disadvantage if the information is to be used in sequence.

Processors

The processor consists of a few storage registers and the logical circuits which operate on them. The registers are used for the arithmetic and as control and order registers. One register is called the accumulator; when an addition or a subtraction is performed, the results appear in this register. Another is used to hold the multiplier and, since multiplication produces a longer number, a double-length register is needed to hold the product; these registers are also used for division. In most systems the operation of these registers is automatic and the programmer need not pay them any attention. The logical circuits are built with transistors, or with the new integrated circuits in which one small block performs the functions of many transistors; and these circuits work so rapidly that designers are beginning to take notice of the speed of light— no signal can travel faster than the speed of light, a fact which sets a theoretical limit on the speed with which a processor of a given size can perform its arithmetic.

Modern processors are no longer limited to the few registers which are their own. They are able to work directly into the store, perhaps adding a number to the one already there. They can work directly into output, or test an input in a buffer store without accepting it. These facilities combine well with the use of multiple processors and modular design, which will be discussed further on.

Input and output

Most computers are fitted with a teletypewriter or electric typewriter (often loosely called teleprinter or Teletype) which allows two-way communication between computer and operator and keeps a clear record of all that has been done. This is convenient, but the computer and its operator are an ill-matched pair, the hare and the tortoise. In this case the fast-working but slow-witted hare must wait for the tortoise to give him its instructions.

To overcome this disparity in speed, most of the user's work is done 'off-line', punching cards or paper tape which will later be fed into the computer. Only relatively fast equipment is used 'on-line', connected directly to the computer. Programs and data are punched on to paper tape; a fast tape-reader can then feed information into the machine at about 60,000 characters per minute, as compared with perhaps the 250 per minute of an operator using a teletypewriter. Card-readers have comparable speeds; and punched cards have become the most common form for input of programs and data on the bigger computers.

These devices are still slow in comparison with the computer which, while a single character is read from the tape, can perform 1,000 operations. Faster input is needed, and the need is being met by using magnetic tape as input; 'key-processors' are coming on to the market, by which information can be typed on to the magnetic tape, sometimes even with a stage of pre-processing during the typing.

Another way of overcoming the mismatch in speed is to provide a buffer store, usually of magnetic cores, to collect and hold information. This allows the computer to work at its own high speed while the input-output equipment works at its own, much slower speed. Another form of buffering is found in the disc-resident systems which have already been mentioned.

Output devices are also too slow for the computer. One way to overcome this, of course, is to have the computer produce just that brief pithy answer which the user needs; we do not print out mathematical tables, only the answer which we need at that time. But for many uses a fuller output is required and for this we must have the faster output devices.

The most convenient general-purpose output is the teletypewriter, which is much faster when controlled by the computer: 600 characters per minute is common, and one modern type is claimed to reach 1,800 characters per minute. The output is easily read in a convenient form for use and filing. For larger installations a faster typed output can be produced by a line-printer which prints a line at a time, 80 to 130 characters long, at up to 720 lines per minute.

Punched tape and cards can also be produced as output, but this is usually done only when the information is to be fed back into the computer at some later time.

Sometimes a picture is worth a thousand numbers, and when this is so we make the computer draw a graph. Sometimes, even, we may use the computer mainly because it can draw the graph for us, doing a little preliminary computation such as the taking of averages; it would be convenient to do this when experimental data has been automatically punched on to paper tape, and must be displayed in a form which can be easily interpreted. Again, we may want the computer to draw a diagram for us, when we can specify the formula but the laying out of the diagram would be time-consuming.

If necessary, a graph can be drawn without a graph-plotter. One version of the teletypewriter, the Alphagraphic 1100, produces not only typed output but also half-tone pictures and drawings. We can even use an ordinary teletypewriter or line-printer to produce graphs and pictures. For example, we regard the successive lines as y positions and let the number of letter spaces along the line correspond to x. Then a program can be written which will space along the line until the number of spaces is equal to x, then type a full-stop or an X to mark the point; and then repeat for successive values of y on successive lines. This would produce an output as shown in Figure 1.4.

Nowadays this expedient is seldom really necessary, since there are a number of graph-plotters which will draw out the required X-Y plot on a sheet of paper, or will draw a long continuous graph on paper from a roll. With suitable programs they can write titles, draw and scale the axes and so on. Unfortunately, many of these plotters cannot produce highly finished work. The lettering is crude; and worse, the pen is controlled by stepping-motors with too large a step, which when required to draw a sloping line will draw it as a staircase. Such work is perfectly satisfactory for the result of a calculation, but if we want a diagram for display we must either get a suitable plotter or be prepared to finish the work by hand or by photographic reduction.

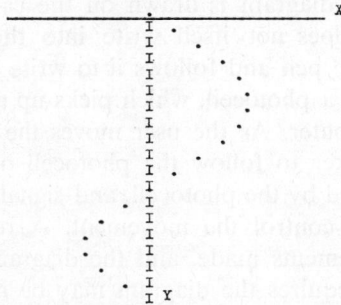

Figure 1.4—*Graphical output from the teleprinter*

Perhaps the fastest output device of all is the cathode-ray tube, which displays the output on a screen like that of a television receiver. These are now available with buffer storage and even with a subsidiary computer to control the display. Such a unit can display a page of alpha-numeric characters, changing the display within fifty milliseconds or so; or it can be made to draw graphs or produce moving diagrams or ani-mated pictures. The display can be photographed if required and the camera can be controlled by the program. (The cathode-ray tube output is often known, perhaps carelessly, as an *oscilloscope*. This is because oscilloscopes, which display pictures of electrical waveforms, soundwaves etc., use cathode-ray tubes.)

Interactive control

With a teletypewriter or with a combination of cathode-ray tube and teletypewriter the programmer can interact with the computer. Although this is slow it is sometimes valuable. The programmer may develop his programs, for instance, by working in what is called the conversational mode. He types his modifications into the machine and the computer types out the results or a diagnosis of program errors. The conversational mode can also be used as an experimental procedure, in which the computer runs the experiment in accordance with the subject's responses. Or the computer can be used as a teaching machine, capable of sophisticated procedures; one such use is for teaching students how to write programs in programming languages such as FORTRAN and ALGOL, which will be discussed in Chapter 2.

In another use which has come to be known as interactive graphics, diagrams are drawn straight into the computer, often in such a way that the computer tidies up as it draws—and of course, the diagram is specified in the computer in a numerical form which can be manipulated by the program. The diagram is drawn on the cathode-ray tube by a 'lightpen'. This pen does not itself write into the computer; instead the computer finds the pen and follows it to write what the pen writes. The pen has on its tip a photocell, which picks up a bright marker cross produced by the computer. As the user moves the pen away, the computer moves the marker to follow the photocell on the pen; errors in the following are sensed by the photocell, and signalled back to the computer to enable it to control the movement. A record is kept in the computer of the movements made, and the diagram is drawn from the record. As the user requires the diagram may be modified, and he can also draw into the modified diagram. For example, he may draw a shape with straight outlines and have the computer straighten out the lines. He can then make the computer move the shape into a new perspective, and again work on the drawing. This is a powerful aid, and many other devices are being developed to perform the same function with less complexity.

Interaction can be extended to the control of experiments. At its simplest, the computer can be used to control an experiment according to a fixed program, using its internal timing circuits as a clock. The next stage is for the data from the experiment to be fed directly into the computer. Digital signals from the experimental apparatus can easily be made compatible with the computer circuits, and converters are available for transforming voltages or other analog signals into digital form for the computer, or from the computer's digital form into an analog form when required by the apparatus. Using these, the computer can run the experiment and at the same time analyse the data from it. Finally, the computer can be made to modify the course of the experiment in accordance with the data so far collected; this interactive mode of working has become known as contingent control of the experiment. This whole topic will be discussed in Chapters 4 and 6.

Time-sharing

One of the great sources of waste in computer use is that the computer is not always available for use when it is needed, yet when it is in use it can work faster than any operator. This is particularly evident in interactive uses, which are not possible in many computer installations. To make economic use of the machines they are operated only by the computer staff, who run the programs written by the users. This system means that one must usually wait until the next day, or even longer, for the results of a program test; and when those results are obtained, all other work must be dropped while the results are analysed, corrections made and the corrected program taken to the computer centre. The user falls into a 24-hour cycle, which disrupts his other work.

These problems are being overcome by the use of time-sharing systems. A number of consoles are provided, through which the user can be in direct communication with the computer, perhaps by teletypewriter. The typewriter is slow and the user is even slower, but the computer need not wait for him. It completes the calculations which he has programmed, and then goes on to work for other users or in controlling experiments or apparatus.

The key to this mode of use is the installation of an executive system on the computer, either as part of the computer design or by suitable programs. Under this system the computer never cedes control to any user's program, but keeps control to itself. At convenient intervals it interrogates the user terminals, and accepts new instructions from them. It then works through the instructions, while keeping them subordinate so that they cannot interfere with other programs or with the executive program itself. To the user, it seems as if he has full control of the computer, with all its facilities to himself. But at the same time, other users are sharing the machine with him, and to them too it seems as if they have the whole use of the machine.

Modular design

A number of modern computers are designed on a modular principle, in which all the components described above, and others, are available as separate units which can be connected by a standard interface—in effect a multipin plug and socket, so that the components are merely plugged together in the required configuration.

In action each of the modules can work independently, according to its function, and can call on other modules when it needs them. For example, the program may instruct a disc store to take a block of data from a specified part of the main store. The disc controller then governs the word-by-word transfer from the main store and organizes its placing on the disc, while the program continues with other work. On the other hand, the processor may reach a point in the program at which it must output a block of characters. It goes into 'master' mode and calls on the teletypewriter console. The typewriter responds by going into a 'slave' mode, so that it is ready for an instruction. The instruction from the processor puts it into a 'continuous output' mode. It then begins to print out the characters while the processor goes on with the program. When it requires a new character, the typewriter interrupts the processor; and when the block has been completed, the typewriter is again available on call as before.

Configurations can be chosen to suit the purpose and changed or extended when necessary. One well-known modular computer system is the Modular One, made by Computer Technology Ltd. In this system any pair of modules can be interconnected, and either module of a pair can act as master for a transfer in either direction. Each module can be connected to several others, to get any pattern of data flow and control; it is even possible to have several processors working each with its own program, calling on the others when necessary, for data or for action.

One possible arrangement is that of duplex operation, in which two processors are connected to the same store. They work in parallel, keeping check of each other's results; and if one fails, the other can continue and cut out the faulty units. In another configuration the system may be designed with a central processor and a high-speed cathode-ray tube display. A display of this sort, incorporating for example perspective transformations of an object as it rotates, may require a great deal of computing. If the central processor is already fully occupied with the main program, we can use a 'satellite' computer with its own program to transform the output into a form suitable for the complex display.

The last system which we shall mention is the PDP-11, made by Digital Equipment Corporation. In this system all modules are plugged into a common line called the bus. The arrangement is rather like that of a suite of rooms with doors opening on to a common corridor; any unit can communicate with any other via the corridor. A module goes into master code and calls for use of the bus; a priority system decides whether the module is to be allowed to become bus master. When given the bus, the module calls by code for the module which it needs; the other module responds and the transfer of information is made. It can be seen that the working configuration of this system is determined, within the limits of the available equipment, by the programs with which it is working.

Because of the ease with which the system can be rearranged to take account of changes in usage, most laboratory computers are of modular design and it is this kind of computer which the psychologist is most likely to operate for himself. He may very likely use other computers by working at a console in a time-sharing mode, but the computer itself will be run by the staff of the computer centre. All who use computers more than casually, however, should know about programming which will be the subject of the next chapter.

Further Reading

Introductory

Cluley, J. C. (1967) *Electronic Computers.*
    Oliver and Boyd Contemporary Science Paperbacks, London. A good introduction to computers, both analog and digital.
Desmonde, W. H. (1964) *Computers and Their Uses.*
    Prentice-Hall, London. An easy-to-read introduction.
'Computers in the Seventies', *Science Journal*, **6**, Special Issue, October 1970.
    Articles on many aspects of computers, their uses and their future.

More Specialized

American Psychologist, **24** (1969). An issue devoted to instrumentation in psychology, with many references to work with computers.
Borko, H. (Ed.) (1962) *Computer Applications in the Behavioral Sciences.*
    Prentice-Hall, Englewood Cliffs, New Jersey. An early anthology of 25 pieces with some particular interest to psychologists.
Siegel, A. I. and J. J. Wolf (1969) *Man-Machine Simulation Models.* Wiley, New York. A description of some models and their use for developing systems in which men and machines must work together. Not for beginners.
Sterling, T. D. and S. V. Pollack (1965) *Computers and the Life Sciences.* Columbia University Press, New York. A good introductory book for biologists.

CHAPTER 2

An Introduction to Programming

John A. Wilson and Geoffrey Barrett

Software and programming languages

Software

It became clear during the 1950s that a computer in hand was not
necessarily a computer in use. Programs must be written to control its
operation and the surprise is that this task which seems so straightforward turns out in practice to be a major undertaking. This realization has led to two developments: first, a multiplicity of programs
having everyday uses and which have come to be known as 'software',
since they are an indispensable part of the machine even though not part
of the 'hardware'; and second, as an important part of the software,
that of the high-level programming languages.

When a computer is designed its characteristic features are determined
by the components which are used and by the way in which these components are connected. But, as we saw in connexion with the Turing
machine, all computers are equivalent; by writing a program and feeding
it into the computer, we can make it perform any task provided that the
task is completely specified. Thus, apart from the hardware of the computer, we need the programs which will suit it to the various kinds of
work. Since so much detailed programming is necessary before we can
get useful work out of a computer, this 'software' has become as important to the user as the machine itself. Its availability may affect the
choice of a machine, and the success of an application.

One important part of the software is composed of programs which
service the running of the computer: programs to read in data, to provide tabulated output, to allocate machine facilities and control the
running of programs for the various users. Another part is composed of
standard programs for carrying out tasks which are often required by
users. The simplest of these would be programs to find the values of
functions, such as the sine of an angle. The more complex would perform complete tasks such as the statistical analyses mentioned in the
section on data processing at the end of this chapter. Finally, there are
the high-level programming languages. These belong to the software, but

27

they have assumed an importance of their own. The use of computers is spreading rapidly, and perhaps the main reason for this spread is the availability of these powerful and easy-to-learn languages.

Programming languages

We have seen that a computer by itself can do nothing; it needs a fully detailed set of instructions. For example, the set of six instructions on p. 12 will cause the computer to calculate the squares of the numbers, 1, 2, 3, . . ., etc., by specifying each individual operation required of the computer. A set of instructions which completely specifies a task is a program; the words and symbols used for writing programs, and the rules by which they are used, are known as a programming language.

Each computer has a language of its own, called the machine language, in which its programs must be written; a simple example was given in the description of the hypothetical computer in Chapter 1. In the machine language every small operation which is to be performed must be specified in the program, and this involves a great deal of work. We cannot dispense with any of these operations; each is a necessary step in the calculation. Yet we often find that a procedure which requires many machine operations can be written briefly and without ambiguity in only a few words of ordinary English. Surely it should be possible to find a way of writing programs in a language closer to that of the programmer. Apart from the saving of labour which such a language would produce, it would be easier to learn than the machine languages and the non-specialist would then be able to use even a sophisticated computer.

To construct a language of this kind is a task which usually requires the combined efforts of a team of programmers, but in principle it is quite simple. Two things are needed: first, a set of instructions which will cope naturally with the sort of problem the user must solve; in their ordinary use these instructions may be loosely used, but for the programming language they must be unambiguously defined. Secondly, we need a set of programs in the machine language, so designed as to make the computer accept each high-level instruction and perform the necessary complex of operations. In this way languages have been developed which are suited to the user, not merely conforming to the machine.

The types of language can be thought of in terms of a hierarchy. At the lowest level are the machine languages. Then come the assembly languages, which use mnemonic symbols such as A for Add, M for Multiply and can use decimal numbers rather than the binary numbers used by the machine, but which otherwise run parallel to the machine language, with one assembly-language instruction for each machine-language instruction. At the highest level of the hierarchy, and far more sophisticated than these assembly languages, are the languages designed to solve specific problems or whole classes of problems, in which one program instruction serves as a shorthand for many machine instructions. Along with these high-level languages are those designed for direct interaction between the programmer and the computer, the conversational languages.

Assembly languages are machine-oriented but are a considerable improvement on the machine's binary code because the symbols are mnemonics which suggest the corresponding computer operation. For example, an assembly language might include the mnemonics A for Add, M for Multiply, J for Jump. ('Jump' is a name often used for Transfer of Control to another instruction. We could insist on the name 'Transfer', and use the mnemonic T.)

In the hypothetical computer described on p. 8ff the corresponding instructions were 02, 04 and 06. It is obvious that the numbers are more easily forgotten, especially by the part-time programmer who spends most of his time on his own more specialized work.

Conversational languages such as Dartmouth College's BASIC and Digital Equipment Corporation's FOCAL have been designed particularly for ease of learning and for the user who wishes to work directly on the computer. These languages enable the user to get immediate feedback of information and results. He can test small sections of the program as he goes along, make trial calculations, correct his mistakes and finally have the machine print out a tidied-up version of the program. To achieve this, the conversational languages are more user-oriented than the assembly languages. They go beyond mnemonics, using symbols and constructions that correspond to everyday language and in which one instruction may represent many machine-language instructions. For example, the three instructions considered above could be programmed in BASIC and FOCAL as shown in Table 2.1.

To evaluate the formula $X = A (B+C)/(D+E)$, an assembly language would require several instructions, perhaps as many as seven. In the

Table 2.1

BASIC	FOCAL
LET A = A + B	SET A = A + B
LET A = A * B	SET A = A * B
GO TO 20	GO TO 1.2

conversational languages it can be written as a single statement: (in BASIC) LET X = A* ((B + C)/(D + E)). Further and more powerful statements are provided which repeatedly perform sequences of statements, print out results in tabular form and so on.

Both FOCAL and BASIC have been developed specifically for mathematical calculations, but their use can extend beyond this. BASIC PLUS, developed by Digital Equipment Corporation for the PDP-11 time-sharing system, has an extended capability for non-mathematical manipulations.

The highest-level languages are both problem-oriented and user-oriented. Most popular in scientific work are FORTRAN and ALGOL, developed for mathematical calculation and using statements very similar to those later used by FOCAL and BASIC. These are powerful languages, but when problems cannot readily be stated in mathematical formulae they tend to become clumsy; for this reason other languages have been developed for this non-mathematical kind of work.

For some of these other languages, useful in psychological work, the central idea is that of list processing, which involves a reorganization of the computer memory. Conventionally, the registers in the store are consecutively numbered, and the numbers serve as addresses. To retrieve an item from the store, its address must be known. With a list memory this is no longer necessary; each register contains not only the symbol being stored but also a link, the address of the register in which to find the next item in the list. This leads to great flexibility in the use of the store, making it easily possible to restructure the problem while the program is running. Items which are found to be related need not be put together in the store, but can be left where they are or put into any available register. The program can gain access as easily as if the list were stored consecutively. To reach the list, only its head item need be known; other items can then be found by using the links.

Specialist languages have also been developed for areas such as Computer-Assisted Instruction, generating animated films and computer control of on-line experiments. Some examples of this last type of language are considered in Chapter 3.

In the last few years there has been some demand for a language to replace all these specialist languages, one which goes beyond them in power and in its capacity to deal with the newer hardware facilities such as time-sharing systems. To meet this demand, the PL/1 language has been developed by IBM. The language is already widely used, for some purposes at least, but it is not yet clear whether it will replace the other languages or merely add one to their number.

The designers of PL/1 claim that its instructions operate at a higher level than was available before. This shows as a simplification of the language and at the same time an increase in the amount and power of computer work performed for each high-level instruction.

To a great extent this is achieved by giving 'responsibility' to the computer, a feature described by the designers as 'default action'. With this feature in the language the programmer is able to shorten his work by leaving his assumptions unstated unless they are unusual. To the programmer using any language various options are available at each step. Current languages usually require that the programmer should spell out his choices; an option left undecided is regarded by the system as ambiguous and signalled as an error. PL/1 acts differently in that a choice left unstated is taken by default to be the usual one. Thus the programmer can work succinctly, and the computer will carry out his unexpressed intentions. Only the departures from the usual need be written out in full.

This new language is a rich one and no effort has been made to keep it simple at the expense of reducing its scope. To compensate for the resulting complexity the language has been designed with a modular structure, so that users need not learn more of the language than concerns them.

Compilers and interpreters

Whatever the language in which the program is written, all the operations specified by the program must be translated into the corresponding operations as described in machine language. The user's program, written in the language of his choice, is called the source program and the final, binary-coded, program is called the object program. It is this object program which finally controls the machine as it executes the task.

Source programs written in assembly language are translated into an object program by an assembler, which is itself a program written in machine language. Source programs written in higher languages are translated by a compiler or an interpreter. These again are programs, often written in the assembly language of the machine. A compiler converts the source program into an object program, specifying all the required operations in machine language; the user can then feed this object program into the computer to perform the required task. An interpreter performs both functions at once: it translates each high-level instruction into the equivalent set of machine-language instructions, and as it translates it controls the computer so as to follow the instructions and thereby perform the required processing. This method is convenient for the user, but it is wasteful of computing time. Each instruction is translated as it occurs in the source program and if the same set of instructions must be obeyed repetitively they will also be translated repetitively. For this reason, compilers are usually to be preferred to interpreters. It is of course possible to use both systems, and one time-sharing system for PL/1 uses a fast compiler for checking programs together with a slower compiler which produces a faster and more efficient object program for long-term use.

Most people working in the behavioural sciences will have access to a computing centre, perhaps in a university or by one of the postal services. These centres and service computers will almost always be equipped to operate with programs written in FORTRAN or ALGOL, which are general-purpose scientific languages, but they will probably not be able to deal with the more specialized problem-oriented languages. These more specialized languages are generally used with a computer which can be dedicated to the specialized uses: many laboratories and university departments now have their own small computer for this purpose. The user will need to learn the language of his departmental machine and, for work which is better done at the centre, he should learn FORTRAN or ALGOL. The high-level languages have much in common, and once one of them is thoroughly mastered there is little difficulty in learning to use another.

A high-level language—FORTRAN

To get a clear idea of these high-level programming languages we shall examine the main features of one of them—FORTRAN. We shall then go on to write a program in the language, and discuss some of the errors and difficulties which arise.

The name FORTRAN indicates the purpose of the language—it TRANslates FORmulae into programs which can substitute numbers into the formulae and evaluate them.

As stated earlier, a program is a set of instructions that completely specify a task for the computer. The instructions are worked through step by step until the task is completed. In FORTRAN the instructions are specified as a list of *statements,* each of which is executed in turn. Each statement is written on a new line which is presented separately to the computer.

With each statement the programmer gives the computer information or gives it a task to perform: he can allocate names to the variables in the program and specify the type of each variable, as for example that it is to be treated as an integer; he can specify that the variable is to be used with subscripts, as x_1, x_2, x_3, ..., x_n, so that the whole of that set of values will be stored together; he can instruct the machine to work out a formula, giving each variable in it the value which is at that time held in its register in the store. Statements can be numbered to identify them; with this facility one statement may direct the program to transfer control to another, as specified by the statement number; transfer of control may be made to depend on logical decisions about the values of the variables, for example, whether the variable is at that time negative or positive. A statement may specify that the same section of the program should be repeated a certain number of times, or repeated until some stated criterion is met. If a part of the task is to be repeated frequently, a subprogram can be written to perform it; this subroutine is called by the main program each time it is needed, and when it has completed its task it returns control to the main program. And, since the organization of input and output makes up a large part of the work of programming, the language provides a powerful set of statements for this task. An additional facility, irrelevant to the program itself but invaluable to the programmer and to the user of a ready-made program, is that of the comment: the programmer can insert comments freely, to explain the workings of the program or how it is to be used. These comments are marked as such so that they will be ignored by the computer, but the programmer who ignores or omits them is likely soon to lose his way.

We shall now consider these provisions in more detail.

(i) *Names of variables.* All the variables which are to be used in the program must be given names. FORTRAN imposes certain limitations on the names which can be used: a name must not be more than six characters long; it must begin with a letter, and the rest of the characters can be any of the 36 alphanumeric characters (i.e. the 26 letters of the alphabet plus the numbers 0 to 9). Within these limitations the programmer can choose names which fit the usual conventions or which call to mind the nature of the variables. For example, SUMX can refer to the sum of the values of a variable X, and STIM1 can refer to the value of stimulus number one.

In some cases, the way in which a number is treated depends on its nature. We can sometimes work in whole numbers; for example, and this is simpler than working in fractions; in the computer simpler and faster programs can be used. But if we do use fractions, then this arithmetic of whole numbers would lead to erroneous results. We must instruct the computer that it must use the more complicated procedures which enable it to deal with fractions. In FORTRAN, this is dealt with by a naming convention: if a name begins with any of the letters I,J,K,L M or N, then it will be treated as a whole number (or integer, e.g. 5, 29, 0, −347, etc.). If a name begins with any other letter it will be treated

as a real number (*real* in the mathematical sense; as applied to computers it means that the number can take on fractional values). If a name
is chosen which does not accord with this convention, it must be 'declared', as real or integer, before it is used in the program. To declare the
name we use a statement which gives the nature of the variable and then
its name. It will then be correctly treated.

To illustrate these conventions we consider the naming of a variable
to represent the mean of a continuous variable X. We can use the name
MEAN; but this name will be treated as an integer, unless we declare
it. We therefore declare it by writing the statement: REAL MEAN.
We could also choose to call the mean XBAR, corresponding to the
spoken form of the conventional $\overline{X}$, and if we did this it would be in
accord with the naming convention and the variable would be treated
as real without the need for declaration.

Declarations can be used for other kinds of numbers. For example, we
can declare a variable to be COMPLEX, and the computer will then
treat it with the kind of arithmetic which mathematicians use for complex numbers. We can also declare an array, which enables us to use
a whole set of numbers with the same name.

(ii) *Arrays.* By putting a set of values into an array it becomes possible
for the program to treat the whole set, or some part of it, as a single
unit. For example, the set of fifty reaction times from each of five
different subjects could all be assigned to the variable RT. It would be
declared as follows:

DIMENSION RT(5,50)

Thereafter, individual values (elements) from the array can be referred
to by using subscripts. For example, RT(3,25) refers to the twenty-fifth
reaction time of subject three. We can work through an array by using
variable subscripts (which must be integers). Thus we can write a
sequence of statements which will perform the necessary arithmetic on
RT(I,J). We can then make the program go through this sequence
repeatedly, setting I and J to new values before each traverse. A program of this sort could find the mean reaction time of each subject, for
example, and then the sum of squares of the differences from the mean.

To a mathematician, these arrays are *n*-dimensional matrices. Some
versions of FORTRAN allow as many as seven dimensions. This ability
to handle matrices is a powerful feature of the language.

(iii) *Arithmetic operations.* Addition, subtraction, multiplication, and
division are represented in FORTRAN as $+$, $-$, $*$, and $/$, respectively.
Exponentiation, i.e. raising to a power, (a^b), is represented as $**$.

To make the computer perform a calculation, we write a statement in which we name a variable and then give a formula by which it is to be worked out. For example, we write:

$$X = Y **2 + Z * (Y - (Z/4))$$

This is equivalent to saying that X must be worked out according to the formula

$$X = Y^2 + Z (Y - (Z/4)).$$

Notice that in FORTRAN every operation is specified by the corresponding symbol; it is not enough to write XY, we must write X*Y, and so on. This is necessary, since the pair of letters together is treated as the name of a single variable.

If the operations are performed in the wrong order, they can give an incorrect result. For example, $Y-(Z/4)$ is not the same as $(Y-Z)/4$. FORTRAN performs the operations in the statement in this order— exponentiation, division, multiplication, addition and subtraction—unless some part of the equation is bracketed, in which case the expression within the brackets is calculated first. When there is more than one pair of brackets, the innermost expression is calculated first. For example, in the statement above: first, Y is squared; then Z is divided by 4, and the result subtracted from Y. This result is multiplied by Z, and the product is added to Y^2. This gives the value of the whole expression, and this value is assigned to X.

The statement above looks like an equation and the novice programmer might be tempted to regard it as such. However, it is not an equation; it is an assignment statement. It instructs the computer to work out a value of X from the values of Y and Z which it has in the store. The distinction can be brought out most clearly by considering a statement which uses the old value of a variable to calculate a new value. The statement $N = N + 1$, for example, could not be true as a mathematical equation (unless N is an infinite number). In FORTRAN, the statement instructs the computer to give N a new value, which is obtained by adding one to the old value.

(iv) *Statement numbers.* Statement numbers provide a cross-referencing device that allows one statement to refer to another. In FORTRAN the number can be an integer between 1 and 9999; it is separated from the statement by a single space, as shown:

    34 N=N+1

We could then refer to this statement by writing:

    GO TO 34

This statement transfers control to statement 34, and in this case statement 34 obtains a new value for N by adding one to the old value. One use of these transfers is illustrated in the next section.

(v) *Conditional statements.* We defined a program as a set of instructions to be performed sequentially by the computer. Sometimes, however, sections of a program need to be repeated or skipped according to the values of variables in the calculation. FORTRAN has several kinds of conditional statement which can perform this kind of transfer of control. We look at only one of these.

In one form of statement an operation is performed only if the specified condition is met. We write:

IF (SUMX.LT.100.0) TRIAL = TRIAL + 1

The trial number is increased by one, but only as long as SUMX is less than 100. If SUMX is equal to or exceeds 100, the trial number is left unchanged. Six conditional operations are available:

Less than   .LT.
Less than or equal to   .LE.
Equal to   .EQ.
Not equal to   .NE.
Greater than   .GT.
Greater than or equal to   .GE.

These conditions can be combined into logical expressions, to give a powerful means of choice. In a program for drawing Julesz figures (as described in the chapter on perception, Chapter 6) we might require that the next part of the program should be skipped if X is between 2.0 and 3.0, but only if Y is between 0.5 and 2.5. This would allow a rectangle to be left free of drawing, to be filled in later. We write:

IF (X.GT. 2.0 .AND.X.LT. 3.0 .AND. Y .GT. 0.5 .AND.
& Y.LT.2.5) GO TO 101

If X and Y are within the specified range control will be transferred to statement 101. (The & is used to show that the statement is continued).

(vi) *Loops.* When a program returns to some earlier statement and repeats a sequence of calculations, using new data, this is called a loop. There are two common types of loop. In the first type the operations in the loop are repeated a specified number of times, for example on each of N values of an array. In the second type of loop the operations are repeated until a specified variable reaches a certain accuracy. Both types of loop can be defined by using conditional statements: for the first, we set I to zero, then increase I by one at each traverse through the loop and test whether it has yet reached N. When I = N, we leave the loop by means of a GO TO statement. For the other type of loop we calculate the value of the criterion variable at each traverse, and test whether it has yet reached the desired value.

In FORTRAN the first type of loop can be specified more easily by a single statement: DO 30 I = 1, N. If N has previously been given a value, say 50, then the program will repeat 50 times the sequence of statements from the DO statement until it reaches statement number 30; it will then leave the loop and go on to the statement which follows number 30, to continue with the rest of the program.

(vii) *Subroutines and functions.* It is useful to be able to write a program in separate parts, each of which performs a definite section of the work. This has a number of advantages, the most obvious of which is that it saves re-writing: the same subprogram can be used again and again within different master programs. Such tasks as selecting the largest of a set of values, or calculating the mean and standard deviation of a set of data, are often performed as part of larger calculations and can be written as subprograms or subroutines.

The subroutine is written separately and is called into operation whenever its particular calculations are required. We might have a routine named MEANSD to calculate the mean and standard deviation of the values of X stored in a one-dimensional array. We call it by the statement:

CALL MEANSD (X, N, MEANX, SDX)

The values inside the brackets are called the *arguments* of the subroutine. They form a line of communication between the subroutine and the main program. In this case, X is the array of N values; X and N must be given values before the call is made. The subroutine performs its calculations and gives values to MEANX and SDX which can be used by the main program after the call.

Another kind of subprogram used in FORTRAN is the *function.* The function is a single value which depends on the values of certain specified variables. It is defined by writing the program which gives it a value; then the value can be used in other calculations by simply naming the` function, just as if it were an ordinary variable. FORTRAN has a number of standard functions, e.g. SQRT(X), which works out the square root of X. This could be called by name within an assignment statement, as in calculating Student's t:

STUDT = ERXBAR * SQRT (OBS − 1.0)/SDX

The user can write his own functions. For example, to draw the
spirals shown in the chapter on perception (Chapter 6 Figure 6.1) it was
necessary to calculate the angle to which each spiral is rotated relative
to the first. Only a few statements are needed, but they are needed in
several places. It is therefore convenient to define a function DIVCCL,
to 'divide the circle'. The function is called by name when we need the
value of the angle. For example, when we want to put THETA equal
to the angle of rotation of the fourth spiral of ten, we write:

THETA = DIVCCL (4,10)

If we want to use the cosine of THETA, we can use our own function
within a standard function for the cosine:

X = R * COS(DIVCCL(4,10))

(viii) *Comments within the program*. Notes can be made within a
program by using a comment marker for each line of comment. Comments are invaluable for giving verbal definitions of the names which
have been chosen for variables, and for describing the purpose or
method of different sections of the program. Comments are written in
natural language; to make the compiler ignore them, we label each line
of comment with the letter 'C' in the first column. It is useful to follow
the 'C' with six dashes so that the comment lines stand out from the
program statements in the print-out of the program. For example,
the complex logical statement in section (v) could be explained by the
comment:

C - - - - - - DRAW SQUARES, BUT LEAVE A BLANK
C - - - - - - RECTANGLE
            IF (X.GT.2.0.AND. . . .) GO TO 101

The comment is ignored by the compiler, the IF statement is compiled
and executed. Comments will be used liberally in the program which is
described later in this chapter.

(ix) *Input and output*. To read information into the computer, or to
print it out, the statements READ and PRINT (sometimes WRITE)
are used. For reading it is necessary to specify the arrangement of the
data on the card and how this data is interpreted in the program. For
output it is necessary to specify the conversion from data in the machine
to the printed characters, and the layout of the output on the printed
page. For both these purposes a FORMAT statement is used. Thus
the READ or PRINT statement will specify two items: the variable
which is to be read or printed and the number of the format statement

which is to be used. For example, an integer N could be read into a FORTRAN program using the two statements:

    READ 10, N
10 FORMAT(I5)

The 'I' in the FORMAT statement tells the computer that the variable to be read is an integer, and the 5 indicates that the number to be read is in the first five columns of the data card. Thus the number on the card can have any value between 0 and 99999. The READ statement will cause the card to read, and will set the value of variable N to the value which it reads from the card. This is only the simplest form of the READ statement. FORTRAN allows many powerful forms of reading, for long sequences of input of complex data.

The FORMAT statement for output of results includes a facility for printing out text and for controlling the spacing of lines: as a simple example, we can space one line and print out the letters NX, followed by a few spaces, by putting '6H _ NX _ _ _' into the brackets of the statement. '6' specifies the number of characters, 'H' that they are to be printed out; the first character is taken separately as an indication of line spacing: blank, as shown, for single spacing; 0 for double spacing; and so on. The remaining five characters, 'NX' and three blanks, are printed out as they stand. The method of indicating the format of numbers is the same as for input. Thus, for example, if we had an integer variable NX in the computer, with the value 54321, we could print out the name and the value by using the statements:

    PRINT 11, NX
11 FORMAT (6H _ NX _ _ _, I5)

The print-out would be:

    NX   54321

The input and output statements given here refer only to use of a card reader and line-printer. Other methods, such as use of magnetic tapes, paper tape and discs, require statements of a form which depends on the particular computer system or installation.

Writing a computer program

The writing of a program can be separated into four stages.

(i) Formulation of the problem to be programmed and its analysis into parts which can be treated step by step.

(ii) Preparation of a rough flow-chart, showing in outline the steps of the program from start to finish. As the problem becomes clearer this rough chart will be transformed into a definite picture of the program as a whole.

(iii) Preparation of a detailed flow-chart, showing each step to be executed in the program.

(iv) Coding the steps of the detailed flow-chart into the programming language.

The first three of these operations are relatively independent of the language which is to be used for the program; they depend on the problem rather than on the way it is to be coded for the computer. This difference between the logical operations of the first three steps and the coding operations of the last step corresponds to the two types of error which might occur in writing the program.

Workers investigating behavioural processes which are complex and subtle may find particular difficulty in reducing their problem to the logical form which it must have before a program can be written. This difficulty must simply be faced by the worker concerned; the program described here is for a problem more easily formulated.

The problem

It is intended to carry out an experiment on short-term memory for decimal digits in strings of between one and nine digits chosen at random, e.g. 7, 543, 754631712, etc. These strings, the stimuli, must be presented in random order and equal numbers are required of each of the nine different lengths of stimulus, say five of each. A string should not commence with a zero, since that would be read by the subject as a shorter string. We wish to program the computer to produce these strings of random digits.

At first sight the problem may appear trivial; we could get the numbers from a table in less time than it takes to write a program. Once written, however, the program can be used time and time again. The program as written here produces only one list, but needs only two extra statements to make it capable of producing a set of different lists, one for each subject. Another advantage of using the computer is the ease with which lists can be made to conform to one or other form of constraint, as for example the avoidance of long runs of the same digit. Finally, the computer print-out can be used directly, as stimulus and as an answer-sheet on which the subject can record his responses—each subject, of course, having a different list of stimuli on his sheet.

The rough flow-chart

We reduce the problem to order by first deciding on a method of tackling it, then developing the method in the form of a flow-chart. As the problem is analysed the parts are laid out on the chart which shows the sequence in which the computer must work. It is usual to set each operation on the chart into a box, using lines with arrows on them to show the flow of control from one box to another. Another convention is to work from top to bottom and from left to right, wherever this is possible.

For any problem there are many possible methods of reaching a solution, and for each method there are many ways of writing a program. We aim to find only one method, not necessarily the best but one which produces a correct result and is easily used.

Let us consider the sequence of stimuli in the way shown in Figure 2.1.

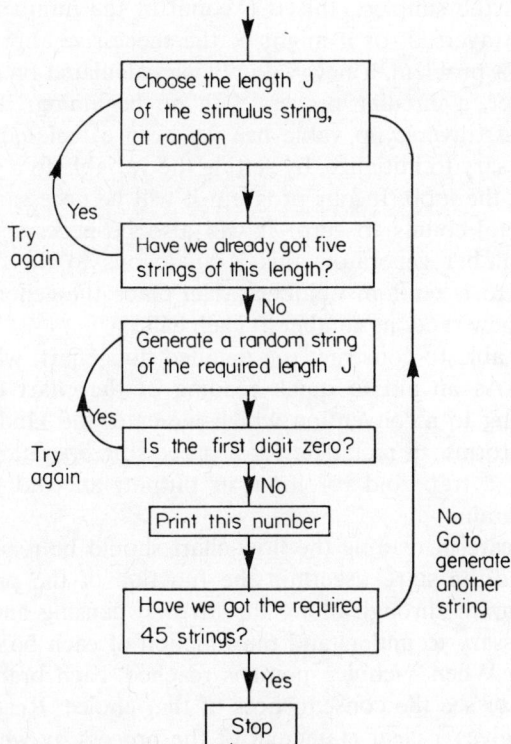

Figure 2.1—*Flow-chart showing the method to be used to produce strings of random digits*

The detailed flow-chart

We should now construct the detailed flow-chart, but before we can proceed we must clear up two points. We shall need random numbers, and we must recognize the need to initialize variables before entering the loops in which they are used.

Our program requires, at a number of stages, a number selected at random. Most computing systems have available a program which will output a random number within the range specified by the programmer. These random number generators can be used quite simply, without the need for a full understanding of the operations involved. For those who have to go further, Chapter 9 in Green (1963) describes some principles for the generation of random numbers. In the following, we use a standard program available in some versions of FORTRAN.

The second point, initialization, is an essential aspect of the use of program loops. Somewhere in almost every loop is a calculation which uses a variable the value of which was calculated on a previous traverse of the loop. At the simplest, this is a count of the number of times the loop has been traversed; or it might be the successive approximations to the solution of a problem, a new value being calculated on each traverse. This is, however, a circular process with no beginning; it can be seen that on the first traverse no value has yet been calculated for the variable. It is necessary to initialize, by setting the variable to a suitable value before entering the loop. In our program it will be necessary to initialize by setting several counts to zero; it will also be necessary to initialize the random number generator; this is analogous to the choosing of a point of entry to a random number table. Once the generator is set, it will produce a new random number at each call.

We are now able to construct the detailed flow-chart, which is shown in Figure 2.2. As an aid to quick reading of the chart the boxes are shaped according to a convention which indicates the kind of operation which each performs: a rectangle for a processing operation; a diamond for a decision; a trapezoid for input or output; an oval for beginning and end of program.

For a more careful reading the flow-chart should be read very slowly, as follows: find the start, ascertain the function of the program. Then follow the program through along the arrows, pausing and puzzling as long as is necessary to understand the function of each box before going on to the next. When a choice point is reached, each branch should be followed so as to see the consequences of that choice. Read in this way, the flow-chart gives a clear statement of the process by which the problem is solved.

The form of the chart is relatively independent of the programming

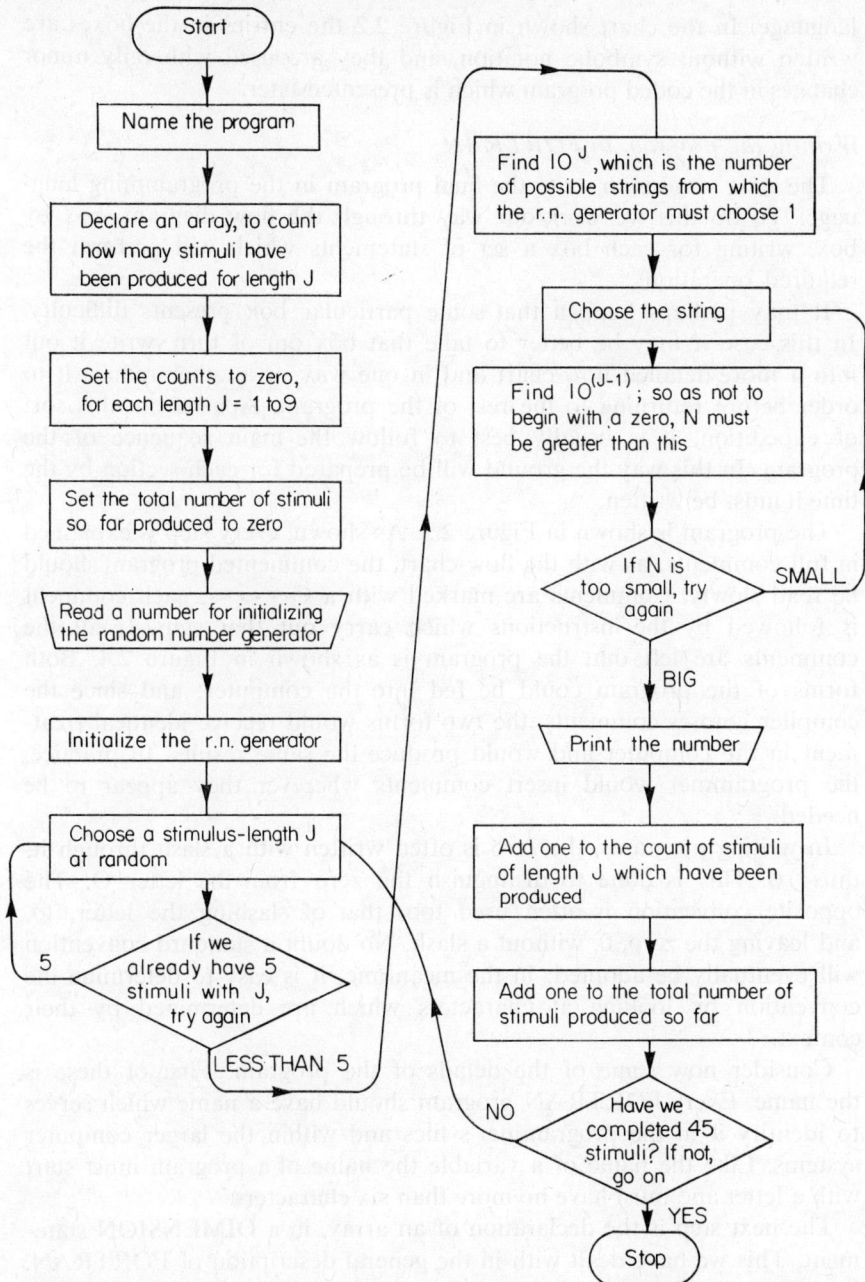

Figure 2.2—*Detailed flow-chart for a program to generate stimuli in the form of strings of random digits. 45 stimuli in all, 5 each of length one to nine digits. The first digit in each string must be non-zero*

language. In the chart shown in Figure 2.2 the entries in the boxes are written without symbolic notation, and they are used with only minor changes in the coded program which is presented later.

Writing the program in FORTRAN

The next stage is to write the final program in the programming language. To do this we work our way through the flow diagram, box by box, writing for each box a set of statements which will perform the required operation.

It may perhaps happen that some particular box presents difficulty. In this case it may be better to take that box out of turn, write it out into a more detailed flow-chart and in one way or another reduce it to order before returning to the rest of the program. Apart from this sort of expedition, it is usually best to follow the main sequence of the program. In this way the ground will be prepared for each section by the time it must be written.

The program is shown in Figure 2.3. As shown, every step is explained in full comments; as with the flow-chart, the commented program should be read slowly. Comments are marked with a C- - - - - -; each comment is followed by the instructions which carry out that step. If all the comments are left out, the program is as shown in Figure 2.4. Both forms of the program could be fed into the computer; and since the compiler ignores comments, the two forms would receive identical treatment in the computer and would produce the same results. In practice, the programmer would insert comments wherever they appear to be needed.

In writing programs, the zero is often written with a slash through it, thus: $\emptyset$. This is done to distinguish the zero from the letter O. The opposite convention is often used too, that of slashing the letter, $\emptyset$, and leaving the zero, 0, without a slash. No doubt a standard convention will eventually be adopted; in the meantime, it is easy to determine the convention by looking at characters which are determined by their context.

Consider now some of the details of the program. First of these is the name. Every FORTRAN program should have a name which serves to identify it in the programmer's files and within the larger computer systems. Like the name of a variable the name of a program must start with a letter and must have no more than six characters.

The next step is the declaration of an array, in a DIMENSION statement. This we have dealt with in the general description of FORTRAN, but another point arises here: the name of a variable or an array. We have seen that convenient names can be chosen for variables; in this

```
      PROGRAM RSTIM1
C........ DECLARE AN ARRAY, TO COUNT HOW MANY STIMULI HAVE BEEN
C........ PRODUCED FOR EACH LENGTH J.
      DIMENSION NWITHJ(9)
C........ SET THE COUNTS TO ZERO, FOR EACH LENGTH J = 1 TO 9.
      DO 1 J = 1,9
      NWITHJ(J) = 0
    1 CONTINUE
C........ SET THE TOTAL NUMBER OF STIMULI SO FAR PRODUCED, TO ZERO.
      NSTIM = 0
C........ READ A NUMBER FOR INITIALISING THE RANDOM NUMBER GENERATOR.
      READ 2, INISH
C........ INITIALISE THE RANDOM NUMBER GENERATOR.
      CALL IMFRIN(INISH)
C........ CHOOSE A STIMULUS LENGTH J AT RANDOM, FROM 1 TO 9.
C........ THE RANDOM NUMBER GENERATOR WILL GIVE FROM 0 TO 8, SO WE ADD 1.
    3 CALL IMFRDN(9,I)
      J = I + 1
C........ IF WE ALREADY HAVE FIVE STIMULI WITH J DIGITS,
C........ GO BACK TO STATEMENT 3 AND CHOOSE A NEW VALUE FOR J.
      IF (NWITHJ(J) .EQ. 5) GO TO 3
C........ FIND TEN TO THE POWER J, WHICH IS THE NUMBER OF POSSIBLE
C........ STRINGS FROM WHICH THE R.N. GENERATOR MUST CHOOSE ONE.
      NPOSS = 10**J
C........ CHOOSE THE STRING.
    4 CALL IMFRDN(NPOSS, NREQD)
C........ FIND TEN TO THE POWER (J - 1); IF IT IS NOT TO BEGIN WITH A ZERO,
C........ NREQD MUST BE GREATER THAN THIS.
      NBTM = 10**(J - 1)
C........ IF NREQD IS TOO SMALL, GO TO STATEMENT 4 AND TRY AGAIN.
      IF (NREQD .LT. NBTM) GO TO 4
C........ PRINT THE NUMBER.
      PRINT 5, NREQD
C........ ADD ONE TO THE COUNT OF STIMULI OF LENGTH J WHICH
C........ HAVE BEEN PRODUCED.
      NWITHJ(J) = NWITHJ(J) + 1
C........ ADD ONE TO THE TOTAL NUMBER OF STIMULI PRODUCED SO FAR.
      NSTIM = NSTIM + 1
C........ HAVE WE COMPLETED THE LIST OF 45 STIMULI?
C........ IF NOT, GO BACK TO STATEMENT 3 AND PRODUCE THE NEXT.
      IF (NSTIM .LT. 45) GO TO 3
C........ WHEN 45 STIMULI HAVE BEEN PRINTED, STOP.
      STOP
C........ FORMAT CARDS KEPT TOGETHER AT THE END,
C........ FOR EASY REFERENCE.
    2 FORMAT(I5)
    5 FORMAT(1H ,I10)
C........ INFORM THE COMPILER THAT THE END HAS BEEN REACHED.
      END
```

Figure 2.3—*A program to generate stimuli in the form of strings of random digits. 45 stimuli in all, 5 each of length one to nine digits. The first digit in each string must be non-zero*

program, we choose the names as they are needed, making them as descriptive as possible. All the variables which we use are integers; to avoid the necessity of declaring them, we choose names which identify them as such, i.e. they all start with one of the letters I, J, K, L, M, N. Thus NWITHJ is the name of a variable meaning 'the number of strings with J digits'. Since J may vary from one to nine, we declare an array with nine places, as DIMENSION NWITHJ(9). Whenever NWITHJ is specified in the program it will be necessary to specify which of the nine is meant: is it one digit, or two, ... or nine? We can do this by writing NWITHJ(3), for example, to specify three digits. Or we can write NWITHJ(J), which can be any of the nine, depending on the value of J at that stage of the calculation. If J has the value three, then it

FORTRAN IV PROGRAM RSTI..

```
                                    90803
                                       70
      PROGRAM RSTIM2                63508
      DIMENSION NWITHJ(9)             67
      DO 1 J = 1,9                     8
      NWITHJ(J) = 0                 24914
    1 CONTINUE                      34291
      NSTIM = 0                   1355152
      READ 2, INISH                 25095
      CALL IMFRIN(INISH)             5591
    3 CALL IMFRDN(9,I)          207993389
      J = I + 1                        7
      IF (NWITHJ(J) .EQ. 5) GO TO 3  234
      NPOSS = 10**J              3402075
    4 CALL IMFRDN(NPOSS, NREQD)       932
      NBTM = 10**(J - 1)         6951470
      IF (NREQD .LT. NBTM) GO TO 4  3558
      PRINT 5, NREQD                9032
      NWITHJ(J) = NWITHJ(J) + 1       14
      NSTIM = NSTIM + 1             8436
      IF (NSTIM .LT. 45) GO TO 3 97760272
      STOP                      502701633
    2 FORMAT(I5)                   337093
    5 FORMAT(1H ,I10)            6542966
      END                            22
                                53412793
                                       1
                                 4786895
                                  239398
                               652857754
                                     417
                                    1167
                                     552
                                     360
                                73513338
                                       6
                               425353119
                                       3
                               949161427
                                      12
                                  236897
                                77722283
                                99134086
                                  196094
                                  555487
```

**FORTRAN ** STOP

Figure 2.4—*The same program as in Figure 2.3, without the comments.*
(a) The program   (b) A set of stimuli, as printed out by the computer

becomes NWITHJ(3), and so on. In this way we can use a single statement to treat all the nine values of the array in turn.

To operate on all the nine values in turn, we use a DO statement. As
we have seen, this statement serves as a loop. The number after the DO,
in this case 1, is the number of a statement which comes later in the
program. In this case the statement is CONTINUE. (CONTINUE is a
dummy statement, used because it makes alterations easier; the computer
merely carries on with the program as specified by the other orders.)

When the computer reaches the DO statement it sets J = 1, and carries
on, using the value 1 whenever the program specifies J. When it reaches
the end of the loop, in this case the CONTINUE statement, control is
returned to the DO. This now sets J = 2 and goes through the loop as

before. The sequence is repeated until it has been done the full nine times. In this case this means that all nine values of NWITHJ(J) have been set to zero.

The READ statement has already been explained, and the FORMAT statement which goes with it, specifying an integer number occupying five columns of the card. The FORMAT statement for printing, statement number 5, specifies (1H_, I10). As explained in the section on input and output, the '1H_' has the effect of producing single spacing of the lines. The 'I10' prints out an integer number of 10 digits; if the number has less than ten digits the preceding places are left blank, so that the column of numbers will be lined up on the right.

The random number generator has two types of call: the initializing call, equivalent to choosing a point of entry into a random number table; and a call which is equivalent to reading a number from the table, and which produces a random number.

The generator is initialized by giving it a number with the call. We have named this number INISH (INISHializer). We use the call: CALL IMFRIN(INISH). Once the initialization has been performed, we can get a sequence of random numbers by calling: CALL IMFRDN(N,I). Each time we use this call, we get a random number called I with one of the N possible values $\emptyset$, 1, 2, 3, . . . , (N−1). For example, CALL IMFRDN (2,I) will give I the value of $\emptyset$ or 1 at random.

If we want to run the program again, and yet have a different sequence of random numbers, we can read in the value of INISH from a data card, as in the program shown; a new data card can then be used for each run of the program, with a value chosen arbitrarily or perhaps from random number tables. If on the other hand we want to obtain the same sequence of random numbers as before, we can initialize the generator with the same value of INISH as before. This was necessary, for example, in generating the Julesz figures (Figure 6.6, p. 160; these figures have a random pattern, but the pattern is the same for both members of the pair over most of the figure.

Coding the program

If the programmer has direct access to a computer, the program can be typed into the machine by its own teletypewriter. In other cases, the program must be coded, usually on to punched cards. The columns of the card are used in different ways for different languages. In FORTRAN, the usage is as follows.

Each card is punched to represent a single line of the program; this is either a single program statement or a line of comment.

Column 1 is the comment column. If the letter C is punched here, the rest of the card is ignored by the compiler. The line is printed out with the rest of the program, so that it can be read by the user, but it does not affect the execution of the program.

Columns 2–5 are used for statement numbers. By quoting these numbers in other statements, control can be transferred or reference can be made to particular statements, e.g. FORMAT statements.

Column 6 is the continuation column. Any symbol punched here will cause the card to be treated as simply a continuation of the previous card. This is necessary when a statement becomes so long that it cannot all be punched on one card.

Columns 7–72 are used for the FORTRAN statements. The program shown in Figure 2.4, without comments, would be punched in these columns; each new statement would start in column 7 of a new card. Only the statement numbers fall outside this range; all those in the program shown are single-digit numbers and would go into column 5. None of the statements needs to be continued, so column 6 is left blank.

The final eight columns of the card are free for any labelling which the programmer may require, as for example the numbering of the program cards in their correct sequence. These columns are not used in the computer.

Programs are commonly written on coding forms which are a direct representation of the 80-column card. The code is transferred to the cards by the programmer or by a card-punch operator. The resultant set of cards is called a program deck and this deck is stacked together with such data cards as are necessary and with a set of control cards. The complete pack is then fed into the computer. The control cards serve to organize the computer; they specify the programming language which is being used, which peripheral devices such as tape readers, magnetic tape, etc., are being used and so on. These control cards differ from one computer installation to the next, and in times of change may differ from one week to the next. The wise programmer will get to know his computer system.

The representation of numbers

When working in a high-level programming language such as FORTRAN one need never realize that the representation of numbers in the computer is not in the familiar decimal system. The decimal system, derived from our ten fingers, is not really suitable for machines which are built of switches and relays; as we saw in Chapter 1, a binary system is much more useful. Although it is no longer necessary to work in the binary system, a programmer should be aware of the binary system and of some of the other systems which are in use, especially if he is to use one of the smaller laboratory machines.

Decimal: the system which we normally use. There are ten digits: 0, 1, 2, . . . , 9. The value of a digit is determined by its position, counting from the right as units, tens, hundreds, etc. For example in the number 235, counting from the right, the digits have the values: $5\times1=5$; $3\times10=30$; $2\times100=200$. Adding these, we get $200+30+5=235$.

Binary. The system normally used inside the computer. There are only two digits: 0 and 1 (corresponding to *off* and *on* of a switch, *absent* and *present* of a hole or electrical pulse, etc.). The value of a digit is determined by its position, counting from the right as units, twos, fours, eights, etc. Thus binary 1 is decimal 1; binary 10 is decimal 2; binary 100 is decimal 4. Binary 111 is decimal 7 as follows: binary 111 = binary $100+10+1$ = decimal $4+2+1$ = decimal 7.

Octal, a system commonly used for programming. There are eight digits: 0, 1, 2, . . ., 7. A three-digit binary number is equivalent to one octal digit, and a binary number can be read 'in threes' as an octal number. Thus binary 110 is octal 6, binary 111 is octal 7; binary 110111 can be read in threes as octal 67 (decimal 55).

Octal numbers look like decimal numbers, but the values are different: units, eights, sixty-fours, etc. Thus octal 6 is decimal 6, but octal 66 is decimal $(6\times8)+6=54$.

Hexadecimal, commonly used in programming, to produce a compact printed number which can be simply derived from the binary. There are sixteen digits: 0, 1, 2, . . ., 9, A, B, C, D, E, F. The value of a digit is determined by its position: units, sixteens, two hundred and fifty-sixes, etc. Thus hexadecimal 9AF is decimal $(9\times256)+(10\times16)+(15\times1)=$ 2479. With large numbers, the saving in length is much greater.

Floating-point, a system for getting very large and very small numbers into the computer, and for typing them in a format which is easy to read. The number is stored in two parts; one gives the significant figures of the number, and the other gives the position of the decimal point as a power of ten (i.e. the point is allowed to float, and its correct position is stored separately).

Thus for example: 170 is 1·7 ** 2;
　　　　　　　　　　0·17 is 1·7 ** −1;
　　　　　　　　　　170 000 000 is 1·7 ** 8.

In the conventional scientific notation, these examples would be: 1.7×10^2; 1.7×10^{-1}; 1.7×10^8.

Program testing and programming techniques

Contrary to what is often said, it is quite possible to write programs which will work correctly when they are first run. To do this, however, requires practice and extreme care during the analysis of the problem, the writing of the program and the preparation and checking of the punched cards. Several techniques are useful in avoiding error and these will be discussed below; perhaps they can be summed up in the remark that it is better to be clear than to be clever.

For the testing of any but the smallest programs it is best to work systematically. Some of the most important points are noted here:

1. Will the proposed method of calculation work? Will it produce the desired results? This must be checked.

2. The program should be written in small parts which can be checked separately. Either they can be run by themselves for testing or the program can be written so as to print out intermediate results which will enable the programmer to locate the stage at which the program goes wrong.

   The use of subroutines and function programs helps to split the program into sections. Often standard programs can be used—computer systems are equipped with a set of system subroutines and functions and also with a library of subroutines. The system routines and functions can simply be called in the program; the compiler will automatically include them in the compiled object program. To use a library routine, the programmer obtains a copy of the program cards and includes them in his program deck. Again it is important to know your computer system; there is much unnecessary duplication of effort in computer programming.

3. The programmer must make sure that he has eliminated the traps into which a program may fall: Loops must be properly set up, variables initialized, so that the machine does not get stuck in a loop or miss the loop. Dividing by zero is an inadmissible operation, and such a possibility must be ruled out by proper writing or by writing into the program a test which will avoid the division if the divisor is zero. Numbers must not be allowed to get too large for the machine or too small for the required accuracy. Rounding-off errors must be kept within bounds. One such error occurs when the required result is a small difference between large numbers; the error

may be so large that the correct result is lost completely. A different method should be used to avoid this danger; it is usually possible to find the difference when the numbers are small, so that the errors are not multiplied up.

4. When the program is written, it will often be wise to work through it on paper or with a desk calculator, to see that the program gives a correct result; or perhaps known results are available and the results produced by the program can be checked against these. It is often useful to perform these checks with values of the data which may be critical in one way or another.

5. The calculation can be done by some other method at key points, by hand or by writing check programs which will reach the same result by an alternative route. Results from the program can be plotted as graphs, inspected for plausibility, etc. The point to notice here is that the program may work happily, may print out results, yet the results may be in error. Results must be suspected until they are proved correct.

6. There are many places inside a program where checks are useful and these should be written into any except the smallest programs. We must suspect that the calculation will not go as the programmer expects, and insert checks, for size of numbers, sign, zero, and so on. We must check also for possible faults in the data read-in, for data outside the expected range, and for other faults outside of the program itself which might creep in with the data.

7. Programs should be written to be as general as possible. The possible re-use of programs is one of the great advantages of computers, and by writing the program in a general form we make it available for uses other than the original one. Programming time is saved and opportunities for error are reduced. Perhaps the simplest way of giving a program generality is to use a variable wherever the specialized program would have a constant. The values of the variables can then be read into the program from a data card, and it is a simple matter to prepare a new data card if different values are to be used.

This writing for generality can be carried too far, however. It is often better to write the program, when it is first needed, in a fairly specialized form. This can be done relatively quickly and gives experience of the problem and of running it on the computer. When the program is needed again, for a slightly different problem, the more general program can be written with the benefit of hindsight.

8. Finally, a word directly to the reader who is new to programming: when you are testing a program remember that the computer is never at fault. It is your program that is wrong, difficult as it is to believe. There are exceptions, but this is a good rule nevertheless.

Documentation

The most important part of computer programming is the adequate documentation of the program. This documentation should be done at the time of writing the program, for to neglect it is to fall into chaos, a litter of unusable bundles of punched cards. Documentation makes the program available to users other than the writer of the program, and it is also necessary for the writer himself. It is astonishing how soon one can forget the subtleties and even the most obvious features of a program which at the time of writing seemed quite simple.

Documentation requires first of all a name for the program and a statement of the problem which the program is designed to solve. With these it can be classified and indexed; the index gives other users their first access to the program. There must be an adequate description of the program: the method which it uses to solve the problem, the limits of accuracy, the amount of store used, input-output media, and any special requirements. An example of input data should be shown, and the form of the output. A copy of the program should be provided, with full comments to explain its action and flow diagrams to make the pattern clear. A set of punched cards should be kept as a library copy which can be duplicated to provide a working set of cards. All this enables the user to obtain results with the minimum of effort.

Data processing for the psychologist

The ability of the computer to handle vast quantities of data has enabled psychologists to be more ambitious in their experiments. They can now study more subjects, more variables, more data on a single variable from the same subject, etc., with no need for a great increase in the time and effort spent processing the data. Even the time spent by the experimenter, either preparing coding sheets of data for the card-punch operators or punching the data himself, can be saved if the results of an experiment are automatically punched on paper tape. The data can then be read directly into the computer in this form or, if necessary, transferred by machine on to punched cards and then read into the computer.

We shall discuss four categories of data processing:

1. Analysis of the data for the purpose of making statistical inferences.
2. Calculation of the statistical parameters of the data. (Descriptive statistics.)
3. Graphical or tabular representation of the data.
4. Sorting and scoring of data, perhaps to derive guidelines for further experimentation.

For the last three of these applications the computer is always valuable but for the first, that of statistical inference, it can easily be misused. It is not lack of familiarity with computers which leads to misuse, but lack of consideration of the statistical implications of using more subjects in bigger and supposedly better experiments. Meehl (1967) has argued in some detail that the practice of behavioural scientists is faulty in this respect. They adopt directional hypotheses, for example that condition A will produce a greater score than condition B. There must however be many differences between the conditions other than those which are related to the particular hypothesis which the scientist wishes to investigate. If the experiment is made powerful enough, say by increasing the number of subjects, then one or other of these differences will show up as significant, and it is as probable as not that the difference will be in the predicted direction. If the scientist regards this result as confirmation of his hypothesis, then an error will be made. According to Meehl, then, if a relationship is sought with sufficient persistence a relationship will be found. Herein lies the danger of the computer, that it enables the experimenter to extend his search and at the same time it provides a technical distraction which might numb his critical sense.

Perhaps the problem is that statistical data processing is too easy. An experimenter must resist the temptation to collect more data and must consider carefully the statistical implications of his experimental design.

These comments on statistics and data processing are intended as a warning but not as a deterrent. The computer is indispensable for complicated factor analyses, analysis of variance, correlations, etc. Moreover, the psychologist wishing to analyse data is in the fortunate position of being able to use programs which have already been written and tested by experienced programmers. These programs can be used without knowledge of any programming language, by following the instructions given. The programs may be found in 'packages', such as the Biomedical package (Dixon, 1968) and the IBM SSP 3 package. The Biomedical package includes programs for Analysis of Variance, Analysis of Covariance, Discriminant Analysis, Principal Component

Analysis and Regression on Principal Components. The IBM package is a collection of 355 subroutines of which those falling under the following general headings are useful in psychology:

    (i) data screening

   (ii) correlation and regression

  (iii) design analysis

  (iv) discriminant analysis

   (v) factor analysis

  (vi) time series

 (vii) non-parametric statistics

(viii) distribution functions

  (ix) matrix manipulation.

The package includes also a program translation of Siegel's book on non-parametric statistics (Siegel, 1956).

A package designed for use in the social sciences is that produced by Nie, Bent and Hull (1970). An attractive feature of this package is the ease with which the data can be organized and the calculations controlled, by means of control cards. A second feature is the ability to compensate for data which has been missed during the experiment or survey. Most computer centres have statistical packages of this type —if no suitable programs are available the psychologist can always send his data to a data processing service, of which there are many.

The statistical programs provided in packages, or from any other source, should not be used indiscriminately. The psychologist must, as always, ensure that the program performs an analysis which fits his experimental design and that the program calculates statistics appropriate to his hypotheses. In addition to these packages, the journal *Behavioral Science* prints a series of computer program abstracts.

It is possible that a psychologist may wish to process data using a statistical test for which no program is available. He can then ask a programmer from his computer centre to write the program or he can write it himself. Writing programs for parametric statistics is fairly easy for they require only a straightforward translation of computational formulae into the computer code. Non-parametric programs can be a little more difficult, especially where ranking procedures are involved. Nevertheless, a person who can perform the computation should be able to write a suitable program. For statistical programs documentation is particularly important; it is very likely that these programs will be useful to other workers.

Computer programs for Factor Analysis are given in a book by Horst (1965). The methods described in the book are accompanied by almost a hundred programs in FORTRAN II. (FORTRAN IV is more commonly used in computer centres, but the difference between the two languages is small, and at least one of the programs from the book has run successfully when translated into FORTRAN IV.) Another book giving programs specifically for the behavioural sciences is by Veldman (1967). Authors of all textbooks on statistics should be encouraged to include programs in the text, where these are available, or at least to give references showing where the programs may be obtained. As stated in the programming section of this chapter, there is too much duplication of effort in program writing.

For the processing of data to derive descriptive statistics, there is a collection of programs known as 'Multiple Variate Counter' (Gurmukh Singh, 1968). The programs are designed to perform data transformations and groupings on the original data and then compute summary statistics. These statistics include frequency distributions, sums, means, standard deviations, chi-square and contingency tables. This system is ideal for data obtained from surveys, however complex.

The use of the computer to draw graphs is straightforward once the user has mastered the series of subroutines which control the movement of the graph plotter. These routines differ from installation to installation, so to make full use of the graph plotting facility the programmer must be familiar with the system he is using. If a graph plotter is not available, the ordinary computer print-out can be used for plotting graphs, as described in Chapter 1; but this is not usually as satisfactory nor as versatile as the graph plotter.

Plotting of histograms and tables is easily done, by writing a program to sort the data into the appropriate categories and print them in the required form.

Finally, the sorting and scoring of data requires no more than a program which uses conditional statements to compare the data with criteria set by the experimenter. If an item of data meets the criterion it is sorted into the associated category, or a score is kept by adding one to the previous score for the category. When the item does not meet any of the criteria the program passes on to examine the next item in the list.

Information retrieval and literature search

A use of computers very different from these should be mentioned— that of information retrieval or literature search. Several commercial organizations now prepare magnetic tapes carrying an index of scientific books and articles in journals. These tapes can be searched by computer, to print out a bibliography of the latest work on any specified subject. The cost of this service is now within the reach of a small research team or even of a lone worker.

Such a search is of course not perfect. Articles are missed, either because they have not been put on the tape or because they are indexed in one way and searched for in another. The contrary fault also occurs, that articles are listed which are not wanted; in a badly designed search these irrelevant articles may be so many as to swamp the user and sink the few articles which might have been useful. To avoid these opposing faults, search procedures are used in which a detailed specification is made in a complex logical statement. A single search, for example, might ask for articles by a *named author, and* any articles concerned with *learning* of *mazes, not* concerned with rats.

Information about these services may be obtained from libraries or from advertisements in the scientific and technical press.

Further Reading

Working Manuals, with which a person can learn practical programming and which he will then keep to hand. A manual of this sort is a necessity for any working programmer. Only a small selection is given.

Farino, M. V. (1968) *Programming in BASIC. The time-sharing language.* Prentice-Hall, Englewood Cliffs, New Jersey.

Griswold, R. E., J. F. Poage and I. P. Polonsky (1968) *The SNOBOL 4 Programming Language.* Prentice-Hall Englewood Cliffs, New Jersey. A Bell Systems language for working with strings of characters which may represent sentences, lists, data, etc.

McCracken, D. D. (1965) *A Guide to FORTRAN IV Programming.* Wiley, New York.

McCracken, D. D. (1962) *A Guide to ALGOL Programming.* Wiley, New York.

Pollack, S. V. and T. D. Sterling (1969) *A Guide to PL/1.* Holt, Rinehart and Winston, New York.

Scriber, T. J. (1969) *Fundamentals of Flow-charting.* Wiley, New York. An elementary textbook which shows in detail the methods by which flow-charting develops into a solution of the problem.

About Programming Languages

Foster, J. M. (1967) *List Processing.* MacDonald, London, and American Elsevier, New York. Computer monographs. A brief but comprehensive introduction to the subject.

Higman, B. (1967) *A Comparative Study of Programming Languages.* MacDonald, London, and American Elsevier, New York. A short and useful study.

Sammet, J. E. (1969) *Programming Languages: History and Fundamentals.* Prentice-Hall, Englewood Cliffs, New Jersey. A detailed study.

CHAPTER 3

Computer Languages for Experimental Control

Geoffrey Barrett

Introduction

Computers are often used for the off-line processing of data from experiments; but a quite different and more spectacular use of the computer arises when the computer receives information directly from experimental apparatus, for example through a lead from a subject's response button connected to the computer. If the computer also directly controls display apparatus through connecting leads, then it is possible for it to take complete control of the running of experiments on-line. In this chapter the software techniques available for psychologists wishing to use computers in this way will be examined. Examples of the use of computers in actual on-line experiments will be given in Chapter 4.

Psychologists whose experience of computers is limited to the use of machines housed in University computing centres are probably unaware of the routine operations required to run a program. This is because the program is run 'in secret' behind the closed doors of the computer room. As indicated in Chapter 2, the language of the computer is not FORTRAN IV or ALGOL but consists of instructions in binary code, and therefore the steps of each high-level language program have to be translated into the corresponding steps in binary code so that the computer can then recognize the required operations. The psychologist with direct access to a computer for running on-line experiments soon becomes aware of the need for this translation and of the hierarchy of programming languages considered in Chapter 2. This hierarchy runs from the language of the machine (binary code) through a machine-oriented assembly language to conversational and high-level languages. The machine-oriented nature of assembly language (i.e. each range of machines has its own specific language) makes it distinct from other programming languages. Although every computer uses binary code and, given adequate storage and the appropriate intermediate programs, can use conversational and high-level languages, each computer must have its own assembly language.

An indication of the difference between languages at different levels in the hierarchy is given in Table 3.1, taken from d'Agapayeff (1970, p. 94). It is obvious however from this table that the symbols used at all levels are far removed from the language used by experimenters in psychology. Very few computer users in any field program

Table 3.1—*Three forms of the same calculation*

(i)	in binary	101011–001101001 110111–001011001 101101–010110110
(ii)	in assembler code	F–C41 A–C54 S–D06
(iii)	in ALGOL	X: = B + C;

The calculation is to take the contents of the variable B, add it to the contents of C and place the sum in the location referred to as X. In (i) and (ii) the letters or digits before the hyphen refer to the operation code (i.e. Fetch, Add and Store) while those after the hyphen are the addresses of the variable in the computer store.

in binary code, for obvious reasons—errors are easily made and the programming process is lengthy. Therefore, assembly languages in which there is a one-to-one relationship between the symbols of the assembly code and the operations of the computer have been developed. This relationship is achieved by using a language composed of mnemonic symbols, which thus aid programming. The specific mnemonic language of the Digital Equipment Corporation PDP–8 family of computers is called PAL (Program Assembly Language). Examples of these mnemonics are:

DCA   Deposit and Clear the Accumulator
JMP   Jump
ISZ   Increment and Skip if Zero
JMS   Jump to Sub routine.

A program written in assembly code must be checked for grammatical errors, in terms of the language, and translated into binary code before it can actually run on the computer. This is done by 'passing' the program tape through the computer a number of times, the number of 'passes' being determined by the computer in use and the amount of store available. The original program tape is called the source program and the resultant binary coded tape is called the object program. When the source program is passed through the computer, there is another program, called an assembler, in the store of the computer. The assembler performs a one-to-one translation of the mnemonic code into binary numbers. Different assemblers require different numbers of passes to generate the object program. For example, the PAL assembler mentioned earlier is a two-pass assembler where 4k of core store is available, while the Computer Technology Modular One machine uses an assembler that also operates in 4k of store but requires only one pass for translation. During the first pass most assemblers detect grammatical errors in the source program. Any errors detected are printed out with a description known as a diagnostic, and the program must be corrected in order to run properly. The main purpose of the assembler is to provide the user with the object program. This tape can be read into the computer whenever the user wishes to run the program. These operations involving paper tapes only apply where a small computer, with a minimum amount of core store and no backing store, is being used. When backing store is available, for example on disc, or magnetic tape, the intermediate programs and final object program can be stored on these media, thus eliminating the problem of handling paper tape.

It is apparent that programming a computer to run an experiment is not simply a matter of writing a program, feeding it into the computer and starting the experiment. Instead, there are a number of necessary operations required before the experiment can be run. There are more operations involved when the control program is written in a high-level language rather than assembly language because the program has to be checked for errors, reduced to an intermediate code (usually the assembly code of the machine) and finally translated into binary code to give the object program. The total number of operations involved is dependent upon the efficiency of the intermediate programs and the amount of core store and backing store available. A program written in FORTRAN for a PDP–8 with 8k of core store requires three passes to obtain the object program, while a similar program requires two passes on a Modular One with 8k of core store and only one pass on the same machine with 16k of core store.

The psychologist wishing to run an on-line experiment is apparently faced with two equally unattractive possibilities. First, he can learn the complicated assembly language of the computer, which has symbols related to the operations of the computer but not to the operations of the experiment. Programs writtten in this language can be quickly implemented on the machine once proficiency has been acquired. Secondly, he can learn a more 'meaningful' high-level language such as FORTRAN. However, this type of language still uses operations unrelated to the language of psychology experiments. FORTRAN and ALGOL were both designed for mathematical operations. Therefore, in the same sense that assembly languages are machine-oriented so FORTRAN and ALGOL are said to be problem-oriented, but they are not oriented towards the particular problem of programming experiments.

Fortunately for psychologists, the irrelevance of these languages has not been disregarded and a number of solutions have been provided by individual workers, specialist groups and industry. The solutions have taken into account the special requirements of psychology experiments run on-line, and are therefore problem-oriented. However, to be strictly correct, a number of the solutions have been developed specifically for particular computers and consequently the languages are only suitable for use on the computer concerned or identical models. These languages are also, therefore, machine-oriented.

The most important distinction between a computer used for data processing and a computer used to run on-line experiments is that experimental control takes place in real-time, i.e. the time scale of computer operation is critical and is dictated by the requirements of an environment external to the computer. In more concrete terms this means that every response must be recorded and every stimulus presented at the appropriate time and by the appropriate equipment. This indicates four important requirements of a language for on-line control:

(i) timing of events must be easily specified, i.e. when an event is to occur, when an event occurred, and the repetitive timing of events.

(ii) equipment definition must be easy, i.e. the programmer must be able to specify all the peripheral equipment preferably by name.

(iii) a wide variety of data types must be allowed, e.g. strings (sequences of characters, contained within quotes, which can be treated either as variables or constants) and lists (values connected by links rather than by sequential order in the store of the computer, see Chapter 2, p.30). These data types are not normal in FORTRAN and ALGOL.

(iv) the programmer must be able to interact with the ongoing program.

The abilities of different languages and other programming solutions to deal with these and other requirements are considered below.

There are basically three different solutions to the problem of programming a computer to run on-line psychology experiments.

(i) use of languages specifically written for controlling psychology experiments, e.g. PSYCHOL (McLean, 1969), PSYCLE (Creelman, 1969), ECL (Francis and Sutherland, 1969). These may be called problem-specific solutions.

(ii) use of languages specifically written for psychology experiments, to be used in conjunction with a specially designed interface, e.g. SCAT (Grason-Stadler Co., 1970), ACT (Millenson and LVE Staff, 1969). These may be called problem-specific, dependent solutions.

(iii) use of FORTRAN with assembly language subroutines, e.g. Haber *et al.* (1970), or FORTRAN with FORTRAN subroutines, e.g. Restle and Brown (1969). Any other general purpose, high-level language could be used instead of FORTRAN. These may be called non-specific solutions.

Problem-specific solutions

PSYCHOL was developed at Carnegie-Mellon University for use on a Honeywell DDP–116 computer, with 16k words of core store and a disc as backing store. Because of this large amount of core, a source program requires only two passes to be translated into the object program which is stored on the disc. The language has also been implemented on a PDP–9 computer. PSYCHOL is based on ALGOL but has been extended especially in the area of allowed data types.

The programming of timing is straightforward and comprehensive. In the same way that statement numbers can be assigned to statements in FORTRAN to facilitate transfer of control and repetition of certain parts of a program (Chapter 2, p.35), ALGOL uses 'labels'. A label can be an identifier, i.e. a combination of alphanumeric characters (the letters A to Z and the numbers 0 to 9) not beginning with a number (cf. 'variable name' in FORTRAN), as well as a statement number. Thus meaningful labels, such as TRIAL, BLOCK, SET1, etc., can be used for transferring control within a program. These labels are used in PSYCHOL for relative timing within a program. This is done by automatically associating with each label the time at which control last passed that point. Constraints on the time at which events are permitted can then be applied by referring to a 'temporal label' associated with the event. For example, if the label LIGHT is associated with a procedure for switching on a stimulus lamp, and control passes this label at a particular time thus lighting the lamp, then a subsequent label LIGHT+ 500MSEC cannot be passed by control until 500 milliseconds after it has passed the label LIGHT. This ensures that the stimulus lamp stays on for at least 500 milliseconds. If control reaches the label LIGHT+ 500MSEC before the 500 msecs. have passed, the program will be held up until the condition has been met. The time expression may be an arithmetic expression so that the time delay can be variable, depending, for example, on previous responses.

Another timing feature is use of the command WAIT. The use of this instruction allows the program to wait for a specified period of time or to wait for a period of time after the passing of a label (cf. the temporal label), e.g.

WAIT 3 SECONDS;
WAIT UNTIL LIGHT+5 SECONDS;

(Unlike FORTRAN which does not use an end-of-statement symbol, ALGOL, and therefore PSYCHOL, uses a semi-colon to identify the end of a statement.)

A third timing instruction allows the repeated execution of a statement until a particular time, e.g.

UNTIL LIGHT+300MSEC DO . . . .;

This instruction could be used in an experiment where a subject was required to count the number of auditory pips presented whilst a light was on. Thus in the construction above, the statement after the DO command would switch on an auditory stimulus to be presented at a pre-set rate during the first 300 msec. of a visual stimulus.

The final timing feature is the presence of a function CLOCK. This is used in recording the latency of responses in such a way that they may be used in arithmetic expressions, and also, when requested, gives the length of time since the beginning of the experiment.

The timing features of PSYCHOL obviously fulfil the requirements of a language for on-line control outlined earlier, i.e. timing of events is easy using the command:

WAIT UNTIL 'label+time';*

The repetition of events is achieved using the construction:

UNTIL 'label+time' DO . . .;

The timing of responses is easy using the function CLOCK, which also provides the result in a form that can be used in arithmetic expressions. The names of all these constructions are associated with time so that their utility is easy to understand.

The second requirement of an on-line language, equipment definition, is closely related to timing of events and event definition, because these

* In the constructions given throughout the chapter, words typed in lower case and enclosed between apostrophies describe the type of statement to be inserted.

events are either presented by, or received from, the equipment. The varied nature of stimuli and responses used in psychology experiments prohibits the use of the standard input and output statements READ and PRINT. These statements are especially limited for the input of information because a subject's response will not always occur at the same time as the READ statement in the program. On many occasions the program will have to wait for the subject to respond and in some cases the subject may not respond at all, for example in a signal detection experiment—in which case a limited period of time for accepting the response has to be specified or the experiment will stop. Similarly, provision must be made within the program for accepting responses only at relevant times. For example, in a reaction-time experiment, anticipation responses (i.e. responses that occur before the stimulus has been presented) must not be included with the set of correctly timed responses.

PSYCHOL provides a number of commands for dealing with responses in a manner determined by the experiment. Let us suppose that the required response in a reaction-time experiment, using stimuli presented around absolute threshold level, is a button press. The button used is recognized by assigning a name to it (identifier) and also naming the subject interface being used; the interface may be thought of as an experimental room. This prevents confusion between buttons with the same name but in different locations. The name of the response medium and the experimental room are declared at the beginning of a program in the same way that variable types REAL and INTEGER are declared in FORTRAN and ALGOL programs. Thus:

RESPONSE button FROM room1;

defines the response medium 'button' in 'room 1' where RESPONSE and FROM are declarations (cf. REAL and INTEGER) and 'button' and 'room 1' are identifiers (variable names). Because of the liminal nature of the stimulus in this experiment it is possible that the subject will do one of the following:

 (i) anticipate the stimulus and respond too early;

 (ii) react correctly to the stimulus;

(iii) not respond at all.

In the first case it is necessary to ensure that the response will only be accepted after the stimulus has been presented. This is achieved by using the command:

PERMIT 'response identifier';

The command must be obeyed immediately after the stimulus has been presented. Associated with the PERMIT command is the PROHIBIT command which prevents responses from the identified medium being accepted. Thus in the example being considered the statement:

'label': PERMIT button;

allows a response from the button to be accepted, while the statement:

'label': PROHIBIT button;

prevents a response being accepted. Thus if the subject responds before the stimulus is presented the response will not be recorded. Presumably some mechanism for detecting that a response has been made will be programmed so that the response can be recorded as 'anticipated' and control returned to the appropriate section of the program.

In the second case, where the subject reacts correctly to the stimulus, the latency of the response may be obtained by simply requesting it in the form:

time: =LATENCY OF button;

This statement assigns to the variable 'time' the elapsed time in milliseconds since the last PERMIT of the response 'button'.

In the third case, the construction:

AWAIT button FOR n SECONDS;

can be used. The value 'n' may either be a constant or an arithmetic expression. Execution of the program continues automatically either after n seconds or after the response occurs, whichever is the sooner. Thus, if the subject does not respond to the stimulus within the alloted time, the trial will be recorded as receiving no response and the program will continue accordingly.

The AWAIT command can also be used without the temporal modifier, FOR, to suspend execution of the program until the response is made. Thus, the statement:

AWAIT button;

while not suited to the reaction-time experiment considered above could be used in a fixed-choice experiment where the subject is forced to make a response without the decision time being important.

Simple stimuli are presented according to the arrangement of 0's and 1's in an output register which is usually one computer word in length. It is possible that, although there are a large number of possible arrangements of 0's and 1's in the register, only one 'on' (1) bit will be needed to control a stimulus. For example, this gives 16 possible stimuli for a computer with a 16 bit word length, and in such a computer the arrangement:

0000000000001000

might be connected to a stimulus lamp. Individual bits in the register can be set and reset according to the 1's in the respective commands:

TURN ON 8;
TURN OFF a+b;

The TURN ON command will set the output register to the binary equivalent of 8 which is the arrangement shown above, and thus the command will turn on the stimulus lamp. The TURN OFF command turns off any bits corresponding to the 1 bits in the sum a+b, leaving other bits unchanged. Thus, if the sum of a and b is 25, the first, fourth and fifth bits of the output register will be turned off, because the binary representation of 25 is 11001.

The TURN ON and TURN OFF commands operate on individual bits of the output register; another command, OUTPUT, is provided for setting the entire register to the value of an expression or variable, e.g.

OUTPUT c;

Any of the stimulus commands may have a temporal modifier that states the time at which the operation will be reversed or, in the case of OUTPUT, all bits will be set to zero; e.g. the instruction:

OUTPUT a FOR 5 SECONDS;

sets the output register to the contents of the variable 'a' for a period of five seconds and then resets the register to all zeros.

The requirement of easy presentation of stimuli and recording of responses is adequately met by the commands of PSYCHOL. As with the timing of events, the commands used are explicit and appropriate to the language of the on-line experiment.

Another requirement of an on-line language is that it must be able to recognize and manipulate a variety of data types. Single integers or letters are rarely used as stimuli in psychology experiments whereas strings of integers and letters, often in combination, are frequently used, for example in memory experiments. High-level languages like FORTRAN and ALGOL cannot handle strings and lists as standard data types, so the following possible data types and declarations have been added to PSYCHOL:

(i) strings—these are used for the representation of alphanumeric information as text which can be used, for instance as stimuli in memory experiments. A text string may be associated with an identifier by declaration or, when enclosed within single quotes, as a string constant. These strings can be used for response checking as well as stimulus generation and would be particularly useful in the Socratic method of Computer-Assisted Instruction (see Chapter 10, p.252).

(ii) lists of integers—these are ordered sets of integers that can contain any integer values in a specified order.

(iii) string lists—these are lists of arbitrarily long strings of text that are associated in an order.

(iv) task list—this is a list of portions of executable program that can either be performed in the order listed or in random order. For example, the list can include stimulus generators such as random number generators and normal distribution functions, for creating stimuli or variables internal to the main program.

(v) historic variables—these are integer variables that keep a record of information for a specified number of trials within the experiment. The variable is associated with a particular label, such as LIGHT in the example on p. 61, and each time control passes this label the contents of the variable are pushed one step into history and a new storage register is made available for the next value of the variable. The variables are stored as a finite list where the length of the list is specified by the experimenter. As an illustration, in the threshold reaction-time experiment described earlier, the experimenter may wish to keep a list of the stimuli that were missed by the subject. The list can then be interrogated when it contains the specified number of trials. The nature of the values in this list gives an indication of whether the subject's threshold is changing during the experiment and any of the missed values can be selected for re-presentation to the subject.

Associated with the five additional data types are manipulations appropriate to the presentation of stimuli and recording of responses.

Strings—specified sections of strings can be presented as stimuli or used to check responses. Three constructions may be used to divide a string in different ways. For example, the following statement declares that the identifier 'text' is a string made up of the letters abcdefg.

STRING text: =abcdefg;

The expression:

text BEFORE 'd';

gives the string abc.

The expression:

> text AFTER 'd';

gives the string efg.

The expression:

> text TO 'd';

gives the string abcd.

The identifier before the command in any of these expressions may refer to an item from a string list. These constructions are useful, in learning experiments, for presenting lists of paired associates.

Lists—each list has a pointer associated with it that determines the currently referenced item. The pointer may be moved along the list or reset to the top using the following commands:

> NEXT OF 'listname';
> INITIALIZE 'listname';

Items in the list may be referenced by the special construction:

> 'arithmetic expression' TH OF 'listname';

The 'arithmetic expression' determines which value of the list is referenced. The 0th item is the current item and any positive value refers to the item in that position of the list, where the first value in the list is item 1. Negative numbers are allowed and refer to the value taken backwards for the defined number of steps from the current pointer item. The list is considered to be circular so that the last item in the list effectively precedes the first. The use of this construction is demonstrated in the following example:

> INTEGER LIST values: = 1, 2, 3, 4, 5, 6, 7, 8, 9, 0;

This statement declares the identifier 'values' to be a list of integers and assigns the numbers 1, 2, 3, 4, 5, 6, 7, 8, 9, 0 to the list. The expression:

> 6TH OF values;

gives the value 6. However, the values given by the expressions:

> 0TH OF values; . . . . (i)
> −3TH OF values; . . . . (ii)

depend on the location of the current pointer. If the pointer is at 4, expression (i) has the value 4 and expression (ii) the value 1. If the pointer is at 2, expression (ii) gives the value 9.

These commands and constructions can be used for selection of stimuli from a list according to a subject's response because the response can be used in the arithmetic expression that determines the list item to be presented. For example, in a computer-assisted instruction program, hints can be stored as a list of text strings and the appropriate hint may be referenced according to the subject's mistake or request.

Although the language provides suitable data types for experimentation, the constructions for the manipulation of the data types could certainly be more comprehensive. A list of constructions necessary for real-time control of operations will be discussed later.

A declaration is a statement that identifies a variable as a member of a particular class. For example, in FORTRAN and ALGOL variables are declared as either INTEGER or REAL. Two special declarations are provided in PSYCHOL:

(i) event declarations—these can be used by the experimenter to record the order of progress of an experiment, by making a suitable mark in the output of the experiment. This feature is very important in on-line experiments because the computer generally controls the order of presentation of stimuli and the experimenter is unaware of what the subject has responded to until he examines the output. Appropriate marks on the output assist the experimenter in his analysis and description of the experiment and the subject's performance.

(ii) response declarations—these were dealt with earlier on p. 63. They are used to identify a variable name as a piece of response equipment and to identify the location of the equipment.

The experimenter is able to interact with the running program only if suitable provision has been made. The nature of the interaction is that the experimenter is able to type in values for initialization of an experiment, or a run within an experiment, whenever queried by the teletypewriter. This interaction is facilitated by including the command PARAMETER associated with the variables to be set, at the appropriate point in the program. Thus, the construction:

  PARAMETER trials, limit, intensity;

can be used in the threshold reaction-time experiment described earlier, to set the number of trials, the maximum length of time to wait for a response and the initial stimulus intensity.

The language also has provision for writing subroutines (see Chapter 2, p. 37) separate from the main body of the program. These subprograms are called TASKs and, as stated earlier, are useful for generating stimuli and performing other routine tasks within the experiment. If PSYCHOL does not have suitable commands for a particular operation the operation can be coded in assembly language.

The PSYCHOL language is considered in detail because it is the only language at present reported in detail in the literature that is specifically written for the control of general psychology experiments.

Another general language, called PSYCLE, was originally written for the control of psychoacoustic experiments using a PDP-8/S (Creelman, 1969), but has since been extended for use in a real-time, time-sharing system on a modified PDP-9 (Taylor and Forsyth, 1969). This language allows the user to describe processes in the experiment in terms closely approximating to natural language. An instruction such as:

start the tone 5secs after button A is pressed

is typical. Programs are written in sequential blocks which cannot be nested. The blocks may or may not be labelled and the experiment is controlled according to conditional statements within the blocks. The full details of the implementation on the time-sharing system are complex because user's programs have to be protected from interference by other programs, and the operation of programs in both 'foreground' and 'background' has to be controlled.

Another language, ECL (Experimental Control Language), has been developed primarily to control animal experiments in a time-sharing environment. The implementation is on an Elliott 4130 with 32k of core store, 24 bit word, and a 4 million character disc as backing store housed at the Laboratory of Experimental Psychology, University of Sussex. As in PSYCHOL, the language is based on ALGOL with a number of exceptions and additions.

Two additions to the language are the provision of records and tables.

Records

General purpose arrays (cf. Chapter 2, p. 34) are one of the ALGOL features excluded from the ECL language. However, the function of storing and outputting data is performed using the RECORD declaration. The declaration sets up an area in the store of the computer to accommodate the value(s) of the identifier. Within the same statement is a definition of the format for printing the record at the end of the experiment. The programmer must declare the largest number that he wishes to store with each record item. For example:

RECORD PRESSES MAX 500;

causes the number held in PRESSES to be printed on a single line at the end of the experiment, the number must not exceed 500.

If there are several items to be recorded in cells of different sizes the terms ABOVE and LEFTOF can be used to form a construction of the following type:

RECORD X MAX 20 LEFTOF Y MAX 30 ABOVE Z MAX 50;

this causes X to be printed to the left of Y on one line and Z on the next line, at the end of the experiment.

Although arrays, as such, are not catered for in the language, they are effectively formed by declaring the number of times an item is repeated within a record. To allow for print out of long records, the user can state whether the record is to be printed DOWN or ACROSS. For example, the declaration:

RECORD A MAX 35 BY 100 DOWN ABOVE B
MAX 10 BY 5 ACROSS;

causes the 100 items of A to be printed down the page, above the five values of B printed across the page. The term BY specifies the number of times an item within a record is repeated.

The RECORD declaration can be extended to store and print data in groups as well as multi-dimensional arrays. A further useful feature of the declaration is that it can be used to construct histograms; i.e. instead of simply entering a number into a record, a number which is already stored in a record is increased by 1. Histograms are declared by writing INC after the maximum allowed size, e.g.

RECORD HIST MAX 200 INC, BY 10 DOWN;

While a program is in operation entries are made to records using a RESULT statement. The system of recording items is made flexible by allowing the name of a record to act as a variable so that data can be manipulated before storage. For example, the average of a series of trials can be recorded rather than each individual item, thus saving much storage space.

The following example shows how the RESULT statement is used, together with some other constructions not considered here in detail. Let us suppose that a histogram of response latencies is required with each column ('bin') representing 5 seconds, all responses over 30 seconds being stored in a seventh bin and a maximum of 40 entries per bin. The histogram, identified as LAT, may be declared by the statement:

RECORD LAT SEC 40 INC, BY 7 ACROSS;

The term SEC is substituted for MAX, indicating that times are to be recorded in seconds. The following statement can be used to store the data:

RESULT LAT[1+(CLOCK−OLDCLOCK)/5];

where CLOCK is an identifier associated with the present time and OLDCLOCK is the value of a previous time. Therefore (CLOCK−OLD-CLOCK) is the response latency. One is added to the quotient because the index number of the first item in the histogram is 1 and not 0. The value inside the square brackets is rounded down to the nearest integer and stored in the associated bin of the histogram. Thus, the first bin of the histogram represents latencies from 0 to 4·9 secs., the second bin represents 5 to 9·9 secs. and so on until the seventh bin, which represents all latencies of 30 secs. and over. The RESULT statement automatically references the final bin if the maximum specified response latency is exceeded.

The comprehensive nature of the RECORD declaration and its associated constructions distinguish ECL as a language eminently suitable for controlling animal experiments, because large amounts of data can be specified and presented in an appropriate manner with comparative programming ease. This is particularly necessary in a system which interrogates 96 response lines every 16msec!

Tables

The declaration and use of tables is very similar to that of the integer lists of PSYCHOL (p. 67). The term 'table' in ECL is specifically defined as a list of integers used for determining stimulus settings from one trial to another. These may be accessed in either cyclic or random order. A table is set up using the following declaration:

TABLE name: 1, 2, 3, 4, 5, 6, 7, 8, 9, 0;

a suitable identifier is substituted for 'name'. Values are retrieved from the table using the statement:

GET name [N];

which sets the identifier 'name' to the Nth value of the table; or the statement:

GET name;

where the entry fetched is dependent on the previous GET statement in the program. If the previous statement specified a subscript the same entry is fetched, otherwise the next item is taken cyclically.

The timing of events in ECL uses constructions of the WAIT statement.

When a WAIT statement is encountered, the program halts until the event specified occurs, e.g. the construction:

WAIT TILL response;

causes the program to halt until the specified 'response' occurs. The statements can be constructed so that the program will restart when any one of a number of specified responses occurs.

When it is necessary to wait for a fixed time interval to elapse, the following statement is used:

WAIT FOR n SEC;

the time waited is dependent on the value of n.

It is also possible to write a statement that will cause the program to halt for an absolute time rather than a fixed time from the last event. For example, consider the following short section of a program:

$$A: = CLOCK + 30 \ SEC;$$
$$REPEAT: \quad WAIT \ UP \ TO \ A$$
$$ELSE \ TILL \ RESPONSE: \ (INC \ COUNT; \ GO \ TO$$
$$REPEAT);$$

The construction WAIT UP TO . . . ELSE TILL . . . ; has a similar effect to the AWAIT . . . FOR . . . SECONDS; construction of PSYCHOL (p. 64). CLOCK is a special variable that takes the current value of the real-time clock and can be referenced at any time during the experiment. The first statement assigns to the identifier A, the present clock reading (in 1/64ths of a second) plus $30 \times 64 = 1920$. Together these specify the value of the clock reading in thirty seconds time, because the clock counts in 64ths of a second. The second statement causes the program to wait either until the value of A is reached, or a response is made. If a response is made within the time limit the value of COUNT is INCreased by 1 and then control is returned to the previous statement because it is associated with the label REPEAT. The effect of this section of program, therefore, is to count all the responses called RESPONSE occurring during a 30-second interval.

The control of output lines is very similar to PSYCHOL (p. 65) except that the terms SET and UNSET are used instead of TURN ON and TURN OFF respectively. For example, the statement:

SET REWARD;

opens an output line for delivering a reward.

As stated earlier the language is well suited to controlling on-line animal experiments. It is easy to understand and uses terms and constructions which relate to the language of the psychology experiment.

The timing of events is easily specified, as are input and output lines. There are fewer data types available than in PSYCHOL but strings and textual information are not normally required in animal experiments. Probably the main feature of the language is the provision of the comprehensive system for recording and producing data. The language is only in its first stages and a number of additions both for enhancing the properties of the language and for improving the time-sharing facilities are in hand.

Problem-specific, dependent solutions

The second solution to the problem of programming psychology experiments involves the provision of special hardware as well as a special control language. The language SCAT (State Change Algorithm Terminology) is associated with a specially designed interface for connecting to a PDP-8/I computer with 8k of core store. The system is designed to run in a real-time, time-sharing mode. The ACT (Automatic Contingency Translator) language is also designed to run in this mode, again via a purpose built interface, and has been implemented on PDP-8 and PDP-9 computers (Millenson, 1970). Both languages consist of user-defined states and transitions (state changes). A state is represented by the stimuli output to a subject, e.g. a light or a bell. Transitions between states are determined either by subject-initiated inputs, e.g. a bar press, or by factors defined in the program. These factors may be the passage of specified times, e.g. 'after 30 seconds, give stimulus 1', or computed events, e.g. 'if the 5th trial with stimulus 3 has been given, give stimulus 4'.

The main purpose of the SCAT language is to provide a suitable notation for describing a control sequence. The general form is:

state name: state description clause; state change clause'

The *state name* is symbolized as:

Cnn:

where the 'C' indicates a control state statement, 'nn' is an integer which provides the name of the state, and ':' indicates that the state name is over and the state description follows.

The *state description clause* can consist of two types of structure involving presentation of stimuli and recording of data. The stimulus commands take the form:

S1,S2 . . ., S12

and generate signals to apparatus connected to the specified stimulus line(s).

The language can gather data in a number of easily specified forms. For example, the construction:

R(m, n)

is called a logical counter and holds up operation of the program until m type n events have been received; e.g.

R(20,1)

will hold up program operation until twenty type one events have been received. A type one event may be a bar press, in which case the suitability of the language to conditioning experiments is immediately apparent.

The construction:

(t)SEC

suspends operation of a program for a period of t-seconds.

SCAT provides a number of 'data elements' useful both for program control and for storing data ready for output in a suitable form. As stated earlier in the discussion of ECL, this feature is particularly important when controlling animal experiments which are notorious for producing almost unmanageable amounts of data.

Five different types of data element are defined as follows:

(i) *Counters*—there are ten of these per program and they are designated as: CTR1,..., CTR0. Each Counter holds a number which may be set by the program or by experimenter interaction through the control teletypewriter.

(ii) *Constants*—ten Constants per program are allowed, named: CON1, ..., CON0. Constants are functionally identical to Counters in that they may be set either by the program or by user interaction.

(iii) *Clocks*—ten Clocks per program are allowed, named: CLK1,..., CLK0. Each Clock holds a number designating a time interval measured in seconds. Although the Clocks never stop running they can be set by the program or by user interaction.

(iv) *Histograms*—ten independent Histograms are allowed within the program, named: HIST1,..., HIST0. Unlike the three previous data types, Histograms can only be filled by the program. The expression HIST(x,n) causes the value of x to be added to the appropriate bin of the nth Histogram; where x is a number, the name of a data element (e.g. CLK1), or an arithmetic expression involving several data elements, and n is a positive integer less than 10. The command: ZHISTn is used to zero all bins of the nth Histogram.

(v) *Lists*—functionally these are sets of individual storage cells which act in a similar way to Counters except that the contents can be output as a list. The number of cells in a List is limited only by the amount of store available to the user. List cells can be manipulated using the form: LIST(nn) where 'nn' is an integer, a data element or an arithmetic expression. Unlike the 'lists' used in PSYCHOL and the 'tables' of ECL, the SCAT Lists are used for data collection rather than stimulus presentation.

Data elements are filled by setting them to an expression; e.g. the statement:

$$CTR5 < (CLK4+CON2)$$

puts the sum of the values in Clock4 and Constant2, into Counter5. (The symbol $<$ performs the same operation in SCAT as the equals sign '$=$' in FORTRAN, and the assignment symbol '$:=$' in ALGOL.)

The *state change clause* describes the conditions for leaving that state defined by the state name and the state description clause. The general form of the clause is:

(condition) $>$ (state name)

which may be translated as: 'If and when the specified condition is satisfied, go to the named state.' The symbol $>$ performs the same transfer of control operations as the 'GOTO' statement of FORTRAN (Chapter 2, p. 35).

Exits from the state are caused by events falling into one of the four categories:

(i) signals received from the outside world; e.g. $R(20,3) > (20)$, i.e. 'when twenty type three events have occurred, go to state 20'.

(ii) the lapse of a specified time interval; e.g. $(5)SEC > (50)$, i.e. 'after five seconds have passed go to state 50'.

(iii) tests on data elements; e.g. $(CTR3.E.CTR5) > (10)$, i.e. 'if the content of Counter 3 equals the content of Counter 5 go to state 10'.

(iv) the absence of any conditional phrase causes an unconditional exit; e.g. $> (20)$, i.e. 'go to state 20'.

Complex clauses may be constructed from state change phrases; e.g. the construction:

$$R(5,2) > (10), (CLK2.E.CTR4) > (20), (20)SEC > (30)$$

reads 'if five events of type two have been received, go to state ten; if the content of Clock 2 equals the content of Counter 4, go to state 20; if twenty seconds have elapsed, go to state 30'. The construction is scanned from left to right and the decision to go to state 10, 20 or 30 is determined by which condition is satisfied first.

The address, or state, to which control is transferred can be the contents of a Counter, Clock, Constant or List, or the result of an arithmetic calculation as well as an integer; e.g. the constructions:

    (20)SEC > (CON4)
    R(6,3) > (CLK5+CTR3)

are both allowed.

The *state terminator* is an apostrophe ' ' ' which indicates the end of a state in the same way that the semi-colon ';' indicates the end of an ALGOL statement.

The language includes standard arithmetic and logical operators (cf. Chapter 2, p. 36) as well as three functional statements that can be used for presenting stimuli. These functions are:

(i) RAND which produces a uniformly distributed random number between 0·0 and 0·99. The value may be used in determining stimuli or state changes.

(ii) NORM(x,y) produces a random variable generated from a normal distribution about mean y, with standard deviation x.

(iii) RANDSET(x) resets the random number generator to the xth term in the random series, allowing for repetition of the series.

Before running a program in SCAT, the Histograms and Lists used in the program have to be declared. The declaration statement is of the form:

    Dnn:

where 'nn' is an integer. Histograms are declared as:

    Dnn:HISTn (xx, yy, zz)'

where xx is the lower bound of the Histogram, yy is the bin size, and zz is the upper bound of the Histogram. Thus, the construction:

    D10:HIST6(2,0·5,5)'

declares that the range of Histogram 6 is from 2 to 5 in steps of 0·5; i.e. it defines a set of bins with the following bounds:

Bin 0: for values less than 2,
Bin 1: for values greater than or equal to 2 and less than 2·5,

.   .
.   .
.   .

Bin 7: for values greater than or equal to 4·5 and less than 5,
Bin 8: for values greater than or equal to 5.

Lists are declared as:

Dnn: LISTxx'

which states that the List exists and has 'xx' data cells.

Data is output from the computer using 'report commands' which
are declared in the program after the term:

Rnn:

The TYPE statement is the most important report command, and can
be used in the same way as PRINT is used in FORTRAN (Chapter 2,
p. 38), with the exception that FORMAT specifications are not
required in SCAT; e.g. the construction:

R20: TYPE 'TOTAL NUMBER OF RESPONSES TO STIMU-
LUS', TYPE CON3, TYPE 'WAS', TYPE CTR6, ...

causes the following print out if the content of Constant 3 is 1, and the
content of Counter 6 is 73:

TOTAL NUMBER OF RESPONSES TO STIMULUS 1·0 WAS 73·0

The command:

TYPE LIST

causes the List values to be typed out beneath each other down the
page.
The command:

TYPE HISTn

causes both the absolute value of each bin of the Histogram n, and the
accompanying percentage of the total count of the Histogram, to be
printed out.

A fixed ratio reinforcement schedule experiment (ten responses of
type 3), to be terminated after 100 reinforcements and to print out as
data a Histogram of the times spent in state 1 (i.e. the time spent making
the 10 responses) could be programmed as below:

D10: HIST3(0·5, 1·0, 20·0)'
C10: ZHIST3,CTR0 $< 0; > (15)$'
C15: S1, CLK2 < 0; (CTR0.E.101) $> (30),R(10,3) > (20)$'
C20: S2, HIST(CLK2,3), CTR0 $< (CTR0+1)$; (3)SEC$> (15)$'
C30: OUTPUT(05)'
R05: TYPE HIST3, RESTART 10'

Two new types of statement are used in this program, but otherwise all the constructions have been dealt with. The new statements are:

OUTPUT (nn)'

which causes transfer of control to the nnth report command; and:

RESTART nn'

which causes the program to restart at the nnth state name.

In the form presented above, the program will run until stopped from the teletypewriter by the experimenter. This is one form of user inter-action allowed by the system; another form is facilitated by typing in CHECK followed by a specified Counter, Constant or Clock. The system responds with the current value of the Counter, Constant or Clock and the user can either type in a new value or leave the original value. The current value of a specified Histogram may also be requested from the teletypewriter but cannot be changed.

The SCAT language has been described in some detail because it is quite different from any of the languages dealt with so far. The main difference, and probably the greatest disadvantage of the language, is that the experimenter cannot use meaningful names for identifiers and variables. As mentioned earlier, a language for controlling psychology experiments needs to be problem-oriented, but programming is easier if the language is also user-oriented: i.e. the programmer can be idio-syncratic in the choice of variable names. Thus, although SCAT is oriented to the problem of experimental control it is not user-oriented. For example, the programmer has to remember whether a green stimulus lamp is S1 or S5 rather than being able to specify it as 'GREENLAMP'. The timing of events is more difficult than in the other languages be-cause constructions such as the 'WAIT UP TO identifier' command of ECL have to be programmed using the values of Clocks and Counters. When referring to the following program for a fixed-ratio schedule:

C1: S1;R(15,1) $> (2)$'
C2: S2;(3)SEC $> (1)$'

Stadler (1969) states, 'The program is admittedly a trivial one, but it does illustrate dramatically the simplicity of the language, the ease of using it, and its appropriateness, because it does describe the experiment precisely in the way the E would if he were engaged in a conversation with a colleague. In this instance, the colleague happens to be a computer.' The language is simple but it is certainly unable to describe an experiment in the same way as programs written in PSYCHOL or ECL. A richly commented SCAT program is easier to follow. However, it is not the comments of a program that do the work but the instructions, and these should be self-explanatory.

The ACT language works on a similar state change principle to SCAT but involves more statements constructed from English. For example, the ACT construction:

> AFTER K CLOCK UNITS GO TO S2

is equivalent to the SCAT statement:

> . . ; (CLK1.E.CON1) > (2)'

where the content of Constant 1 is K, and state name 2 refers to S2. The ACT language appears, therefore, to be more user-oriented than SCAT, while both are best suited to animal experimentation.

Non-specific solutions

The third solution to the programming of psychology experiments involves the use of a high-level language (FORTRAN) and appropriate subroutines written either in assembly language or FORTRAN.

The paper by Haber *et al.* (1970) describes an experiment run on a PDP-8 computer with 4k of core store housed at Rochester University. The program makes use of the machine's ability for FORTRAN programs to reference assembly language subroutines using a simple PAUSE statement followed by a number defining the starting address of the subroutine. The assembly language, PAL, is used for important real-time operations, such as the timing of events, presentation of stimuli and recording of responses, because the execution time of a typical PAL instruction is 0·003 msec. compared with an average of about ½ msec. for a FORTRAN statement. In addition, coding some of the program in assembly code saves storage space, which is important in such a small configuration. The section of the program for presentation of stimuli is reproduced below with the program comments. (N.B. A semicolon written after a statement number separates the number from its statement in the same way that the space separates a statement number from a statement, as described in Chapter 2, p. 35.)

7;DO9J = 1,IEVENT LITE = LTCODE(J) ITIME = IDURAT(J)	For each event in sequence get code and duration of event.
Pause 3472	Jump to subroutine to execute event.
Pause 3488	Jump to subroutine to count out the duration of the event.
IF(J-IEVENT)9,8,9	If all events are not completed, do loop again.
8;LITE = 0	If last event is done, then turn last event off (set light code to 0).
Pause 3472 9;Continue	Jump to subroutine to execute event.

The subroutine associated with the number 3472 operates a stimulus light, while the subroutine associated with the number 3488 is responsible for counting the duration of an event in milliseconds, specified by the main program as IDURAT.

The program illustrates the unfortunate FORTRAN convention, for the experimenter, that integer variable names must begin with one of the letters I through N. Variables with names such as ITIME and IEVENT seem to be divorced from their meaning in the experiment merely by the addition of the letter 'I'. The program has been written in general terms so that a number of similar experiments could be performed using the same program. The identical experiment could be presented using auditory instead of visual stimuli merely by connecting loud-speakers to the interface instead of lights.

This solution to the programming problem is good for the type of installation involved, i.e. a comparatively small system. However, it involves the learning of two languages with purposes quite remote from the control of psychology experiments. The efficiency of such a system could be increased by having an extensive library of assembly code subroutines. A user could then include relevant subroutines in his FORTRAN program without the need to learn assembly code. The use of a library of this kind poses a problem, because it introduces a certain mystique concerning the operations of the language controlling the computer. This mystique is less likely to be present when a user, particularly a psychologist, can program in a language which he fully understands because its terminology is relevant to the operations that he wishes the computer to control.

The system at Indiana University, described by Restle and Brown (1969) is a time-sharing system capable of running seven different experiments at the same time on both human and animal subjects. It is obviously at the other end of the size scale to the Rochester system just described, for computers running on-line experiments. The system is implemented on an IBM 1800 computer with 24k of core store, 16 bit word, and a disc as backing store. Unlike the PSYCLE time-sharing system, the Indiana system is not a truly real-time system because the internal timing arrangements preclude accurate reaction-time measurements. This results from the way in which core store is allocated to users. In the PSYCLE system each user has a certain amount of core store dedicated to his program and access to the bulk of core when required, according to a system of priorities. In the Indiana system each user's program runs in core with a set priority, so that if a higher priority program requires the store the lower level program will be dumped on to the disc. Obviously this could happen at a crucial moment in a reaction-time experiment.

Programs responsible for controlling experiments whilst running are written in FORTRAN. Ease of writing such programs is facilitated by the use of subroutines for operating input and output equipment. For example, in order to turn on Event Light 3 in Booth 4 in the SP (Slide Projector) room (Room 2), the programmer writes:

CALL EVN2(4,3)

This statement calls subroutine EVN2 with arguments 4 and 3 (see Chapter 2, p. 37). The first argument, 4, indicates that booth 4 is being referenced, and the second argument, 3, determines that light 3 is to be switched on. Similarly, to select a slide, number 25, in the slide projector in the SP room, the programmer writes:

CALL SEARCH(25)

The subroutine converts the argument to a binary pattern suitable for controlling the slide projector to select slide 25.

An important variable in a control program is called IWHER. Values assigned to this variable during the running of the experiment are used for transferring control within the program according to the required order of operations in the experiment. Because the programming language is FORTRAN, IWHER is limited to integer values which are not as meaningful to the programmer as the labels of ALGOL and PSYCHOL (p. 61).

Two subroutines are used for performing similar operations to the PSYCHOL commands PERMIT, and PROHIBIT (p. 63). These are:

LETGO(I,J)

4—TCIP   *   *

which permits responses to be recorded from booth J of room I; and:

NOGO(I,J)

which stops recording of responses from booth J of room I.

The whole method of writing these programs is oriented around the use of a wide variety of subroutines and this itself plays an important part in slowing down response times within the system because, even though experimenters' programs have the highest priority level over routine, system control programs, it nevertheless takes time to transfer control to and from a sub-program.

The criticisms of FORTRAN as a language for controlling psychology experiments apply to this system just as to the Rochester system. Restle and Brown report that any student gaining reasonable mastery of FORTRAN is able to write his own experimental programs.

One great disadvantage of FORTRAN is its inability to handle textual information efficiently, in lists and strings. This and some other requirements of an on-line experimental language are finally considered below.

As stated earlier (p. 60), the most important distinction between a computer used for data processing and a computer used to run on-line experiments is that experimental control takes place in real-time. The peripheral equipment controlled by an on-line computer is also more varied than the standard teleprinter, card reader and magnetic tape units that are interfaced to data processors. These two factors alone, i.e. those of real-time control and equipment definition, demand special provisions in a language designed to program on-line control sequences. The on-line control of psychology experiments is only one of many real-time applications of the computer, and in 1967 a British Computer Society specialist group prepared a report projecting, in some detail, a language for real-time computer systems (BCS Specialist Group, *On-Line Computers and their Languages,* 1967). Some of the recommendations of the report are given below, and it is apparent that they are appropriate for inclusion in a language for controlling psychology experiments. Of the languages considered in this chapter, PSYCHOL includes more of the recommended programming features than any of the others.

The language suggested by the group, RTL (Real-Time Language), is based on ALGOL. Suggested additions to data types permitted in ALGOL are:

(i) strings—the value of a string variable can be any sequence of characters contained within string quotes " ". A string named 's'

would be declared as: *string* s and a value would be assigned to s
using the statement: s: = "abcd";
Strings are particularly useful in psychology experiments using text
because, provided with relevant operators, much comparison of
responses and presentation of stimuli can be accomplished. The string
operators in the BCS report are ideal for this type of manipulation.
Strings can be treated in the following ways:

(a) *con*—concatenation. The pair of statements:
   s1: = "abc";
   s2: = "def" *con* s1;
assign the value "defabc" to s2.
(b) *isin*—this statement compares two strings to see whether the
second contains a sub-string identical to the first, and defines appropriate transfer of control operations; e.g.
   if "a" *isin* s *and* "b" *isin* s *then* . . .
This construction could be used in a Socratic CAI program where
spelling or syntax is not important (see Chapter 10, p. 252).
(c) =—two strings are equal if they contain exactly the same
characters in the same order. This construction could be used in
the Socratic system mentioned above where spelling or syntax is
important.

Other operators for splitting strings according to their contents and
also for taking the first and last character of a string are suggested.

(ii) binal variables—these contain a declared number of bits, each able to
take the value 0 or 1. They are particularly useful for the output of
stimuli because, as shown previously, (p. 64) stimulus output can be
readily controlled by the arrangement of bits in a computer word.
Binal constants are also allowed as a sequence of 0's and 1's preceded
by the symbol *b*. E.g. *b*11011 is a binal constant equivalent to the
decimal number 27.

Two other powerful features of the suggested language are provisions
for dealing with further data types and for writing sections of program
in assembly language or any other available language. The former
allows the user to program experiments with a wide variety of stimuli,
while the latter allows the programmer to use a code other than
the programming language either where necessary or where it is advantageous from a programming viewpoint.

In conclusion, it is unfair to state categorically that every computer
in a psychology laboratory must be able to use a language for running
on-line experiments. However, it is fair to say that where conditions of

storage allow, the use of a psychology-oriented language is to be encouraged and, preferably, the same language should be available for use on every suitable computer. The present problems of exchanging programs are immense; in many cases by the time a borrowed program has been adapted to run on a computer the program could have been written from scratch (Moray, 1969). The standardization of documentation would facilitate program exchange which is important in preventing duplication of effort in both psychology and programming. Moreover, the replication of experiments within psychology becomes easier. Previously this might have proved difficult owing to differences between controlling equipment in different departments.

It has been emphasized throughout this chapter that a programming language for use in psychology must be user-oriented. This is particularly true when the psychologist with little knowledge of computers wishes to write a program to control an experiment. When the programming language includes words and constructions related to the language of the psychologist, the task of programming is much easier than when the language is composed of single letters, or words and constructions, unrelated to experimental control. The claim of Restle and Brown, that any student gaining reasonable mastery of FORTRAN is able to use the Indiana system, is interesting in this respect; i.e. if a language, both psychology-oriented and user-oriented, were used instead of FORTRAN, the number of people who would be able to use the system might increase.

In the light of the evidence presented here, the development of a high-level, psychology-oriented language capable of implementation on any system, either time-shared or dedicated, with 8k of core store and a rapid access disc (as large as finances allow) as backing store, must be encouraged if more psychologists are to take advantage of the versatility of the digital computer.

Further reading

Sammett, J. E. (1969) *Programming Languages: History and Fundamentals.* Prentice-Hall, Englewood Cliffs, New Jersey. A comprehensive overall view of more than one hundred higher level languages with a wide range of applications. No examples of languages designed to control on-line psychology experiments are included.

CHAPTER 4

The Computer in Psychology Experiments

Godfrey Harrison

Introduction

Mathematicians sometimes have to accept, at least for a time, existence proofs. They have proof that a solution to a problem exists, but they cannot prove what that solution is. This chapter may at times seem as provoking as an existence proof. In most psychology experiments some use could be made of a computer. Even when a computer is not available for *running* your experiment, it may still be possible to use a computer in *setting it up*. In many parts of the world today, access to large computers serving many users is available. Using these machines to set up experiments will often give better stimuli, obtained with less effort. Consider, for example, the importance of randomization in designing experiments. Pseudo-random generators, which are a standard facility of large machines, enable one to employ more demanding designs while dispensing with the use of printed tables of random numbers or random permutations.

If large undedicated machines may be used in setting up experiments, running experiments by computer typically involves the use of a small laboratory computer which can be dedicated to this task. The choice between large undedicated machines and small dedicated ones is not logically forced on us, for a large machine, or some part of it, could be dedicated to on-line experimental use. Some computer-assisted instruction systems illustrate this principle. Equally, small machines can be used for preparing stimuli for experiments that will not otherwise involve a computer. But in practice the first of these uses is uncommon and the latter can often be done better on a large machine as line-printers and graphical outputs are less commonly found on small machines than on large ones. The second section of this chapter, therefore, will concern the experimental possibilities afforded by large undedicated machines and the third section will deal with those afforded by small computers used in on-line work. Neither section can be

85

exhaustive, but examples from a variety of fields will be found in part II of this book.

This chapter seeks to indicate the sorts of tasks computers can be usefully put to, rather than to enumerate their successes. Indeed, enumeration would almost be contrary to one of the most central characteristics of computers: they are machines intended to be arranged and re-arranged into other machines. This characteristic holds so well that any list of particular uses for a computer will always be an incomplete one. The skill in seeing how to use computer possibilities in setting up and in running experiments lies in seeing how the general logical and practical facilities of a given machine can be applied to individual empirical enquiries. No writer can know precisely how to do this, instance by instance—being ignorant of those enquiries and of the configurations of many computers. Fortunately people who wish to acquire this skill seem to generalize from examples quite quickly. That is why three sections of the chapter present examples. The final section sounds a note of caution, not for the sake of safe respectability but because the manipulative fascination associated with these machines may be psychologically sterile. One can rephrase Bartlett discussing statistics (1932, p. 9), and say, 'From beginning to end the psychologist user of computers must rely on his psychology to tell him where to apply and how to interpret computer possibilities.' In illustrating the field most of the examples chosen have directly involved the writer. The work described comes primarily from the efforts of psychologists starting to use computers for their experiments. Some of it has been concerned with exploring situations not feasible without very sophisticated and psychologically novel apparatus. The examples are chosen to elucidate basic notions and to persuade the doubtful or timorous that using a computer in psychology experiments is not difficult or irrelevant and can be fruitful. One experiment cited has been repeatedly and successfully carried out by first year undergraduate students and both they and those engaged in research in that area found the results interesting.

Experimental possibilities of large undedicated machines

This section attempts to illustrate how, by using computers, an experimenter can obtain stimuli for his studies. It is particularly about the use of computers when other methods of equivalent precision or thoroughness would be impracticable. The first three topics considered, namely, *calculation, collation* and *generation of displays,* are of wider relevance than the last two—*synchronization* and *precision drawing.* The five topics differ also in how amenable they are to satisfactory completion in an operator-controlled system, i.e. in a system controlled by a full-time member of computer staff and not just by a current user. It is unhelpful of a user needlessly to take up the time of an operator who could be usefully running other programs. If synchronized stimuli or animated visual displays are sought, special access and help from the computer installation staff will be needed, usually at a rather higher level than from an operator. Any help with the first three topics will centre on actually writing the program—not on running it.

Calculation

Increasingly, psychologists have available tables of data on material that can be used in experiments, or on their subjects. Standardization data on psychological tests, tabulations of drug dosages, developmental profiles and measures of verbal learning materials, are typical examples. Mostly such tabulations make controlled experimentation more simple. To be able to consult tables to find that a note of a given frequency will be audible at an intensity of 55 decibels is better than having to carry out rough preliminary studies on audition. When values of the required sort are not presented for the particular case of interest, the possibility of calculation may still be open. If we know the luminous intensity of a light we can calculate the illumination of a point at a given distance from the light. If it is not possible to calculate, this may be because the relations upon which calculation depends, such as additivity, do not hold. A runner's time for a mile cannot be found by adding his times for two runs of half a mile. An obvious laboratory example comes from drug dosage data. These are commonly given in units of capacity (or weight) per unit of body weight. Even when such a rate is stated, limitations may be hinted by the table but not specified. If dosages for rats are given over a range about the average weight for adults then to interpolate an exact dose for a large but immature animal may be misleading. In this simple example justified calculations, say for an adult animal of normal weight not specifically given, could be done on a slide rule or even mentally. In other cases, when reliable explicit formulae are not to hand, intuitive interpolations (guesses) have their place. Where the problem is to calculate many possible values and then choose the best of them using precise criteria, computer methods will be best. To illustrate an apt calculative use for a computer we describe an iterative program.

Iterative calculation is repeated calculation of an expression, usually with a systematic ascription of values to its variables. It is made to attain a value for the expression, that has some required characteristic. For example, one might start to obtain the square root of a (positive) number iteratively. This can be done by arbitrarily choosing a number and squaring it. If this product is smaller than the number whose root is sought some larger arbitrary number will next be tried. Such increasing choices are continued until the product is too large, that is, larger than the number whose root is being sought. The succeeding choice is then smaller than its predecessor until again the product becomes too small. This alternating scheme can be repeated until any discrepancy between the current product and the number whose root is sought is as small as one desires, allowing that it will usually be non-zero.

Any full appreciation of tactics in iterative calculation has to be gained from writings on numerical calculation combined with practice. The calculation described below, however, serves to show how iterative calculation can be relevant in starting to produce experimental material.

Conrad (1964) produced data indicating that the misrecall of letters presented in an immediate memory situation is related to their acoustic confusability. The letter P sounds similar to the letter B, and P is often recalled after a B has been presented in a list; this is so especially when both letters are members of the set from which material is drawn. Conrad (1965) has further claimed, from later data, to have pinpointed the same source for recall errors in which two presented items are reproduced in each other's original positions. This common source, acoustic confusability, must obviously be controlled by anyone interested in such transposition errors and in trying to relate them to other independent variables. Helpfully, Conrad (1964) has published a confusion matrix for the whole of the English alphabet. This shows the frequencies with which each letter was identified as itself, or as another letter, when all letters were being auditorily presented in a long equiprobable sequence and against a background of noise. In one experiment (Harrison, 1967, pp. 163–95) lists were not to include vowels and were to be made up from a set of only six letters. Further, all the possible acoustic confusions among the remaining six consonants were to be equiprobable, or nearly so. Clarke (1957) had produced a tested formula to obtain confusion data on subsets of items from larger sets (and *vice versa*). His Constant Ratio rule gives the probabilities of correct and incorrect recognition. After converting the frequencies of Conrad's table to probabilities it was possible to derive a confusion matrix for 20 letters: the consonants less Y. The principal computer calculation was to obtain one of the thousands of sets of six consonants specifiable from the 20 remaining letters. The set required would have its error probabilities spread over a very small range. This set was determined iteratively—by repeatedly calculating the standard deviation of the error probabilities for confusion matrices for sets of six letters.

In the program the initial value for this variable was arbitrarily taken as 1,000. This value is obviously ludicrously large; it was replaced by the standard deviation from the first calculated matrix of six letters (B, C, D, F, G, H). This replacement occurred because the newly calculated value was less than the value previously stored; and after it had happened the corresponding matrix was printed out in full along with the value of the standard deviation. No further output was printed until a still smaller value for the standard deviation was calculated.

After more than 2,000 calculations of matrices and their error probabilities, standard deviations all the sets of six letters including B were exhausted. The 'best' set at that point was B, F, H, J, M, R, which had a standard deviation of $\pm 0\cdot 0219$ and the mean probability of confusion was also small: 0.0237. That matrix was the first one printed out for over 100 matrix calculations. This seemed a conveniently large run without other output, and calculations were then ended. Obviously more calculations could have been made with other sets (e.g. the next step would be to exclude B and examine all sets containing C), but the values already found seemed acceptable and the computer then in use was a slow one much in demand so the set listed above was the one used in the cited experiment. As the overall probability was not very great (and, more important, the distribution of error probabilities was in a small range) the force of the acoustic confusion account of transposition errors, still prevalent in the experimental data, is small. The reasoned if somewhat arbitrary decision to stop computing is illustratively important: not all the decisions need to be programmed in calculation—merely the ones that save work. To devise some general strategy in the program for ending its calculations would have been needlessly elaborate here. One did not know the rate at which improved values of the standard deviation would be found during the run, nor at what rate it might itself change. If the standard deviation value finally produced had not been so low it might have seemed appropriate to wait until 200 matrices had been calculated since any previous output, in the hope of getting an acceptable (i.e. low enough) value from the additional 100 calculations. If, then, no other output were produced, a reassessment of what was low enough might have had to be made. The stopping strategy here was not explicit and one falls back on the comment 'some correction is preferable to none', and the cost of a better correction did not promise to be worthwhile.

Collation

This use of computers in preparing material is related to the one just discussed. There it was necessary to extend or select from a given table.

Here the problem is to find a set of items showing several attributes, each separately available with all of them being acceptable in some specified way. Suppose one has found a set of 20 words, all with nearly equal probabilities of acoustic confusion. These words may still differ in various other experimentally relevant ways. One of these words may be very infrequently used according to Howes' word count for spoken American English (1966). The distribution of their initial letters may be far from rectangular and from the distribution of initial letters of words in a dictionary. In others of the 20 words the letter digram frequencies may be atypical according to the count of Baddeley, Conrad and Thomson (1960). Some of the words may be ambiguous if presented in isolation, such as *seal* or *match*; some may be ambiguous to the ear and transcribable in different ways, such as $\overline{rut}$ (write, wright, right, rite) or $\overline{at}$ (eight, eyot, ait, ate). The variety of attributes of single words relevant to their perception in adverse presentation conditions is legion. Pollock *et al* (1958) pointed out the ineffectiveness of controlling one relevant variable in intelligibility studies. In undertaking studies of words out of context, selecting experimentally useful sets seems a thoroughly arbitrary process. It can however be made a less arbitrary and briefer process by using computers, and a general strategy on which to base programs for computer collation may be helpful. This strategy is concerned with reducing the time to produce required sets. That is, it is concerned with the time for the whole solution rather than with the times for particular sets that have to be considered on the way to that solution. It supposes that for any set of items, and for all attributes deemed germane, there is available a tabulation of data from which can be calculated some statistic allowing acceptance or rejection of the set's values on that attribute. Here a pairing of attribute and corresponding statistic will be called a criterion.

In general the statistic will reflect the balance (bias) of item values on an attribute. For example, word frequency may be thought experimentally relevant but has not been chosen as an independent variable and must therefore be controlled. Suppose a table of word frequencies is available, the associated statistic might then be x^2 and one would want the overall distribution of word frequencies in the experimental material to be not significantly different from those in the word count, as shown in the table of word frequencies. Alternatively and more simply the statistic might be the number of words (N) in the set occurring less than once in 10,000 words and the basis of acceptance or rejection could be staightforwardly abitrary: say, if N is greater than two then reject the set, otherwise accept it. Or again acceptance may follow the use of a test of proportions and the common statistical conventions on significance.

The strategy begins by dividing all the selected criteria into two kinds: those with which experimental sets must comply, and those with which one would like them to comply. Within these divisions the criteria are ranked from most quickly to least quickly applied. In collation these rankings are used to order the application of the criteria, with the application of necessary criteria preceding that of desirable ones. On failing a necessary criterion a set is rejected and a new set selected for checking through the necessary criteria—again starting with the quickest. For sets surviving all the necessary criteria, several options are open when applying the desirable criteria. A simple one counts the number (m) of desirable criteria that each set meets after applying all the desirable criteria. If the current value of m at least equals m for the retained set satisfying fewest desirable criteria, then retain the current set, otherwise reject it. There are two exceptions to this last rule. The first exception applies when m is less than that for the retained set with the lowest value of m. If the number of sets currently retained is less than the number needed for the experiment then retain the current set. The other exception is when m is greater than that for the retained set with the least value of m and there are enough retained sets for the experiment: in this event discard the retained set with the least m value, replacing it with the current set. A strategy stopping rule is: stop collating *either* when you have enough sets for experimental purposes which satisfy all necessary criteria and some arbitrary specified number of desirable criteria, *or* when all possible sets have been exhausted. In this latter case, if more sets are being retained, that satisfy all necessary criteria but an insufficient number of desirable criteria, than are needed for the experiment, then print the required number and stop. Do this print out starting with the sets that satisfy most desirable criteria. Otherwise, in this latter case, print out all the retained sets then stop.

The strategy given above is certainly not a universally optimal one. What is optimal for a situation will take into account aspects not considered here. More generally, to divide criteria into necessary and desirable ignores any relevant patterns of attributes among the desirable criteria. Again the arbitrarily specified number of desirable criteria to be met by the experimental sets is a difficult value to guess sensibly, and some calculation of its value, depending on how many sets are currently usable, might be preferred. The main justification of the outlined strategy lies in indicating the sorts of considerations that must be included rather than in drawing together all those to be found in any particular and efficient collation.

Generation of displays

Once one has got some set of items to use in an experiment the actual experimental stimuli can be drawn from them. This will very often involve stating some constraints, which may reflect experimental variables, and making selections which are random within those constraints. This strategy will be illustrated, but first note the scope of computer output possibilities. In a printed book it is convenient to cite examples from verbal learning. To continue to use such examples as if complex visual displays, like those described in Chapter 6, and even auditory ones were not to be had from large computers not dedicated to on-line work would be misleading. The oscilloscope outputs of large machines, their graph-plotters and even their line-printers and loudspeakers can provide material for experiments on other topics than verbal learning. Some details of these uses and others will be introduced later. Our concern here is with sequences and dependencies among runs of stimuli *of any kind*. Today computers cannot systematically produce stimuli for olfactory studies, but it would be perfectly possible for a computer to output a schedule specifying the characteristics of olfactory stimuli from some relevant set so that the specified run would be random within stated constraints. For those experimental materials which the computer can output directly, schedules like those *output* for olfactory stimuli can be used *within* the computer to structure its output of stimulus material. Put simply: a computer can virtually always output a particular table of numbers that are random within certain constraints although sometimes this is unnecessary; the table's contents can be applied inside the computer and its output will then be the experimental stimuli.

Switching has been an important notion in the study of attention. The present writer once made lists of the names of eight colours with four of them always named in French, though not always the same four, and four in English. The experimental variable was the number of changes between languages. This ranged from one switch, when all the items in one language preceded all those of the other, to seven switches, when alternate items were in different languages. Two other patterns of alternation provided three and five switches. The following constraints applied: there were the same number of lists with each of the four alternation patterns; each colour was named once in each list; in each list four colour names were in each language; half of the lists started with an English colour name, half with a French; over all the lists the four alternation patterns occurred in random order. The overall scheme of the program that produced such lists had ten main points:

1. Read the letters of the 16 names of colours into the computer: one

letter to a computer word. Do this allowing seven computer words for each colour name and its succeeding space character, for shorter words than YELLOW include extra space characters on the right until seven characters are obtained for each name. Have all letters and spaces from the eight English colour names stored consecutively in a block of 100 computer words—ignore the unused words in the block. Store the French colour names translating the English ones in a similar 100 word block starting immediately after that for the English. Order the names of colours in the same sequence for both languages. (This last sentence is an instruction to the program user, and not a job for the program.)

2a. Read the number of lists required with each number of switches.

2b. Calculate related values for counts used in establishing if the total number of lists required has been produced, and for similar tests.

3. Set up seven counts at zero: four to be increased by one on choosing a particular alternation pattern for the next list to be produced, unless the value of the count exceeds the appropriate terminal count (calculated in 2b); two to count the number of lists starting in English and in French; the other count to stop the program after printing enough lists.

4. Produce a random permutation of the integers 0 through 7, using a pseudo-random number routine.

5. Decide whether to try for a list of 1, 3, 5 or 7 switches, using a pseudo-random number routine.

6. Discover if there are already enough lists of the kind selected in 5,

(a) If there are repeat 5

(b) If there are not decide, using a pseudo-random number routine, whether to start the list with an English or French name *unless* the appropriate count for the indicated language is already too large (i.e. greater than or equal to half the required number of lists) in which case opt for the under-represented initial language; in either case increment by 1 the count for the initial language used.

7. Consequent on the decisions from 5 and 6b set up an appropriate structure (for the kind of list required) in terms of the addresses of the computer words holding the initial letters of the colour names being in the first 100 such computer words or the second 100.

8. Use the structure from 7 and the permutation from 4 to determine which particular colours shall be named first, second, third, etc.

9. Print out the contents of the computer words specified in 8 and increment the appropriate count by 1.

10. If enough lists have been printed stop, otherwise recommence
from 4.

This sort of scheme may seem far from straightforward at first sight but
usually one makes such schemes in one's head and writes them down
as a flow-chart to use when turning the idea into a program to test and
run. Flow-charts make any incoherent parts of such schemes more easily
apparent. However, not all computer users think in flow-charts when
actually working on a problem rather than just ordering a few well-
known themes. Some of those who do not, apparently describe to themselves what a flow-chart would be about. The ten point scheme presented
is one such description. Its main failing is that it does not adequately
convey the working from the middle outwards that is commonly
involved in forming the scheme. Points 4 through 7 are the ones that
came to mind first—and even then not in that order. Once you have
such a scheme, drawing a flow-chart helps to check that it does what it
is thought to and, because of its greater detail, writing the program
from it is relatively simple. Some people do not use preliminary schemes
but preliminary flow-charts instead. It does not matter which one uses
as long as producing a program is made easier. The thing not to do with
a program of any length at all is to write down the constraints and
try to program them straight off! The chances are you will make a
mistake.

The problem just described exemplifies some of the points common
in preparing stimuli on a computer; there are others. That program was
short and the justification for some of its less than rapid methods is
that in short programs, especially when they are to be little used, it is
pointless spending even ten minutes seeking refinements. Suppose you
achieve them: the output systems of the computer will still be the
limiting speed for running the program. Where time-sharing on a large
machine circumvents that limit, for the computer, it will still be difficult
to save more than a second of central processor time. The sort of
occasion when a little time might usefully be spent in getting an efficient
method is when somebody else has carefully programmed a common
well-known problem. One such problem is included in the scheme above
at 4: produce a random permutation. (In a random permutation of the
numbers 1, 2, 3, ..., n, each number appears once in random order.
Obviously before adding a further number to an incomplete permutation
one has to check that it is not a repetition of an earlier one.) There are
primitive ways of doing this that waste time dramatically, even for small
permutations, say of the numbers 1, 2, 3, ..., 30. In such circumstances

it is worth consulting someone with special knowledge of the topic, or a book like the one by Greenberger and Jaffray (1965).

Synchronization and other temporal aspects of stimuli

As early as 1962 psychologists were using a large computer, the Lincoln Laboratory TX–2, to achieve the synchronous presentation of spoken words. Yntema and Trask (1963) had a speaker recite the ten digits and ten other words into a microphone. The microphone voltages were, at intervals of 1/10,000 second, read by an analog to digital converter and the values of the readings were stored in the computer memory. By using the computer simultaneously to access *pairs* of sequences of stored values two digital to analog converters could feed two tape recorder channels. The start of the recordings of pairs of items, one item per tape channel, would then be synchronized to within a minute fraction of a second. Such stimuli are increasingly being used in studying attention (cf. Treisman, 1967) although other techniques have been used to produce them. The automation that Yntema pioneered does require a large machine: one word lasting one fifth of a second would provide 2,000 values, and Yntema and Trask used twenty words. Subsequent work using the computer-stored speech measurements has achieved unnaturally rapid rates by omitting some values when reconstituting the speech (Yntema, Wozencraft and Klem, 1964. This whole topic of speech reconstitution to achieve synchronization or compression, or other effects, has developed in the past few years. One spur to this development has been the ease with which intelligibility is lost. Some sources of loss relate to particular sampling rates or converters. It is not therefore intended to discuss them here in detail but the possibility of synchronizing, and compressing or extending speech offers novel experiments.

Another type of computer-processed auditory stimulus for which temporal control has been exercised is musical sound. Mathews (1963) early developed a flexible system for synthesizing musical sound. A tape recording of output from Mathews' program was used in an experiment of Shepard (1964). His subjects listened to a series of complex sounds, each of many simple tones playing simultaneously and with precisely controlled amplitudes. This series was so ordered that subjectively each sound was higher (or lower, depending on the direction of play of the recording) than the preceding one. Only twelve complex sounds were used in a repeated cycle and one can easily see the aptness of Shepard's analogy with the endless staircase visual illusion, in which each step in a drawing of a castle turret bears the same relation to its adjacent neighbours but no step appears highest or lowest. Computers offer relatively simple means of exploring such analogies. One could discover which variables relevant in one modality, and applying in the other, were also relevant there.

Synchronous visual stimuli are more easily obtained than those for speech. The accurate and easy control of intervals between streams of visual stimuli output on the oscilloscope of a computer can be an improvement over other methods, especially when the delays vary through time. This advantage becomes more readily available as do video recorders.

Precision drawing

The stimuli in some psychology experiments are precision drawings. Their preparation by hand is as lengthy as that of most precision hand work. Especially in drawings with many evenly spaced parallel lines the tedium of drawing board techniques is now unnecessary. Many large computers have graph-plotters and a very few have high precision character-generating oscilloscopes. Either of these devices produces stimuli, say, for studies of illusions. The rare character-generating hardware-controlled oscilloscopes are quicker to use but expensive—some cost over US $250,000. These oscilloscopes can produce runs of drawings for use as precise animated stimuli when recorded on video tape. This form of stimulus has not yet been greatly used even by psychologists with their own collections of sophisticated electronic devices. Indeed, such animations may have little laboratory application. Knowing that some larger computer installations have this facility may, however, assist anyone wishing to study, for example, the ramifications of phi-phenomena.

Experimental possibilities from small dedicated computers

There are at least four general ways of employing a computer dedicated for use in on-line psychological experiments, namely, determinate, contingent, closed loop, and interactive.

To illustrate the four methods given above, examples will be given from a common field—verbal learning—and additionally one example, at least, from other fields will be provided under each heading. The distinguishing characteristics of these rest upon the increasing use made of the computer's responses to a subject, in real-time. The phrase 'real-time' concerns the immediacy a subject experiences because a computer is being used. In flying an airliner, events occur at a certain characteristic rate. In any satisfactory simulation of piloting an airliner they should also happen at that rate. Therefore any computer used in the simulation must be able to put together its simulated events, such as a fuel tank becoming empty in flight, at least as quickly as those events would occur—i.e. in real-time. In a realistic simulation of a tank emptying, a needle could simply move across a gauge irrespective of whether there was any tank. The needle's movement would represent the emptying. In a simulation of this kind, a fixed period of time cannot be represented by some other period: the time to fly between Rome and London has to be the same in simulation as in actual flight. This is because it would give a curious and misleading idea of an indicated airspeed of 400 mph if the projected cockpit view in the simulation changed from the Rome skyline to the Heathrow approach in twenty seconds. Stage plays provide examples of simulation that are not in real-time. Real-time is often relevant to psychological experiments because accurately manipulating a subject's experience of time is difficult and delay is impractical. It would render a reaction time study worthless.

Determinate studies

In a paired associate learning task, like the one reported by Murdock (1966) one might typically present five pairs of common nouns once each and at a fixed rate. Retention could be tested by presenting one of the stimulus nouns and requiring the subject to give its response item. A confidence rating for the response could also be sought and the response latency measured. Responses, ratings and latencies would all be recorded. Using the oscilloscope output of a computer, an on-line teletypewriter and computer 'clock' the experiment could be run on-line. Subjects practised on the teletypewriter would be required or their latencies might be extreme and range widely. In other ways the on-line version is preferable to a memory drum version employing a stop-watch and a tape recorder or pencil and paper recording: summary statistics could be printed out along with the raw data; the hard copy of responses would be easily legible on the teletypewriter roll (though not so on magnetic tape). The presentation and inter-item times would be better controlled than on most memory drums and latencies would be recorded with accuracy similar to or better than that obtainable on many stopwatches. The problem is the teletypewriter: ten characters per second is often the fastest possible input rate. Because of this even though the computer 'clock' is driven by a crystal oscillator dividing time into units of 1/10,000 of a second, the latency recordings will only be as accurate as the input channel is rapid: here ten characters per second. The oscilloscope used for outputting stimuli has, of course, no corresponding limitation on its temporal resolution, at least in the range of times used in paired associate tasks. With very brief presentation times the bright-up and decay times for the oscilloscope's phosphor might conceivably be crucial. Apparently therefore the on-line version of this experiment is not better in all respects than the conventional set-up based on the memory drum but it offers useful advantages.

The on-line experiment sketched above is determined in form, and in the values of its independent variables, before any subject starts a run. The first experimental trial would be strikingly similar to the last one: the actual list used on the last trial would certainly be different and probably the performance of the subjects too, but other clear differences would not be expected by the experimenter. This similarity throughout a session would, of course, be observable in the more traditional version. It is this fixed experimental form which justifies the classification of it as a determinate study. In determinate studies the computer only varies the subject's situation in ways that can be stated explicitly before the run: changing the subject would not change the computer presentations.

The principal benefit of on-line determinate studies comes with their precision, this generally exceeding that obtained with other apparatus. When it does not they have little compelling justification. In his book *Attention* Moray (1969) cites Whelan's unpublished study (1968) of selective attention in vision. Letters were presented to subjects using an oscilloscope output. Their position, duration, and superposition were under computer control. Although some ancillary optical apparatus was used it is the accuracy of Whelan's methods which Moray regarded as crucial. He writes, 'Many of the effects are small, though definite, and precise methods of presentation are required to detect them. The use of slide projectors is far too crude a method.' The precision easily gained in determinate on-line studies is obviously worth having.

Contingent studies

In serial learning a subject is presented with a list of items, after which the complete reproduction of that list is attempted. Presentation followed by attempted recall of the complete list continues until the criterion level of reproduction is achieved. Consider a serial learning task with a subject learning a list of 24 visually presented items to a criterion of one completely correct reproduction of the list. We could introduce knowledge of results in this situation by placing a tick ($\sqrt{}$ to the right of every item correctly recalled on an immediately preceding trial. The control condition would be without knowledge of results. Implementing the experimental condition we might put together the list each subject saw by drawing on two sets of list items: one set with all items ticked, the other with all items unticked. On the initial trial the experimenter would show the list drawn from the set of items without ticks. On following trials items correctly recalled in the preceding attempt would be shown in their ticked form, i.e. these items would now be drawn from the ticked set. (See Table 4.1 for a simple example of what might happen.) Alternatively, a subsidiary display could present the knowledge of results information. This experiment need not demand a computer or even much special apparatus for noting correct responses

Table 4.1—*An example of the provision of knowledge of results in a serial learning task*

	List presented on trial	1	2	3	
	Recall after trial	1	2	3	
L	Item No.1	47	47√	47√	
		47	47	47	
	2	36	36	36√	
I		33	36	36	Third recall attempt is an accurate reproduction of list and list presentation ceases
	3	29	29	29	
S		—	25	29	
	4	77	77√	77√	
T		77	77	77	
	5	58	58√	58√	
		58	58	58	

as they are made if the experimenter is sufficiently adroit. However, the necessarily slow presentation rates and untimed recall interval restrict the depth to which the problem can be investigated. As the rate at which subjects acquire knowledge of results is an interesting topic such limitations are to be avoided, if possible, and special apparatus can often be less quickly built than an equivalent computer program can be written. A computer-controlled study would certainly allow a full investigation of the rate at which subjects acquire knowledge of results. Before explicity stating the general points which this serial learning study exemplifies and which characterize contingent studies it is worth presenting

Table 4.2—*Measures of performance in acquisition of lists of* 24 2-*digit numbers presented at a* 2-*second rate*

	MEAN AND STANDARD DEVIATION	MEDIAN IN RANGE
No knowledge of results Group (N = 9)		
Trials to criterion	16·7 ± 5·8	16 in 18
Total errors	210·9 ± 95·9	221 in 340
With knowledge or results Group (N = 8)		
Trials to criterion	10·4 ± 7·5	12 in 16
Total errors	130·4 ± 45·1	125 in 117

results from the on-line study. These are shown in Table 4.2 and indicate clearly that knowledge of results aids serial learning.

The experiment summarized above exemplifies the formal point: the computer varies subjects' situations during their individual runs. The ticks beside items correctly recalled on an immediately preceding trial were presented under computer control and reflected the subject's earlier responses. Ignorance of a subject's responses in learning precludes one being able to state the exact form of stimuli before the experiment. We can only guess the first trial when, say, six items will appear with ticks. Notice, however, that we can still specify the consequences of a subject's correct and incorrect responses. Even this degree of certainty is lost in closed loop studies which are considered below.

We can cite as another example of a contingent study using a computer some unpublished work of Rabbit and the present writer; twelve subjects were found, who on each of four consecutive days responded to 500 serial choice reaction stimuli. In a choice reaction task one stimulus is presented from a known set. The subject has to respond appropriately, often by pressing one key on a keyboard rather than one of the others, and these others will each be appropriate to another item in the set. A sequence of choice reaction stimuli are presented in a serial choice reaction task. The effects of the duration of the intervals between consecutive responses and stimuli can then be studied. In 24,000 responses of our subjects there was, predictably, a small percentage of errors. That is, subjects pressed a key not corresponding to the presented stimulus. One independent variable was the response stimulus interval (the R/S interval) that is, the interval between subject's response and the following presentation of a stimulus. This interval was specified as being, if the (preceding) response was an error either one millisecond or 200 milliseconds. The chosen value held throughout a run of 500 responses. The R/S intervals after correct responses were also varied. Further, they were varied during a run of 500 responses. Consequently when a subject erred the computer had to displace the R/S interval already chosen to follow a correct response. These R/S intervals were available from values previously read into computer memory. This displacement became necessary because the already available R/S interval might not be the one millisecond, or 200 milliseconds, interval currently stipulated to succeed errors in a run. Our subjects showed the characteristic increase in response latency to the stimulus after one to which the response had been incorrect. The increase was less when the post error R/S interval was 200 milliseconds than when it was one. This finding has implications for theories of error in choice responses and especially for those theories denying subjects the ability to monitor responses during the so-called refractory period. To pursue these implications the reader may consult Rabbit's contribution to the symposium on Attention and Performance reported in *Acta Psychologica* (1967). The importance of our experiment here is to illustrate that contingent on-line studies allow, quite simply, an analysis of errors and their secondary effects which before the advent of computers was impossible even within the life-time of probably the youngest readers of this book.

Closed loop studies

Closed loop studies are an extension of contingent studies. Their form is shown in a schematic diagram (Figure 4.1). The usual hope in a closed loop study is that by altering the value of stimulus parameters as a function of a subject's previous performance, attainment of some criterion performance will be more rapid than otherwise. Briefly, it is

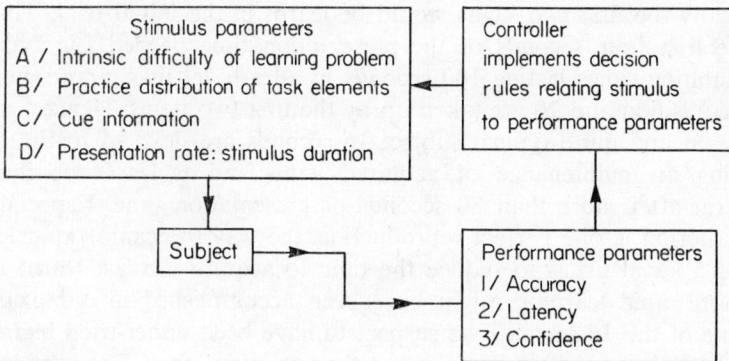

Figure 4.1—*A schematic representation of a closed loop system*

hoped that the system will be adaptive. It will not necessarily be adaptive because the function chosen to alter the stimulus might be inappropriate. In theory this sort of unfortunate choice is easily corrected by trying some new function in the light of the difference in adaptiveness, or maladaptiveness, of earlier ones. Systems that have such higher order selection have been made (cf. Pask and Mallen, 1966). Here we only consider experiments where the form of the controller is specified by the experimenter and there are no higher order rules in the computer program. This specification remains relatively open. The possible relations between the input and output variables are many. One might for example determine cue information as a function of accuracy and confidence, and stimulus duration as a function of latency; other functions are always possible. The chances of confusion by the experimenter are considerable when using complicated functions and the corresponding programming would certainly be time-consuming. Even given the simple controller function used in the example below, the values of the single coefficient can be altered. Obviously non-linear functions with several coefficients provide larger scope. Employing psychologically plausible controller functions is more important than simply seeking the mathematically attractive.

The bowed serial learning position curve suggested the rationale of the closed loop version of the serial learning task referred to in the section on contingent studies. This bowed curve represents the finding that initial items in a list are acquired first, the final items follow them in acquisition and the last learnt items are those in intermediate serial positions. Constant and equal presentation times for list items are widely used and this distribution of presentation times suggests a wasteful consequence. Suppose that in five trials a subject masters a list of ten items each shown for two seconds with very brief inter-item intervals. Typically the first two items would be learnt in the initial trial. That is, in the first four seconds of the presentation time needed for mastery. Presentation times lasting 100 seconds in all are, let us suppose, needed for acquisition and 20 are taken up by the first two items. Hence for our supposed and quite typical subject 16 seconds are devoted to the over-learning or maintenance of acquired items and at least one item is unlearnt after more than 80 seconds of presentation time. Especially if our criterion is one perfect reproduction, the way to ensure rapid learning of a serial list is to reduce the time to acquire the last learnt item. So more rapid learning might have been accomplished in our example if some of the 16 seconds we suspect to have been under-used had been devoted to intermediate items rather than to initial ones. For purposes of comparison this re-distribution would have to be so contrived that the overall presentation time in a trial would be the same as in the situation in which all items appeared for equal periods of time.

This rationale can be implemented in several ways. A cumulative serial position error curve is kept and from it one can calculate the total number of imperfect responses, including omissions, over a whole list. As we have said, the differences among the presentation times of individual items will be so contrived that they reflect the number of errors on particular items while keeping the presentation time for the whole list constant. In terms of Figure 4.1 we have D changing as a

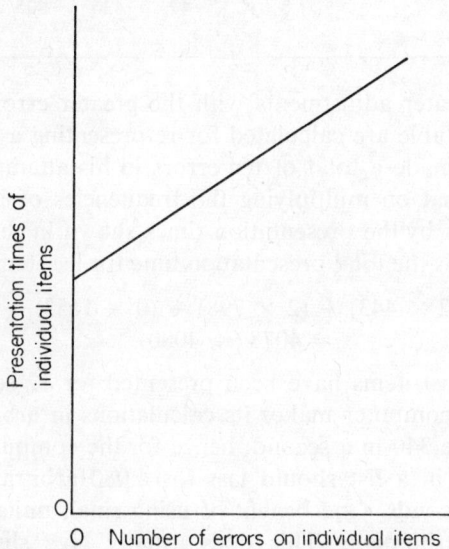

Figure 4.2—*A linear relation between presentation times of individual items and cumulative number of errors on the items*

function of 1. We can most simply illustrate a linear relationship between item presentation times and the number of errors on the corresponding items. Figure 4.2 shows this linear relationship and Table 4.3 presents a numerical version of the same relationship. Plotting either the line of figures marked y or the one marked y' as a function of the line marked x gives a straight line graph. In this table the term error weight needs special comment. Once we have decided to take account of errors the opportunity arises for quantifying how great an account of them we shall take. In the table this is exemplified by showing the values of $+4$ and $+8$ used in the calculation of the individual item presentation times shown. The repartitioning of the constant presentation time for

Table 4.3—*The effect of error weight on presentation times in arbitrary units*

Cumulative no of errors. with an item	x		0	1	2	3	4
Frequency of items with given no. of errors			1	2	2	0	1
Time in arbitrary units for error weights of:	+4	y	88	443	798	1153	1508
	+8	y'	47	426	805	1184	1563

a list involves greater adjustments with the greater error weight of $+8$.
The times in the table are calculated for re-presenting a six-item list to a
subject who has made a total of ten errors in his attempts to reproduce
the list. Notice that on multiplying the frequencies of items with given
numbers of errors by the presentation times shown in the table, the sum
of these products is the total presentation time for list items e.g.

$$(1 \times 88) + (2 \times 443) + (2 \times 798) + (0 \times 1153) + (1 \times 1508)$$
$$= 4078 \; (\simeq 4080).$$

On all trials the list items have been presented for 12 seconds in all. In
our example the computer makes its calculations in arbitrary time units
of which there are 340 in a second; hence for the computer the presentation of all items in a list should last for 4,080 arbitrary units of time
rather than 12 seconds. One benefit of using small units is that one can
employ integer arithmetic. This does usually give slightly inaccurate
results, but it is much quicker than floating point arithmetic and it is
often easier to program when using assembly languages. (The discrepancy between the sum of the calculated presentation times for the six
items and 4,080 is less than 0.1 per cent.) Notice that the graph shown
in Figure 4.2 makes a positive ordinate: items continue to be presented
even when they are always correctly recalled. The Figures also illustrate
the difference between closed loop and contingent studies: the specific
consequences of, say, an error cannot be exactly specified in a closed
loop study. Levels of performance (or latency or confidence), and not
separate events, are used in calculating stimulus changes. Closed loop
studies typically introduce new experimental variables, like error weight
here, that may influence the adaptiveness of the loop. Results
from employing the linear function described appear in Table 4.4.
They refer (as did Table 4.2) to lists of 48 seconds duration and 24

Table 4.4—*Measures of performance in the control and closed loop conditions. Experimental Group A had an error weight of +4, and Group B had one of +8. There were nine subjects in all groups*

	MEAN AND STANDARD DEVIATION	MEDIAN IN RANGE
Control group		
Trials to criterion	$16·7 \pm 5·8$	16 in 18
Total errors	$210·9 \pm 95·9$	221 in 340
Experimental groups		
(A)		
Trials to criterion	$11·4 \pm 3·4$	13 in 9
Total errors	$131·9 \pm 44·4$	132 in 120
(B)		
Trials to criterion	$11·9 \pm 3·0$	12 in 10
Total errors	$152·4 \pm 44·8$	145 in 128

2-digit numbers. Notice that doubling the error weight has virtually no effect on the improvement in the adaptive conditions. Comparison of these results with those cited for the contingent study of serial position effects leads to the suspicion that here the adaptive effect may be ascribed to knowledge of results. Certainly subjects were aware of the general strategy underlying re-distributions, albeit they gained their (partial) knowledge of results from abstrusely coded information. The information on knowledge of results that a closed loop task provides through changing stimulus attributes, is a logical consequence which may sometimes be psychologically relevant.

Keyboard responses have been studied by closed loop techniques for some time, (cf. Pask, 1965), and computer-controlled experiments have been completed. Guest and Sime (personal communication) asked subjects to code visually-presented single letters into keyboard responses. An arbitrary code was used and letters were selected from a limited set of ten. Specified responses included some chords, that is, responses in which two (or more) keys had to be depressed. The extreme rapidity of computer information processing compared with that of subjects raised clear problems in scoring. In non-computer experiments on this skill these points might have been overlooked or obscured, rather than resolved. The definition of a chord response normally involves the simultaneous depression of more than one key. In the computer study whenever its keys were depressed the keyboard required the computer to discover the state of its keys. Even on a slow computer this requirement could be formulated and dealt with by the processor in a fifth of a millisecond. This time is so brief that even a highly skilled operator would be very unlikely to depress two keys within it. In effect, the computer's assessments of chord responses would then be overcritical and chord responses virtually unattainable. Guest and Sime therefore had to specify their own acceptable working definition of a chord response. They specified the duration of the interval in which constituent keys of a chord could be depressed. They also decided that all and only the constituent keys were to be held down together at some time in the chosen interval. The structure of these decisions, more precisely put, was included in the program controlling the experiment.

In the overall rationale used by Guest and Sime to achieve closed loop control, ten random selections (with replacement) were made from the set of ten letters. From this randomly derived set a letter was chosen for display. Initially this too was done randomly but subsequently according to the following scheme. After each response, and allowing for the differing presentation frequencies of the ten letters, the overall arithmetic mean of response latencies to the ten different letters was calculated. If the response to the last letter shown was slower than the mean, the selection of the next letter to be presented was made from the set of letters used immediately before. The effect of this is that letters with slower than average responses are particularly likely to be re-presented. If the response to the last letter shown was not greater than the mean the selection of the next letter was from a newly constituted set of ten letters, again randomly selected, with replacement, from the ten in use. The effect of this is that letters not slower than the mean are not particularly likely to be re-presented.

Guest and Sime also used an open loop control situation. There they simply made random selections from the set of ten letters irrespective of response latencies to particular letters. In the closed loop condition the described feedback system undoubtedly affected the statistical properties of the letter sequences seen by subjects. There was, however, no significant difference in the levels of skill of subjects in the two conditions (closed loop and open loop) after equal numbers of responses. This result shows that not all closed loop studies are adaptive. After describing the previous example of a closed loop study, knowledge of results was mooted as a possible contributor to the adaptive character. The changes that Guest and Sime introduced through their closed loop control were obscure and probabilistic and it may be suggested that their subjects were unable to decode the signals carrying the knowledge of results information.

The closed loop paradigm can be realized in a variety of situations and at many levels of complexity. We shall not discuss any others here but one recently described by Wolfendale (1969) is particularly worth brief reference. He has devised a program that so alters the values of several independent variables that the one dependent variable is optimally described. The ingenuity and potential of this approach are best appreciated on reading his article.

Interactive studies

These studies are more varied than the others of this section but they are clear examples of on-line work. The novel characteristic of these studies is that subjects actually make decisions about what the computer should do. In other situations information has been provided for the computer to assess and thence to influence subsequent stimuli. However, subjects have not decided particular stimulus attributes or determined their own general situation in an experiment. Any study where a subject has such possibilities is interactive.

Some years ago (cf. Brown, 1959, and Crossman, 1960) it was suggested that short term memory for item position in a list was independent of that for identity. To investigate this distinction between order and content information presents practical problems, apart from any attendant conceptual difficulties. Gibson (1970), helped by the present writer, ran an on-line experiment with display facilities sufficiently flexible to allow an attempt to investigate the suggested independence of order and content information; this experiment was interactive.

Subjects sat, individually, before an oscilloscope output and at the console of an on-line teletypewriter for all three conditions. One was very like an ordinary memory span situation. In this and the other conditions Gibson presented lists of eight different consonants other than Y. Immediately after the word READY a list appeared horizontally across and halfway up the screen. Presentation was for four seconds, and immediately afterwards subjects tried to type the list items on the teletypewriter keyboard. The typed letters appeared simultaneously on the screen and the teletypewriter paper. If a subject wished to omit an item the space bar of the teletypewriter could be tapped. The effect of each tap on the space bar was to move the position of any subsequently typed consonant one place to the right on both paper and screen. In this, and the other conditions, only eight teletypewriter characters (including spaces) could be typed in a recall attempt.

In a second condition when subjects typed letters, after list presentation ended, the computer ensured that the consonants entered were displayed on the screen in their list positions. This, of course, meant that the sequence of letters on the screen would not always correspond with that on the teletypewriter paper. In this condition it was hoped that the subject need only remember content information. Tapping the space bar

reduced the number of letters recalled. Tapping a key corresponding to
no list item produced no letter on the screen.

In the other condition it was hoped only order need be stored. Immediately after a list presentation ended, its items, that were to be recalled
in order, appeared in a different order at the top of the screen, again
being in a horizontal line across it. The subject had to tap the teletypewriter keys corresponding to the list items and do this so that the
letters were entered in their original order. On tapping a key the
corresponding consonant was displayed halfway down the screen and
ceased to be shown in the upper line. The first letter whose key was
tapped appeared on the extreme left of the screen and subsequently
tapped letters were positioned progressively to its right. This effect is
illustrated serially in Figure 4.3. Tapping the space bar in this condition
did not position letters because the entry of teletypewriter characters
was limited to eight, and so some letters remained at the top of the
screen after a recall attempt with space bar taps. This happened rarely.

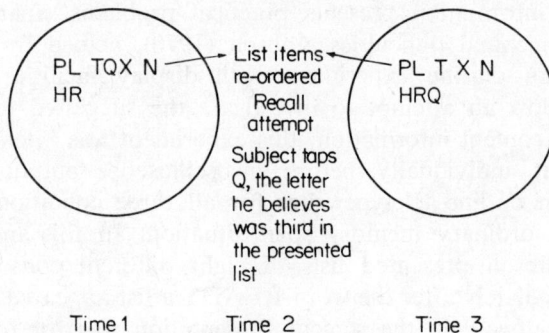

Figure 4.3—*The manipulation by the computer, of list items ordered in
recall by a subject*

The experimental results did not support the independence hypothesis
but watching subjects was intriguing. Enquiry confirmed what observation suggested: the facilities of the order only condition were sometimes
used to exclude certain letters from later recall, and when there was
little confidence in the correctness of some keyboard entries, with the
attempt having to be completed, subjects effectively used the computer
to remove items of whose position they were doubtful. This allowed
them to deal with items presented on the right and of whose position
they were less uncertain.

This on-line experiment is an apt example because it shows how a
subject may produce information for a computer to respond to, or

be directed by, and also because it produced a clear problem of a kind found in other early on-line work, as well as in this study by Gibson. The programming did what it had been specified to do when the experiment to be implemented was conceived, but unfortunately the chosen method for re-presenting consonants confused subjects in the order only condition. This confusion arose, they clearly if less concisely informed us, from the re-presentation being itself a list. Apparently having obtained richer possibilities by devising an unexplored situation one has to explore it to ensure that it is not only logically apt but also subjectively appropriate. To cite a parallel case: the Marathon is logically suited to discovering the best of a number of long distance runners but does so only if they all know the chosen route. (For anyone continuing Gibson's study we suggest re-presenting the list consonants in a circle around the place where the list is to be re-constituted.)

The well-known 'Project Grammarama', reported by Miller (1967) and less accessibly, if more fully, by Miller and Stein (1963), is another interactive study. Subjects had to produce letter strings that met generation rules specified in the computer's programming. They were told the letters in use, but not the rules: these they had to induce. They typed their letter strings at an on-line teletypewriter. After typing a string they supposed admissible they pressed the teletypewriter's blank key and the computer responded by typing RIGHT if the string infringed none of the rules and WRONG otherwise. A deletion facility was provided obviating errors the subject recognized, say, mis-typings. When a letter outside the prescribed set was entered the computer promptly reminded the subject of the prescribed set and other legitimate entries. One of these was the word FINISH which the subject typed when he had some confidence in his knowledge of the appropriate rules. It marked a subject's decision that the computer should give a short test of how well the rules were acquired. The session ended with the computer printing the test score, asking for the name of its respondent and the date and expressing its thanks. This automated experiment of 1963 is elegant, original, and obviously interesting.

Interactive studies of choice in rich environments hold some promise. To illustrate this, consider specifying displays of dots on an oscilloscope output. Among other stimulus parameters one can vary the number of dots in a display, its duration, the number of separate displays in a set, any biases from random in generating the coordinates of the points at which the dots appear, and whether or not each separate display shall move during presentation. One choice situation asked individual subjects, familiar with the experimental situation and its parameters, to type input values for producing displays they found pleasing and for displays they found displeasing. Some serious, busy, and industrious technicians were content to play for minutes at a time in a situation like the one described. Such appeal hardly characterizes those studies of choice that utilize bags of poker chips. The record-keeping accuracy of a computer affords some hope of a study of choice sufficiently fine grained to elucidate rather than obscure making decisions in other than impoverished environments.

Some practical considerations

The preceding sections have sketched some ways an experimental psychologist might use a computer. Some main points about work on undedicated machines have been mentioned in previous chapters and the use of well-known programming languages, such as ALGOL and FORTRAN, is covered in a wide introductory literature. The previous chapter has reviewed languages for on-line work. It remains now to introduce some concepts necessary to carry out a full range of on-line experiments. They concern the program organization and using the peripheral equipment needed in experiments. The most important concepts are: *interface, priority level,* and *interrupt,* but *re-write* and *re-set* times are also mentioned. Particular machine peculiarities are beyond this book but some typical problems are within our scope; for example, the concomitant effects of instructions and problems from ohmic resistances. Some other points of practice are recommended and the section ends with an illustrative outline of how a program on knowledge of results and simple reaction time was made to work, which brings together some of the preceding material.

Interfaces

Using computers for calculations involves carefully designed input and output devices built to fit in with the logical processing parts of the machine. These teletypewriters, readers, tape transports, and punches, etc., are relatively constrained information channels between the computer and the world. They are usually limited to eight binary digits at any one time. The related symbolic codes allow, at most, 256 distinct single symbols and several of the common pieces of peripheral equipment operate at low speeds. In contrast the computer's central processor and memory registers handle more information at a time and operate much faster. The variety of events that *can* be made acceptable to, or controllable by, computer is fortunately much wider than that provided by the standard data peripherals of small machines. To exploit this greater scope interface units must be used. The importance of interfaces in on-line work is stressed not because the standard data peripherals lack interfaces but because it would make little difference to someone carrying out only calculations if they had never heard of them. That is not true for an on-line experimenter. Interfaces translate. An input interface accepts voltages at the wrong level for the computer, or which are ragged functions of time, and provides from them acceptable signals still containing the intended digital information of the original signal. An output interface takes computer signals and amplifies them or extends their duration, or both, and perhaps changes their level, to drive slower devices, such as relays, or power devices, such as tungsten filament bulbs.

Among the units most commonly interfaced to a computer are analog to digital converters (ADC) and their inverse: digital to analog converters (DAC). An ADC is an input device to the computer that supplies effectively instantaneous digital readings of voltage. These can be taken at high speed. Commonly an ADC can take 60,000 readings per second from some continuous voltage, say that related to the galvanic skin response (GSR). These readings are conveyed as binary numbers, often with an accuracy of better than 0.1%, to other parts of the computer system, usually the central processor. A DAC takes a series of digital values each distinct in time and produces from them a corresponding continuous output voltage from the computer. A typical use for DAC is producing the x, y deflexion voltages for the plates of an oscilloscope output; without these voltages it would display a stationary dot. A DAC also operates at much higher speeds than paper tape devices.

An ADC or a DAC will often have its own interface built-in but not always. These converters may need an interface because the digital voltages they deal in are different from those the computer uses. Devices like keyboards built in one's own workshops are generally not worth interfacing individually and as they produce digital information an ADC is unnecessary. For such devices a digital interface is appropriate. An example of the use of digital output interfaces is the driving of displays of discrete lights for experimental purposes.

There are numerous potential sources of information to a computer that can be transduced into continuous voltages by strain gauges or photo-electric cells or simply potentiometers. By using an ADC, such variables as pressure, opacity, and temperature become directly readable by computer. There are, too, a sizeable number of sources that can display information to subjects when driven by voltages produced by the computer. These sources, along with devices supplying digital inputs, obviously circumvent the limitations of tape systems but they all require interfaces, which is why it is worth knowing in detail the interface

facilities on the computer you use for on-line work. If you are fortunate
a technician will solve your interfacing problems for you.

Priority levels and interrupt

A computer can accept and direct information to and from a large
number of peripheral devices. None of the many operations involved
are infinitely fast. Even a computer carrying out a million instructions a
second needs time to obey each one. In real-time, events occur independently of the computer's state: a subject tensing a muscle to press a
key in response to a computer-presented stimulus normally does not
know when the computer can accept his response or measure the
accompanying changes in muscle potential. Even more obviously a
crystal oscillator clock cannot miss a pulse when the computer is busy.
Sometimes devices have to queue for service by the central processor
but the examples just given illustrate that some devices demand a briefer
queue.

It is to accommodate such problems of simultaneity or overlap that
computers suitable for on-line experiments provide levels of program
with orders of priority, or some equivalent facility. In the example
above, the subject responded to a computer-presented stimulus by
pressing a key and a simple computer program assigns that response
input to the highest level of priority. This is done by connecting the
interface unit of that key to a 'level one priority interrupt'. An interrupt
is a signal of an event external to the computer processor and affecting it.

Consider a simple psychological task: judging when two lines are of
equal length. This task can be presented on-line. For example, our
subject could be seated in front of the oscilloscope output of a computer. On the screen are displayed two horizontal lines with the mid-
point of one line vertically below that of the other. One line is of a
standard length and does not change during a trial. The other line when
first shown is less than two thirds of the length of the longer one. This
initial state is indicated by the additional appearance on the oscilloscope
of: READY? To show his readiness to make a judgement the subject
presses a key held in the left hand and as the computer responds only
the lines remain displayed. The shorter line then starts to grow longer:
both of its end points moving slowly apart.

When the subject judges the two lines to be equal in length he presses
a key held in his right hand. This latter key-press signals the computer
to measure the length of the growing line when judged equal to the
standard one. The trial is then complete; obviously we could have more
like it.

The role of the oscilloscope and keys, and the form of the subject's situation should now be clear and the programming point which justifies this example can be made. The most important component of the system is the key held in the subject's right hand. It is the pressing of that key which indicates the instant at which the subject believes the two lines are of equal length. Accordingly it is at that time that the computer has to record the length of the growing line. Delay could lead to error because the growing line might grow more in the interval. Anticipation in the computer noting the length of the growing line will defeat the purpose of the experiment for the subject will not have made a judgement. In wording commonly used when describing on-line computer work: the interrupt provided by the key-press on the right hand key must switch the computer to obeying the instructions on a higher priority level. These instructions when obeyed will register the length the growing line has currently reached. After this record has been obtained the growth of the line could continue or a new trial start immediately. Figure 4.4 illustrates the latter of these two possibilities. Notice that the flow diagram is so contrived that if the subject should inadvertently press his left-hand key while the line is growing the oscilloscope display is unaltered. In practice the return to the lower level will be so rapid that perceptually nothing will happen to the two line display.

Figure 4.4 is not a complete flow diagram for writing a program to run the experiment described. Points it omits are discussed below. Before going on to those more complete examples it may be worthwhile to see how many inadequacies in Figure 4.4 you can note.

The interrupting device may simply produce a change of program level without requiring any transfer of information between processor and peripheral. The oscillator acting as a clock is used this way in an example below. Note that a crystal clock used by a computer is external to the computer processor which is counting the number of pulses from the clock. In everyday clocks the ticking and the positions of the hands are aspects of a single unit—the clock. In the computer we call the pulsing crystal alone the clock; although, for mnemonic purposes, we might in our programs refer to the register in which we keep a count of its pulses as CLOCK. The interrupt may, however, initiate a data transfer; the processor will often input data from the interrupting device; it may also output data on clearing an interrupt, which means returning the device to a state where it can interrupt again.

In the example mentioned earlier, of a subject tensing a muscle to press a key in response to a computer-presented stimulus the effect of our level one interrupt is somewhat along the following lines. When the subject presses his key the instruction currently being executed is

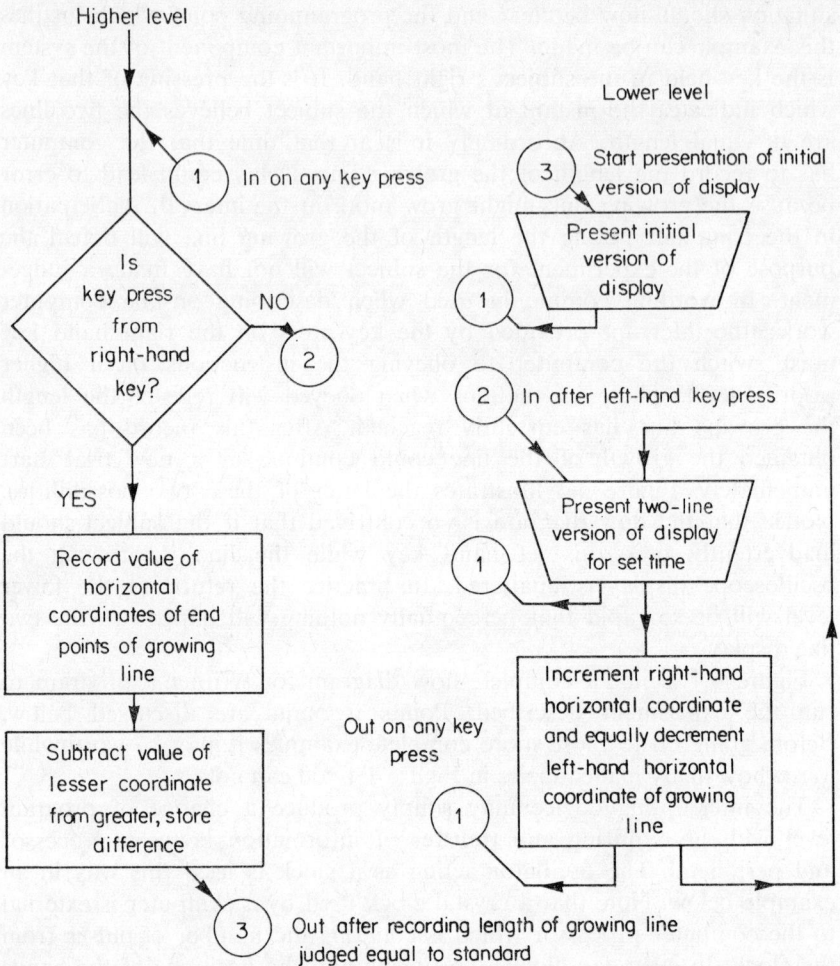

Figure 4.4—*Fragment from a flow-chart to illustrate the relation of program
levels for an on-line experiment on judging line lengths*

finished and the computer immediately starts to execute the level one
program. Presumably in our example, of key pressing, the top level
program could record the latency of the response. This entails referring
to a time measure derived from the clock which is an oscillator. Suppose
it pulses at a frequency of 1,000 hertz. If a register of the computer is
set to zero immediately before presenting the stimulus then time can be
counted in it, in thousandths of a second, by incrementing the register
by one every time the clock pulses. Suppose the stimulus is to be dis-

played until the subject responds, i.e. for an unknown time. The clock pulses have to interrupt the display program rather than wait for it to finish, otherwise reaction times of zero would appear. Putting the clock on level two, the second highest priority level, would be appropriate. This is because a reaction time study hinges on the subject's response and so we allot to the highest priority level the interrupt this response generates. Were the response interrupt brief and the clock on a higher level the subject's latency might go unmeasured and our experiment would be less nearly perfect than we had hoped. Accordingly, we put the clock on a lower priority level than the response.

Even on a slow machine, obeying 40,000 instructions per second, the registration of time produces no disruption of the stimulus visible to the subject. The ADC input from the suitably amplified and interfaced electromyographic measure can be read every hundredth of a second on the same priority level as that on which the stimulus is produced. These readings also use a series of instructions sufficiently infrequent and brief as to avoid any noticeable stimulus interruption perceptible as flicker.

In introducing the effect of the level one interrupt the loose phrase 'somewhat along the following lines' occurred. This looseness comes partly from the range of relevant circumstances in which the interrupt might occur; it also comes from the range of facilities different computers have, to accept interrupts. In counting clock pulses little need happen apart from going to the higher level. There the computer may only need to increment in store, jump back two instructions and then return to the former level. The jumping back is necessary for the next interrupt to increment the clock register again. Without it the entry point would move beyond the timing program and subsequent instructions would be executed. The clock pulses could cease to be interrupts (being on the same level as the program being obeyed) and problems would ensue from missing the return to the former level. These points are illustrated schematically below.

Attempts at a timing program (in words) may be as follows:

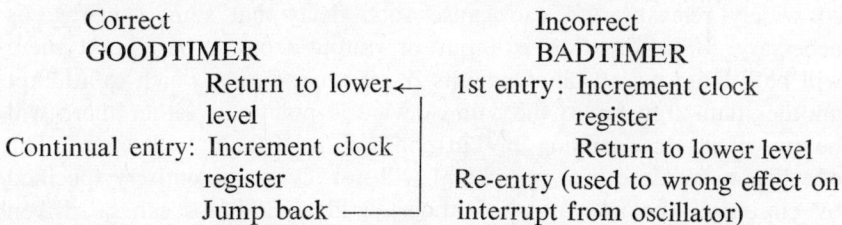

Correct	Incorrect
GOODTIMER	BADTIMER
Return to lower← level	1st entry: Increment clock register
Continual entry: Increment clock register	Return to lower level
Jump back ———⌐	Re-entry (used to wrong effect on interrupt from oscillator)

In a more limited system lacking an increment in store instruction, on going to the higher level the program would need to store the contents of certain registers. In our example we shall protect the accumulator contents in the low level program from higher level loss as follows.

Protecting a register's contents when changing program levels:

LONGTIMER

Return to lower level

Continual entry: Store contents of accumulator

Load contents of clock register into accumulator

Add contents of a register holding +1 to the
Accumulator's contents

Store contents of accumulator in the clock register

Restore contents of accumulator that were stored by
instruction at entry

Jump back six instructions

Protection like this is generally needed when the higher level program uses the accumulator and certain other registers. In some sophisticated computers it is given automatically by hardware, rather than by program when an interrupt occurs. The preceding example points another piece of necessary housekeeping when using priority levels. Somewhere the initial entry points to programs on the different levels must be specified. In general each level has an associated control register the contents of which determine the next instruction to be obeyed. Where there is no such single register there is a functional equivalent. Unless the address of the first instruction for the program of a particular level is stored (or 'planted' as it is sometimes put) in the corresponding control register the effect of changing levels is 'indeterminate', which is a neutral way of hinting chaos.

Hardware and on-line experiments

No adequate treatment can be attempted here but some points are so widely relevant and can cause such delay that some coverage is necessary. If information is input or output from a peripheral there will be a finite period, known as its *re-set time,* during which to attempt another data transfer to the same device is pointless: either there will be no effect or a mixing of current and prior data will occur. The effective re-set time of a peripheral will not always be entirely specified by circuitry. The rate at which tungsten filament bulbs can be driven by a computer controlling the circuit supplying their current will generally exceed the rate at which their changes in brightness can be discriminated: white-hot metal takes time to cool. Conversely, failure to refresh computer-driven displays sufficiently often will produce visual flicker; oscilloscopes are most commonly affected. To decide if such effects may be likely to need special consideration make *rough* calculations based on: the time to write one element of the display, the largest number of elements to be used in the display, and on the period for which an element is acceptably clear after being refreshed. The maximum time for which an element can be left unrefreshed is called its *re-write time*.

Sometimes specially made equipment passes a technician's bench tests but fails to work properly when connected through a usually appropriate interface, that is, one which has worked with other equipment producing the same input or output signals. This is no occasion for abuse. Here are two, among several possible, causes for such a failure. First, the program employing the device is logically inappropriate: an initial control signal may be necessary to 'set up' the device, and if it once got started it would work as expected. Second, the device is being sabotaged by ohmic resistances; this is less common. It means that the minute resistances of some of the connectors used with the device are impeding its working. Earth (or ground) lines are ones to check first. If they are connected to a circuit board or card on a computer with its chassis at earth potential have them re-connected direct to the chassis.

Other points of practice

The end of the previous paragraph was spelt out to show how running on-line computer studies is one proper field for a thoroughly pragmatic approach. When a program will not work, do not ascribe its failure to something or someone else until there are strong evidential grounds for doing so. The speed with which the defeated users run to others to solve computer problems they could perfectly well solve themselves is astonishing. If this rings of advice to young brides it does nevertheless seem useful, and forgivable, to state a few points. Several of these will recall advice already given in Chapter 2.

1. Write as much program as you can in routines—after establishing that they are not already written. (Routines, it will be remembered, are self-contained blocks of program that can be put together in larger programs.)

2. Annotate programs and routines fully. Pay special attention to describing the effects of input parameters and to any parts of the program requiring experimenter intervention, for example which peripherals to connect to which priority levels. This week you may

understand a program; next week no one may, and if you cannot even make it run again, because of being unable to connect all the relevant hardware, possibly no one ever will.

3. Always seek the chance sensibly to reduce a series of pieces of on-line program in assembly (or higher) language to one binary tape.

4. Label all program print-outs, or listings, their tapes, and subjects' data and print-outs of their responses where these occur—do this promptly.

Following these few injunctions will reduce frustration.

The concomitant effect of instructions

Programs for on-line experiments are often written in assembly languages. In these each program instruction corresponds to one computer word, or register, some mnemonics are allowable, and at least some addressing aids are provided for the programmer. The fine control of the machine that these languages give makes them especially suited to on-line work. In FORTRAN or ALGOL, which are compiler languages, one cannot directly instruct the computer to read an ADC or change the pulsing rate of a 'clock'. The closeness of assembly languages to actual machine instructions does, however, have possible disadvantages, apart from increasing the number of instructions in a program. One is the greater scope for the concomitant effects of instructions to subvert programs.

There are computers that shift their accumulator contents left when inputting characters from their photo-electric readers. If the accumulator had been cleared before reading, say, two eight-channel tape characters, one might hope to have them in the accumulator after two reads, the accumulator having more than 16 bits. In fact the quotient register which is used in division calculations is functionally on the right of the accumulator in many machines and its contents too may shift left when characters are input. If the quotient register is not equal to zero its contents may distort the characters input. As the quotient can sometimes be set by other instructions than the shifts, divide, and multiply, which obviously involve it, the concomitant effects of these other orders need to be remembered.

Concomitant effects are not all hardware-determined. In one series of machines, one program can run another with both of them being under what is termed executive control. In the dominant program certain registers are set to permit entry to the other. Unfortunately such entry can be effected directly only once and subsequent direct re-entry is not reliably possible. Why this is so does not matter here. What is relevant is that users have to know this executive characteristic and how to circumvent the concomitant effect of moving between programs.

There are numerous effects like this and it is not possible here to describe them all. What is important is to bear in mind that they will be specified in machine manuals or instruction books. Concomitant effects can often be ignored and sometimes to do so is unwise, not because an error will occur but because an easy solution might be missed.

An example of a program to run an on-line experiment

The experiment investigates if simple reaction times decrease when subjects know their reaction times for immediately preceding responses.

The subject is given a foresignal of specified duration: the word READY presented on an oscilloscope. After a specified brief pause the stimulus (the characters XX) appears centrally below the position of the foresignal. The subject responds by pressing a hand-held response key. This response terminates the stimulus. After anticipatory responses the word CHEAT is displayed for a fixed time and an additional trial given. After responses with positive latencies, in the knowledge of results condition, the reaction time is displayed for a specified time as a four-digit number, the subject knowing this is his reaction time in milliseconds. In the control condition there is no knowledge of results. There is always a pause between the response and the succeeding READY signal. This is specifiable so that the overall length of runs in the two conditions can be comparable. All runs end after 100 reaction times are recorded and these data are then punched out. This unsophisticated experiment is easily set up and promises to indicate the worth of less crude studies.

In designing the program for the experiment, three already written routines were available: one for inputting and a second for outputting signed integers; the other displayed alphanumeric characters on the oscilloscope. The hand-held key was produced during a day by workshop staff and the interfaced crystal oscillator and oscilloscope were well-tried peripherals. The scheme of levels chosen was the one described earlier in this section: the response key was on level one, the 'clock' on level two, and the stimuli were generated on the base level where most of the housekeeping for the program was also done. The following tasks remain for the program to carry out:

Read the parameters specifying: display durations;
pauses between READY and XX;
and the response and READY.

LEVEL 1

LEVEL 2

```
        (Start)
           │
           ▼
    ┌──────────────┐
    │ Read input   │
    │ parameters   │
    └──────────────┘
```

┌──────────────────────────┐
│ Enter on oscillator   │
│ pulse wherever base   │
│ level program is   │
└──────────────────────────┘
          │
          ▼
┌──────────────────┐
│ Increment clock │
│ register by 1   │
└──────────────────┘
          │
          ▼
┌──────────────────────┐
│ Return to base level │
│ exit point   │
└──────────────────────┘

(3)

┌────────────────────┐   ┌──────────────────────┐
│ Plant addresses of │   │ To initiation of   │
│ initial instructions│ │ base level program   │
│ in sequence control │ └──────────────────────┘
│ registers of level │
│ 2 and base level   │
└────────────────────┘

Is response anticipatory i.e. is flag Ø ?

NO

(1)

┌──────────────────────────┐
│ In from base level on   │
│ receiving subject's   │
│ response   │
└──────────────────────────┘

┌──────────────────┐
│ Record reaction │
│ time from clock │
│ register in   │
│ location 'RT'   │
└──────────────────┘

YES

┌────────────────┐
│ Display CHEAT │
│ on 'scope   │
│ for fixed   │
│ time   │
└────────────────┘

Is knowledge of results required?

NO

(4)

┌──────────────────┐
│ To base level to │
│ restart cycle   │
└──────────────────┘

YES

┌──────────────────┐
│ Display value   │
│ of RT on 'scope │
│ for fixed time   │
└──────────────────┘

(2)

┌──────────────────┐
│ To base level   │
│ to record RT   │
└──────────────────┘

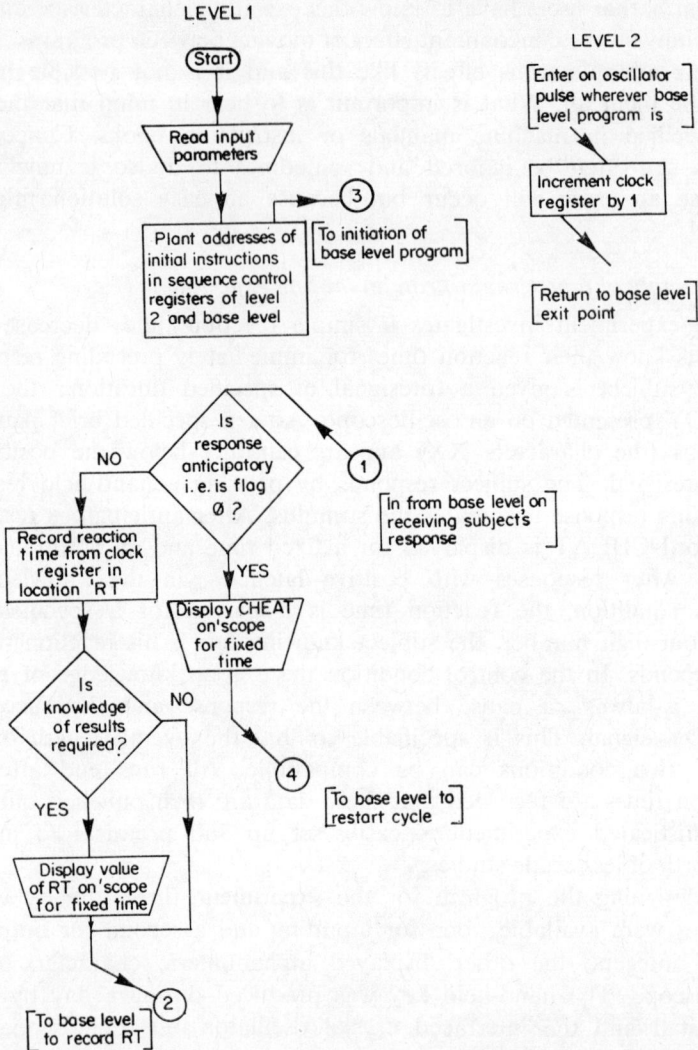

Read the parameter indicating whether Knowledge of Results is to be given.

Plant the addresses of the initial instructions for the lower level programs in the appropriate sequence control registers.

Start a count of how many reaction times have been recorded.

Set the reaction time register to zero.

Set the register to be used to indicate anticipatory responses to zero. (This register is being used as a 'flag').

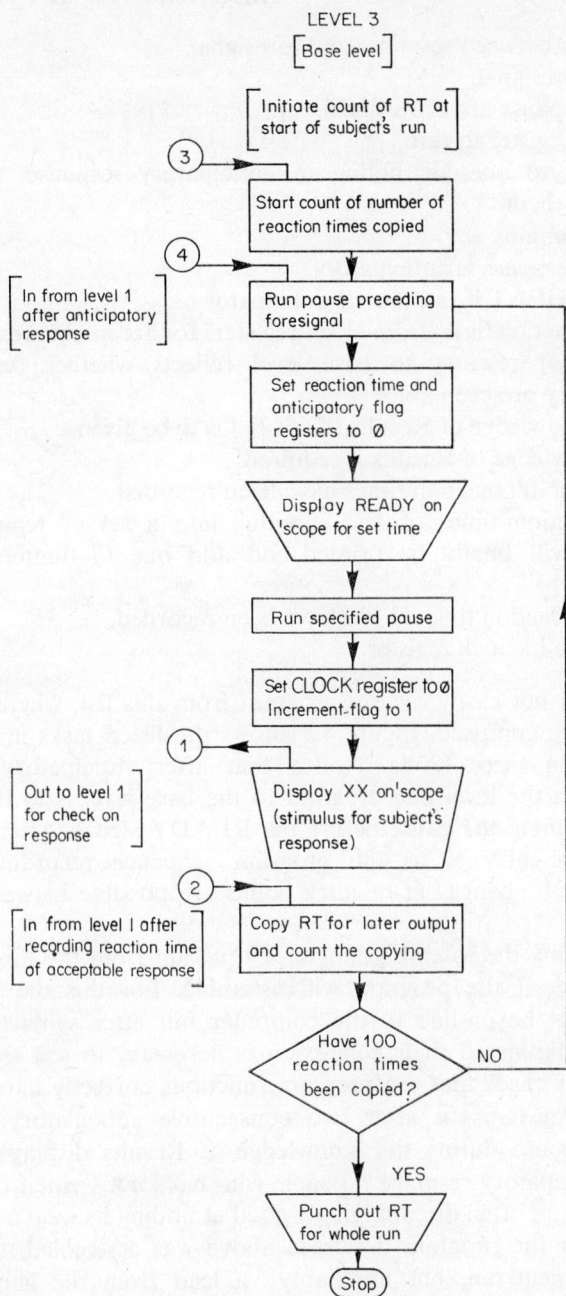

Figure 4.5—*Flow-chart of experiment on the influence of Knowledge of Results on simple reaction times*

Run pause between response and foresignal.

Display foresignal.

Run brief pause after foresignal.

Set clock register to zero.

Increment to one, on noting an anticipatory response, the register indicating them.

Display stimulus.

Check if response is anticipatory.

Display CHEAT if response is anticipatory.

Record reaction time (from clock register) for acceptable responses.

Ensure that re-entry to base level reflects whether response was anticipatory or acceptable.

Find if Knowledge of Results (K. of R.) is to be given.

Give Knowledge of Results if required.

Discover if 100 reaction times have been recorded.

Copy reaction time for last stimulus into a set of registers whose contents will finally be printed and add one to number noted as copied.

Print out reaction times if 100 have been recorded.

Count time in clock register.

One could not easily write a program from this list, where levels and sequences are confused. Figure 4.5 shows the listed tasks arranged in a flow-chart on three levels. Notice that after anticipatory responses, re-entry from the level one program to the base level is to the program sequence running the pause before the READY signal. After acceptable responses, re-entry is to the program sequence recording response latencies. Such changes in re-entry points are possible between any pair of levels.

After writing the assembly language program from the flow-chart one must discover if the program will assemble. For this the 'clock' and key need not be on-line to the computer but after syntactic mistakes have been eliminated their connexion is necessary to test the program. Testing must check that the program functions correctly in odd circumstances. What happens after two consecutive anticipatory responses? Does a response during the Knowledge of Results display count as a normal anticipatory response? People who have not written the program being tested are often discouragingly good at finding its weaknesses!

Soon after the program discussed above was assembled, the reaction time experiment ran, but unreliably: a lead from the hand-held key had a significant resistance. When this was eliminated everything was ready for the subjects. Sometimes things take longer.

On knowing the destination of the bandwagon

There are more possibilities for experimental psychology now that we possess computers than there have ever been before. This is no guarantee that results will be universally entrancing; it is too easy to get lost under computer control.

We not only have new forms for our experiments, we also have the facility to change with unparalleled ease parameter values in any experiment and quite often we can, without much effort, add another parameter or two just to see what happens. Given a modicum of enthusiasm anyone can bury himself in data and paper tape. The opportunities for virtuoso special apparatus are also great.

It seems unchallengeable that easier data acquisition, specialist hardware and advanced programming techniques should be taken seriously. It is useful to be able to understand the work of computer specialists but the beginner might remember how time-consuming such involvement can be and give his main attention to psychology. In the future, some of the interesting problems in computer experiments will be situational, i.e. investigations of the complex environments in which we live.

Not all the results from on-line experiments will generalize to other situations that are not automated. In his work on adult human learning, Kay (1953) remarked the change in response style a piece of laboratory apparatus could occasion in a psychotic subject (who apparently could not complete a task, but who when Kay switched off the attached polygraph recorder, immediately made the final response with some satisfaction). Some subjects in an experiment by the present author typed abuse into an on-line teleprinter and then left the experiment. Such aggressive responses to machines have been mentioned by Conrad (1967) outlining for psychologists the problem of designing machines that uninstructed users could correctly operate on first encounter. Other subjects in on-line experiments have given the impression of idly playing. More subtle situational variables are the little understood ones that produce contrary results in formally similar tasks presented on one occasion on a computer, and on another in some other way. Studies at Sheffield and Uppsala have produced this kind of difference. It has taken a long time for psychology to become widely aware of experimenter effects; it must also be wary of computer effects in on-line experiments.

Discussing psychology Before Computers, Miller (1967, p. 94) wrote, 'I can think of no summary statement more appropriate than that made by a famous American athlete who said, "I've been rich and I've been poor, and believe me, rich is better." Believe me, computers are better.'

Let us remember that in this All Digital era not all those who believe in a Messiah think everything is going to be perfect—even automatically.

Further Reading

Green, B. F. Jr. (1963) *Digital Computers in Research: An introduction for Behavioral and Social Scientists.* McGraw-Hill, New York. Comprehensive, clear and written by someone who as much as any single person showed psychologists why computers were worth knowing about.

Moray, N. (Ed.) (1969) *On-line Computing for Psychology.* Proceedings of a NATO Advanced Study Institute held at the Department of Psychology, University of Sheffield, England. Difficult to obtain but especially worth chasing for its candour on the pragmatics and politics of on-line work.

Uttal, W. R. (1967) *Real-Time Computers: Technique and Applications in the Psychological Sciences.* Harper and Row, New York. A detailed introduction to the field. Presents many technical concepts and points worth knowing.

Chapter 5

The Computer Modelling of Behaviour

Michael J. Apter

This chapter starts with a complaint—a complaint about the English language. Whichever term is chosen to describe the contents of the chapter, it will have connotations which may make it difficult for some people to take its subject-matter seriously. Thus the word 'simulation' is often used to mean 'feign' or 'pretend' and therefore the term 'computer simulation' might be taken to imply that the computer is in some way cheating: either it is not really generating the behaviour which it appears to be, or the methods used are quite dissimilar to those used by organisms in producing similar behaviour, or the behaviour itself is only superficially similar. In the case of any particular simulation the last two possibilities would have to be examined in any attempt at evaluation; but it is unfortunate that the word itself appears to prejudge the issue. A similar point could be made about the word 'imitate'; and the word 'mimic', which has also been used in the present context on odd occasions, not only suffers from the same deficiency but in addition implies an attempt to ridicule on the part of the computer. What about the term actually used in the chapter heading: 'computer modelling'? The problem here is that children's toys are often models, and so the term 'computer modelling' has to some people overtones of play and childishness. The perhaps unconscious, and certainly incorrect, syllogism seems to be: toys are sometimes models, hence computer models are no more than toys. All this no doubt exaggerates the case, but it can be seen that a difficulty of terminology does nevertheless remain.

The belief underlying the following chapter is that computer models can be more than entertaining deceptions or expensive toys. The intention is to show how they can be used seriously, and to advantage, in a scientific psychology. Partly because of this, but for other reasons too, this chapter will be more polemical than many of the other chapters in this book.

Structural and functional models

A preliminary distinction which it is useful to make in discussing

125

computer models is between 'structural' and 'functional' models. Oettinger has discriminated them in the following way:

'A functional model is like the electrical engineer's proverbial "black box", where something goes in and something comes out, and what is inside is unknown or relevant only to the extent of somehow relating outputs to inputs. A structural model emphasizes the contents of the box. A curve describing the current passing through a semiconductor diode as a function of the voltage applied across its terminals is a functional model of this device that is exceedingly useful to electronic-circuit designers ... A corresponding structural model would account for the characteristic shape of the curve in terms that describe the transport of charge-carriers through semiconductors, the geometry of the contacts, and so forth.' (Oettinger, 1969, pp. 21–22.)

It will be argued here firstly that the structuralist methodology has a place in psychology. J. A. Deutsch has also notably argued this and the interested reader is referred to his book *The Structural Basis of Behaviour* (1960). Secondly it will be argued that the computer is a useful medium for structuralist models in psychology.

To some extent functionalist and structuralist methods are complementary, the one concerned primarily with questions of prediction and control and the other with understanding. The situation is of course not clear-cut because the ability to predict and control in themselves may be said to represent in some way an increased understanding, and because understanding the structure of a system may increase one's ability to predict and control.

It should be noted that the terms 'structural' and 'functional' are being used here in the broad sense just indicated. When they are referred to psychology in this chapter they will not be used in the way in which they are traditionally used in psychology to refer to two movements in the early history of the subject, the former associated especially with the work of people like Wundt and Titchener and the latter with the views of Dewey, Angell and others. It is clear that in this broad sense the whole tenor of behaviourist methodology in psychology has been functionalist: the emphasis has been on measurable independent and dependent variables, often stimuli and responses, studied under well-controlled conditions, and the attempt to find lawful relationships between them. The epitome of this approach finds its expression in the work of Skinner and the 'experimental analysis of behaviour' school. Some behaviourists, notably Hull, have attempted to go further than this, but the resulting theories of what happens between stimulus and response have been limited by an understandable fear of moving too far away from the objectively measurable stimuli and responses themselves. And yet for a full understanding of behaviour it may be necessary to move further away. In general, although the functionalist approach can to some extent generate an increased understanding, it may be limited in psychology by the following four closely related considerations.

1. It has become increasingly obvious during the last fifty years that the nervous system does more than act as a switchboard which passively mediates between stimuli and responses, but that it actively *organizes* information. This would appear to be particularly true, of course, of the human nervous system. In support of this one can mention, among other things, the phenomenon of 'selective attention' which is of much current interest and implies that the organism chooses its own stimuli (cf. Norman, 1969); the Gestalt argument that stimuli are typically treated as patterns and that the organism may react to relationships between stimuli rather than to stimuli themselves; the evidence of Bartlett and others for the constructive rather than simply reproductive nature of memory; and the development, organization and modification of attitudes and their relationship to both perception and behaviour. It is true that each of these can be dealt with to some extent in a functionalist way, but the results seem to call more strongly for a structuralist explanation than do the results of simple learning experiments —and already we see many structuralist models being developed for both selective attention and attitudes. In more general terms we begin to see the nervous system being treated as an information-processing system rather than as a stimulus-response connecting system.

   Attention to the way in which the nervous system organizes information, leads one to realize that it is in itself a highly organized system. It is no doubt subject to laws, and one hopes that it will be possible to uncover many of these using functionalist methods; but to understand fully how it works it may also be necessary to understand the way in which various processes, many of them concurrent, are related to each other.

2. The aim of functional approaches appears always to be to find a mathematical formula such that when the value of an input variable is specified, the value of an output variable is also specified. But the assumption underlying this is that psychological systems do indeed operate in such a way that independent variables unequivocally specify dependent variables. This implies that the organism is a rather static system with relatively little going on inside it. But although one may criticize dynamic psychologies like those of Freud and Adler from a scientific point of view, one cannot but be impressed with their insistence that psychological systems are not static but involve continual

dynamic internal interactions. Related to this, dynamic psychologists have also tended to emphasize the need to examine behaviour from a developmental point of view whereas functionalists have tended to assume that the *history* of a system can be ignored: a mathematical relationship which holds at one time is expected to hold at other times too. This overlooks the possibility that stored information may play an important part in governing and changing behaviour. But it is likely, surely, that it does: the organism seems to accumulate, and use, and be subject to the effects of previous experience in a complicated way. Thus Mays (1964) in a powerful critique of probability models in psychology such as that of Bush and Mosteller (1955) has argued that the manifestations of memory 'may be discontinuous and only appear at selected points in the succession of events' (p. 264); he also mentions 'practice' effects and the possible long-range effects of 'trauma' as examples of situations where stored information needs to be taken into account. This is not to say that functionalists are not aware of this kind of phenomenon; but they often choose experimental situations and design experiments to avoid such 'aberrations'. In doing so they could be missing much of importance in the study of behaviour. This leads us on to the next consideration which concerns another form of stored information.

3. The activity of the nervous system may be partly pre-determined before it comes into contact with the environment at all. It should be noted that even if all changes in behaviour (which were more than merely adaptive) were due to learning, something would still have to be said about what kind of structure in a nervous system would allow this to happen. After all, even a mirror, which perfectly reflects its environment, has to have a structure (and in this case a very special one) which brings this about. However, it is extremely doubtful that all changes *are* due to learning, at least in any simple way. This is not the place to discuss the old nature-nurture problem in any detail; it is perhaps enough for present purposes to indicate the evidence collected by ethologists for processes like imprinting. Thus some birds treat whatever moving object they see for a short period after hatching as they would a parent. In the natural state such an object usually is the parent; but under experimental conditions other objects can be substituted. Animals which display imprinting, therefore, have been *pre-programmed* to produce a particular kind of learning at a particular moment. It is likely that other animals, including humans, go through critical periods during which they are especially sensitive to, and able to learn from, particular aspects of their environments.

An anthropologist, impressed by the evidence for such processes, has argued that we must assume a capacity not just to learn but '. . . the capacity to learn some things rather than others, and to learn some things easily rather than others, and to learn some rather specific things into the bargain . . . (the organism) is in a state of readiness—at various points in the life cycle—to process certain kinds of information. This information has to be of a certain type, but the actual "message" can vary a lot.' (Robin Fox, 1970, pp. 36–7). He goes on to point out that while this is not a *tabula rasa* behaviourist theory, neither is it a traditional instinct theory of the McDougall type. Chomsky's well-publicized view that the types of organization of input necessary for language acquisition in the human are pre-programmed (Chomsky, 1957) is in a similar vein: according to this view, although the individual acquires language from the environment he requires a programme, which animals do not have, to accomplish this special feat.

This is all related to the previous main point in that the way in which information is organized may itself depend on instructions built into the nervous system. Certainly it is possible to study phenomena like imprinting using a functionalist methodology—for example, to find the optimum stimulus properties for imprinting to take place and the relationship between certain stimulus variables and strength of imprinting as measured in various ways—but at some stage it would seem to be necessary to reconstruct the program which underlies and gives rise to such relationships.

It should be added that according to ethologists like Lorenz and Tinbergen, besides various learning capacities being available to the organism, whole sequences of species-specific behaviour ('instincts') may also be available to the animal in stored form. These simply have to be 'released' by the appropriate stimuli in the environment including, especially, stimuli from other members of that species.

4. Behaviour appears to be *synthesized* as well as elicited. Until recently the tendency has been in psychology, especially behaviourist psychology, to think of the organism either as passively having responses elicited from it or (more recently, following Skinner) as emitting responses. In either case the behaviour is conceived of as being made up of a sequence of atomistic units, often referred to as 'responses'. Consequently the organism, especially the human organism, may appear simpler than it really is. One does not even need to refer here to human behaviour like creating masterpieces of music or constructing cathedrals. It is possible to make the point with comparatively simple

processes such as producing grammatical sentences. Although sentence-construction is simple in everyday terms, such a process strains the limits of stimulus-response behaviourism. Chomsky (1957) has demonstrated that sentences cannot be built up as a linear string of words and gives cogent linguistic reasons for this. Rather, sentences must in some sense be planned and generated as wholes by the speaker. (The reader unfamiliar with Chomsky's ideas will find more detail in Chapter 7 below.)

If this is true of language behaviour, then it may well be true of other kinds of behaviour too. In other words, the organism may generally be more creative than it is given credit for by behaviourists. It may construct or generate its behaviour as an organized process (even though necessarily it has to be emitted in a temporal sequence), rather than simply emitting responses on a moment-to-moment basis, each response being related to a single (internal or external) stimulus or configuration of stimuli at an immediately preceding moment. This point of view has been developed in particular by Miller, Galanter and Pribram (1960) who believe that the S–R unit is too small to deal with purposeful behaviour and who introduce the concept of 'plans' into psychology, a plan being '... any hierarchical process in the organism that can control the order in which a sequence of operations is to be performed' (Miller, Galanter and Pribram, 1960, p. 16). They go on to say that 'A plan is, for an organism, essentially the same as a program for a computer, especially if the program has a sort of hierarchical character ...' (p. 16). The use of plans gives an organism its appearance of autonomy from the environment and of using this environment rather than being used by it. This consideration is related to the earlier one about internal genetic information, because if the organism does synthesize behaviour, it presumably requires information to do this: information in the form of a set of rules, or a 'structure' or a 'programme'. If this is true, a functional approach to understanding such behaviour and the way it is produced is limited, firstly because the kind of information involved is internal and cannot be 'got at' easily by stimulus-response methods, and secondly because the information in any case cannot usefully be described in terms of relationships between variables.

It will have been noticed that the four general points mentioned here are related to each other in various ways. For example, if information in the nervous system is organized (point 1), so is emitted behaviour (point 4); the fact that sentences cannot be built up on a word-to-next-word basis (Chomsky, point 4) is an example of the need to take the structure of the memory-store into account (point 2); the possession of genetic pre-programs (point 3) may allow the animal to organize information (point 1) and to synthesize behaviour (point 4); and so on.

None of this is intended to denigrate functional approaches in themselves, but rather to criticize those who believe that psychology can progress through functionalist methods alone. It may be that psychology has had to go through a strongly functionalist phase to establish its credentials as a science; but only a limited (if still large) domain of psychological problems can be dealt with in this way in the future. The advent of the computer may help to make it possible to embark on a scientific exploration of more complicated structural problems.

The four considerations outlined lead one to think of the nervous system as an organized information-processing system, governed by programs, able to store and retrieve information, and able to act on the basis of these programs and stored information in a constructive and relatively autonomous way—in other words as something like a large computer with an enormous memory store, complex input-output equipment and organized hierarchies of programs.

The relevance of the computer

Clearly, there are important respects in which computers (at the present stage of development) and brains are different. For example, the brain contains many more elements than any computer yet constructed; it appears not to be entirely digital in its functioning, and it operates in a highly parallel fashion while today's computers operate mostly sequentially. Also, it would seem that memory in the brain may not be totally erasable as it is in the computer, with the exception of those programs which are wired into the computer. And the brain exhibits some degree of plasticity or equipotentiality—if part of it is damaged, other parts of it may be able to take over the damaged part's functions. All of this raises difficulties for those who would wish to draw a precise and detailed analogy between computers and brains, especially at the levels of hardware and physiology respectively. (For a fuller discussion, see Von Neumann, 1958; Sluckin, 1954; and George, 1961.)

It will have been realized, however, that the comparison which has just been made in this chapter is at a rather more general level. At this level both can be regarded as information-processing devices which differ in some respects and are similar in others. The computer is a kind of brain and the brain a kind of computer. Fortunately the computer can be programmed so as to approximate to the brain in various specified ways, and it is of course this feature which makes it useful to the psychologist since he can use it for purposes of simulation. It may have some features, like those mentioned above, which limit the amount of approximation which is possible. But for many purposes of psychological interest these need not matter. For example it does not affect the principles involved in a program simulating, say, hypothesis formation, that the program is to be erased afterwards or that if part of the computer is damaged the program might not work. It is not the aim of the computer programmer to produce an exact copy of the brain in all its complexity. Rather, the aim is to write computer programs to model and therefore make inferences about the programs that govern selected kinds of behaviour; and such inferences are usually about the programs themselves, not about the way they happen to be embodied physically unless this is of direct relevance (as it is in some cases, e.g. Uhr and Vossler, 1963). An exception, of course, is where the program itself is conceived of from the beginning as representing definite events at the neurophysiological level and here it may be necessary to adopt various conventions to overcome computer limitations, e.g. to represent parallel events in sequential terms.

In any case, computer models are useful in studying any kind of process—not just psychological but, for example, economic, military or ecological. This is because they ensure that the theoretical ideas underlying the programs are *precise* and *effective*. It is not possible to write a program containing ill-defined ideas: a program consists of a specific set of instructions, and putting ideas in the form of a program forces the theorist to make his ideas precise. Also to work in the way required, a program must be consistent (i.e. contain no contradictions) and complete: putting ideas in the form of a program ensures that they are effective. Once a program is functioning it brings to life the ideas incorporated in it and may do so in a striking and stimulating manner.

It should be added that functional as well as structural models have been run on computers. The functional models in this case are usually mathematical models, the implications of which are worked out on the computer. (See, for example, the program of Robinowitz described later in this book on pp. 217–8). That is, the computer is used as a data-processor in which the data happen to represent the inputs to some other system and the processing is carried out in terms of mathematical formulae which relate such inputs to outputs of that system. The computer may be a convenient way of making predictions from mathematical or functional models, but is no more than this. It is when we come to structural models, in which the *means* used by the computer to produce an output are intended to model at a general level the means used by the system being simulated, that computer modelling really comes into its own, and takes unique advantage of what the computer has to offer. For the rest of this chapter by 'computer models' we shall mean 'structural computer models'.

The general point of view being expounded here is also of course broadly consistent with that of 'cognitive psychology' as pioneered by Tolman and Köhler. But as Miller, Galanter and Pribram (1960) argue, cognitive psychologists have not gone far enough but have left a 'theoretical vacuum between cognition and action' (p. 11) and this vacuum requires even more cognitive theory: thus according to this argument, Tolman concerned himself with the way in which the rat builds up cognitive maps (Tolman, 1948) but hardly at all with the way in which these maps are used in the actual production of behaviour. In contrast to this, computer models must actually produce 'behaviour'. And this necessity also ensures that the ideas involved are not just vague redescriptions like the words 'insight', 'cognitive maps', 'expectancies', etc., words which sound impressive but do not in themselves necessarily contribute much towards increased understanding.

In the light of the argument here for the need of structuralist research in psychology it is interesting to note that in anthropology a self-styled 'structuralist' movement has been gaining ground in recent years. The most prominent figure has undoubtedly been Claude Lévi-Strauss who may be described as having attempted to uncover the brain mechanisms which underly the generation of social systems like kinship systems, totemic systems and myth systems. His best known single work is probably 'The Savage Mind' (Lévi-Strauss, 1966). Some writers (e.g. Lane, 1970, and Piaget, 1971) have seen structuralism as an interdisciplinary movement in the social sciences which would include also the work of Chomsky and others in linguistics and extend into political science, literary criticism and psychiatry. In psychology, Piaget looks on his own work as being structuralist. In these terms, computer simulation could be regarded as representing a further incursion of the interdisciplinary structuralist movement into psychology.

The role of computer models in psychology

The term 'model' appears to be used in a number of different areas of science and mathematics and whether there is a fundamental similarity between the roles of all such 'models' is a matter for discussion (viz. Freudenthal, Ed., 1961, especially the papers by Apostel and by Suppes). However, in psychology, computer models—at least of the structural variety—take a particular form: they are programs which allow the computer to perform in a way which is similar, at least in certain respects, to the performance of animals or humans under similar conditions. It is then inferred that the principles on which the computer was programmed *may* be the same as the principles governing the generation of the animal or human behaviour modelled. The general situation is represented in Figure 5.1. Input and stimulus have dotted

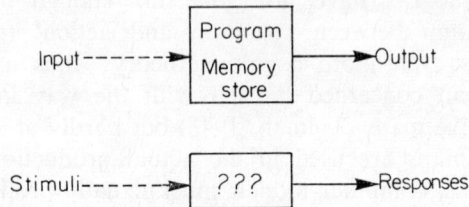

Figure 5.1

lines in this diagram, because in this theoretical paradigm behaviour can be initiated by the program as well as by environmental stimuli. It is interesting to note that, as Freeman (1971) has pointed out: 'Most scientists and engineers simulate for the purpose of obtaining the output or *results* of that simulation. Most behavioral scientists benefit from the *process* of simulation' (p. 104).

There are, of course, computer models in psychology of kinds other than that just described, including models in physiological psychology which are concerned with physiological changes *per se* and need make little explicit reference to overt behaviour (e.g. Rochester *et al.*, 1956) and social psychological models in which the simulation is of a number of individuals in interaction with each other (e.g. Coe, 1964). But, with these exceptions, it is probably true to say that most structural computer models take the form just described.

Sometimes the environmental conditions and the performance will be identical for the computer and the organism. For example, models of pattern-recognition (see Chapter 6) have been programmed so that the computer can identify exactly the same patterns—such as handwritten letters—as an adult human being. Again, a computer can be programmed to play chess against a human opponent and both the human and the computer play the same game (viz. Newell, Shaw and Simon, 1963). At other times, however, the environment has to be simulated as well as the organism and in these cases the computer's behaviour will necessarily be less realistic. For instance, in certain computer models of personality (e.g. the model Aldous by Loehlin, 1968), the output consists of numbers which on a consistent but arbitrary basis are said to represent certain actions and changes in attitudes; events and objects in the environment are also represented simply by numbers and a separate program determines the environmental conse-quences of any action of the model of the organism.

Only statements about models can be true or false—not the models in themselves. There are two kinds of statement that one might want to make about a model. The first is that the *behaviour* produced by the model is in some way the same as the behaviour produced by the organism. (This is not always as easy to decide as it might appear.) The second, which may only become of interest if the first is taken to be true, is that the *method* used to produce the behaviour is the same in the two cases, i.e. that the computer uses the same method or possesses the same 'program' as the organism. Such a statement is of course a conjectural one: because two systems produce similar behaviour this does not necessarily imply that the two systems use similar means to produce this behaviour. But then, this is not a special weakness of modelling: all theoretical inferences in science are in the last analysis conjectural. In psychology, computer models are based on the same kind of information as any other theories. We shall return to these points in the final section of the chapter.

Computer models in psychology are in one respect like organisms and in one respect like theories. They are like organisms in being concrete systems which produce actual behaviour. They are like theories in that they are used in the attempt to understand the way in which behaviour is produced. Indeed, some writers have regarded them *as* theories (Simon and Newell, 1956). But it is probably more meaningful and useful to regard them rather as exemplars of theories. On the one hand they can test theories: they can be used to check whether a theory as already formulated is effective and also whether its implica-tions are of the kind assumed by its originators. On the other hand, a model can be used to lead to the formulation of a theory covering both the model and the organism. Models may help in the latter case by being simpler than organisms and reducing complexity (for example by cutting out details which are irrelevant to the problem in hand) while still operating, it is hoped, in accordance with the same principles.

Another way of putting this is that models mediate between theories and organisms. There are three different ways in which they mediate, as we shall see in the next section of this chapter, depending on whether one's starting point is the organism, the computer program or the theory.

It has been said (Jordan, 1941) that the generality of theoretical statements in physics and chemistry tends to be much greater than that of biology. According to this argument, one can refer in physics and chemistry not only to aspects of *actual* situations, situations which already exist (e.g. the constitution of sea water, the motions of the planets in the solar system), but also to aspects of *possible* situations (e.g. the result of bringing together in pure form certain substances which do not normally meet, or the sending of satellites into space). In contrast with this, biology is concerned mainly with the actual: it is limited on the whole to considering organisms that happen to exist or have existed already. While it can study those still existing under specially created experimental conditions, it cannot consider potential organisms, and far less can it bring totally new animals into existence. Thus the physicist and chemist can consider all possible situations of interest; the biologist tends to consider only that subset of possible animals which are those animals which have actually existed. If this is true of biology it is also true of psychology: the psychologist is concerned with the behaviour of actual animals that do exist, especially the human animal. However, this kind of distinction is beginning to break down in a number of ways. One is through 'biological engineering' of which we see the beginnings today: e.g. directly altering the chromosomes by means of certain new laboratory techniques. Another is through the advent of the use of modelling, including especially computer modelling, in biology and psychology. In the latter case, new or artificial systems can be brought into being which function in ways similar in specified respects to those systems which are usually referred to as 'living systems' but different from them. Possible systems with some of the properties of living systems can be envisaged alongside actual living systems. As we have seen, theoretical statements can be general enough to cover man-made models as well as those naturally occurring systems which they represent. This idea, and implications of it, have been discussed further by the present writer elsewhere. (Apter, 1966, Chapter 1).

Three types of computer models

In the previous section of this chapter the relations of computer models, organisms and theories were discussed briefly. Research in psychology using computer models can start from theory, from organisms or from computer programs (Figure 5.2). Thus computer models of behaviour fall naturally into three categories in terms of their provenance.

Research using computers can start with a theory from which a

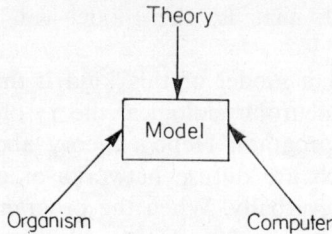

Figure 5.2

particular model can be deduced and its behaviour compared with the behaviour being studied. Alternatively, the researcher can start by observing behaviour, creating a model which produces the same kind of behaviour and then relating the behaviour of both model and organism to a more general theory that covers both. But there is another possibility: research can start from computer programs which have been brought into existence for practical purposes but which do things previously done, or attempted perhaps less successfully, by human beings (especially solving problems of different kinds). This field is often referred to as 'artificial intelligence' an appellation which however embraces hardware devices as well as computer programs. Where such programs exist, it is conceivable that they utilize methods of a kind similar to those of human beings, and may give insight into the latter—in other words, they can be treated as models unless disqualified by using means which are *prima facie* quite different from those used by humans or other animals and intrinsic to the model's success.

There are comparatively few examples so far in the history of computer simulation of the first kind of research, and rather more of the second; but the bulk of computer work up to the present which is of interest to psychologists derives from the third, i.e. computer programs in the field of artificial intelligence. Let us now look at each of these categories.

First, then, there are those programs that are derived from already existing theories in psychology. These may contribute to the evaluation and development of such theories in the following ways. Firstly, they ensure that the theory is stated precisely and they test it for consistency and completeness. Secondly, if the theory is complex, its implications can be worked out more quickly and accurately. At this point it can be seen whether they are those expected by the theorist and are consistent with already existing information. If not the theory may have to be reformulated. If they are, then new predictions for experimental testing can, hopefully, be derived; that is, the model can be used to generate hypotheses.

A good example of a model of this kind is that of Rochester *et al.* (1956) which put the neurophysiological theory of Hebb (1949) into the form of a computer program. Hebb's theory about the way in which 'cell assemblies', which are diffuse networks of cells, mediate learning was described by him verbally. When the program based on this verbal description was run it was found that it did not work in the way expected at all. Because of this the theory was subsequently modified (Milner, 1957) to make reference to inhibitory connexions between neurones as well as the excitatory connexions of the earlier theory.

Another example is a program written by Colby (1963) which is based on Freudian theory and simulates certain features of neurotic behaviour as seen by this theory. The model has programmed into it sets of 'beliefs'. These 'beliefs' are statements, some of which conflict with each other and some of which do not: e.g. 'I must love mother', 'I ought to love people', and 'I hate mother'. The computer compares beliefs and attempts to overcome conflicts between beliefs as they occur. It does this by means of mechanisms which modify or distort beliefs and which are analogs of Freudian defence mechanisms. Eight types of such mechanisms are available to it. Every time it fails to reduce a conflict a number representing 'anxiety level' increases; when this level exceeds an upper threshold the computer moves on to a new set of beliefs to process. If it succeeds in reducing conflict, anxiety is lowered and the computer prints out the new distorted version of the belief which has been changed. It can be seen that this program necessitates putting some of Freud's ideas in a more precise form than is usual in psychoanalytic literature. Having done this, Colby has gone on to derive implications from the model for psychotherapeutic interviewing (Colby, 1965).

Other models of this general kind include Abelson's model (1963) of an attitude system based on Heider's balance theory (1958) and also incorporating defence mechanisms, and the social interaction model of the Gullahorns (Gullahorn and Gullahorn, 1963) which expresses in computer form a theory of George C. Homans (1961).

The second category of model-types proposed was that of models derived initially from observation. Such observation leads to a theory of some low-level kind which is then put in the form of a computer program and in this sense the program expresses a theory. But models in this category differ from those in the previous category in that the research process leading directly to the program starts from observation rather than from some already well-developed psychological theory. In this case computer modelling is brought into the psychological laboratory and tied in closely with a line of empirical research.

An obvious source of information about the mechanisms that generate behaviour (other than the behaviour itself) that can aid the construction of a model of this kind is introspection. Introspection is limited, however, both by its subjective nature and by the fact that the introspecting subject may not be aware of the mechanisms that he is using: how can someone introspecting explain how he generates a sentence, for example? Nevertheless, verbal protocols may have some use.

The best known example of work in this second category must undoubtedly be that of the team of Newell, Simon and Shaw. It should also be added that this work does not represent a pure case of computer simulation since the aim of these researchers has been to develop artificial intelligence for practical purposes as well as to attempt to increase our understanding of human problem-solving. The next section of this chapter is devoted to a description of their 'General Problem Solver' program. It is interesting that their first paper (describing a program called the 'Logic Theorist') was given at the same meeting at which Noam Chomsky made his views on linguistics public for the first time (Newell and Simon, 1956). The paper by Rochester *et al.* already mentioned was also read at this meeting.

Another example of a computer model based on observation is that of Smith (1968). His model was intended to replicate the thought processes of a skilled psychologist making decisions concerning personnel selection and placement. The model was based on the psychologist's recorded verbalization of his thoughts as he evaluated a series of applicants for jobs. The resulting program achieved a high level of agreement with the psychologist in a subsequent set of test cases. Another model of the decision-making process is that of Feldman (1962). The decisions simulated in this case were those made by subjects in a binary choice experiment where the subject had to predict which of two events would occur on each of a series of trials. Use was made, in the construction of the model, of observations of what subjects in fact did in this situation and the reasons given by them for their choices.

Finally, we come to the third and most ubiquitous type of model: the computer program designed primarily to achieve a given end by any convenient programming means at hand but which may, nevertheless, suggest what means are used by humans to achieve the same ends. Of course it is unlikely that everyday computer programs carrying out conventional computer tasks, like working out series of mathematical equations or retrieving business data, will help us much to understand human thinking. The term 'artificial intelligence' refers more to the attempt to make computers *life-like* in their functioning in the sense of giving them the capability to deal with kinds of problems previously regarded as ones that only human beings could deal with (or could deal with satisfactorily).

Most of this work involves the development of 'heuristic' methods. These are methods of dealing with problems which are intended to provide short-cuts to their solution but which cannot guarantee that a solution will be reached at all. They contrast with 'algorithmic' methods which, if followed, guarantee a successful outcome but which may be highly tedious and time-consuming. For example, suppose the problem is to find a given book in a library in which the books are ordered alphabetically in terms of authors' names, but only the title of the book is known. An algorithmic method might be systematically to read each title in turn until the required book is found. Heuristic methods might include guessing from the title who the author might be and checking possible authors first. It can be seen that heuristic methods are in some sense more intelligent, and also more difficult to program on a computer, than algorithmic methods. It is also possible to use them in situations where there is no known algorithm available. For example, there is no known algorithm which, if followed, would guarantee that one would win a game of chess. But there are many heuristics which can improve one's chances. It is quite possible that the general endeavour to develop heuristic methods for computers will eventually help psychology and that artificial intelligence may throw light on human intelligence.

Much research in artificial intelligence is concerned with improving computer and programming techniques in ways that would have immediate practical applications, especially in industry. For example, computers would obviously be much more useful if they could recognize patterns like handwriting or real objects in their environment and if they could understand natural speech. But a great deal of research in artificial intelligence is more playful than this, even though it is still oriented to the achievement of ends irrespective of means and may give insight into ways of improving our computer technology in the longer term. For instance, computers are being programmed to play games like checkers and chess, to compose music, to write poems and to produce visually pleasing objects and pictures.

Let us mention just a couple of examples from this huge field. Many other examples have been described by Hunt (1968) in an excellent review paper.

Samuel (1963) has written a much-publicized program to play checkers (draughts) and to learn how to improve its performance at the game. The computer plays by looking ahead at each stage and evaluating all the board positions which could be reached within a few moves; it then chooses a move on the basis of this information. It improves its performance in two ways. Firstly, it stores all the board positions encountered during play together with their related calculations. Positions encountered frequently are kept in store, those encountered infrequently dropped. When a stored position is met in a game, time is freed for the computer to compute in greater depth. Furthermore if, in looking ahead, a board position is foreseen about which the computer has information in the memory store, its look-ahead capacity is automatically enhanced to that extent. The second way in which the computer improves its performance is more complicated. In evaluating board positions various weighted terms can be used, e.g. terms which represent degree of control of the centre of the board, piece advancement, etc. The computer learns by trial-and-error which terms to use and how much weighting to give each of them. Although it was not intended to do so, the program raises questions and stimulates thought about the way in which human beings learn certain kinds of skills. Are there any fundamental differences between such human learning and computer learning? If so, what are they?

Gelernter (1963) has written a program which successfully proves theorems in Euclidean plane geometry and bears certain resemblances to the General Problem Solver program to be described in the next section. To give the computer the chance of proving the theorems in a more intelligent and less time-consuming way than would otherwise have been possible, two heuristic methods were employed in conjunction with each other. One was to work backwards, thus assuring that every sequence of steps in each attempted proof did indeed terminate in the theorem required. The disadvantage of this is that most sequences generated, while terminating in the way required, would not be proofs of anything. The second heuristic, which helped to overcome this difficulty, was the use by the computer of a diagram against which the sequences constituting attempted proofs could be checked and those not supported by the diagram rejected. In this way a great deal of time could be saved and the search for proofs guided in a fruitful direction. It is interesting that, as Gelernter himself points out, no one would attempt to prove a theorem in Euclidean geometry without first drawing, or at least visualizing, a diagram; and the injunction from mathematics teachers to 'Draw the diagram!' is often heard in the classroom. More generally, the intelligent human problem-solver might use what Gelernter calls 'heuristic filters' which allow him to filter out unpromising lines of thought as the geometry program does by means of diagrams.

One is tempted to ask whether Gelernter's program might not in some ways be a model of the technique used by computer modellers themselves. Thus computer models can, like diagrams in geometry, be regarded as concrete representations of more abstract ideas; and they are intended to act heuristically to guide thought in promising directions. But of course, as discussed earlier in this chapter, computer models may help to guide thought in a number of different ways. Whether any of these particular ways is similar to the use of the diagram by the geometry program is open to debate; but this does demonstrate the way in which artificial intelligence programs can make suggestions of interest to psychologists.

Other examples of models in all three of the categories outlined here will be found in other chapters in Part II of this book.

An example of a computer model

Let us look at one example of a computer model in just a little more detail than has been possible up to this point. We have chosen a classic in the genre: the 'General Problem Solver' (GPS) program of Newell, Shaw and Simon (1959). Although, as we have seen, this program can be classified as belonging to the field of artificial intelligence, it was developed on the basis of observations of the behaviour of human subjects and their verbal reports during attempts to solve problems of the kind with which the program was intended to deal. Newell, Shaw and Simon regard the finished program as consequently embodying a theory of human problem-solving.

Such problems can be described as problems in which a finite number of clearly defined *operators* are available which can be applied to distinct situations or *objects* in the problem-environment to *transform* them in specified ways, the problem being solved by applying the appropriate operators in an appropriate sequence. A number of problems which are superficially different can be reduced to this type—hence the name *General* Problem Solver. (An even larger number can be reduced to this type if one removes the phrase 'clearly defined' and 'distinct' in the previous sentence, although in these cases GPS would not be able to solve them.)

Various kinds of problems have in fact been used with GPS. A typical problem is this: given one expression in symbolic logic, derive a second specified expression. In the terms used in the last paragraph, the first expression is an 'object' which has to be 'transformed' into a second 'object' (expression). The 'operators' available in this case are the rules of symbolic logic, these specifying equivalences between expressions. When expressions are equivalent, one can be substituted for the other. For example, A.(B v C) is equivalent to, and can therefore substitute for, or be substituted by, (A.B) v (A.C). (In symbolic logic '.' stands for 'and'; and 'v' stands for 'or'.) GPS is given access to these rules and to a table which specifies which rules (operators) lead to which kinds of transformations. For example, in the rule cited three kinds of transformations are involved: changing the number of terms, changing the logical connectives ('.' 'v', in this example), and changing the grouping of the terms.

Using this kind of information GPS must start with the first expression, apply an operator to it (or part of it) to produce a new expression, apply an operator to that, and so on until the required terminal expression is reached. In the simplest case only one step may be necessary; in more difficult cases many steps may be required. What GPS has to do to achieve success, therefore, is to apply appropriate operators in an appropriate order. (Remember, there may be a number of different routes to a correct solution.) How does it work out which operators to apply and when?

In order to understand this it must be realized that a hierarchy of goals are involved, sub-goals being generated from higher-level goals and needing to be achieved before the higher-level goal can be. At the highest level there is the goal of transforming the first expression or the expression which the computer has currently reached into the required terminal expression. In order to do this it may be necessary to derive another, intermediate, expression which will be more similar to the terminal expression than the expression in question. Reducing a difference between an expression and the terminal expression in this way represents a sub-goal. When it is achieved a new sub-goal is set up, of reducing another difference. But there are even lower-level goals: an operator may be chosen which cannot be applied to the particular expression in question, i.e. the logical rule may be applicable to a number of expressions but not to the expression to which it is required to be applied. In this case the goal may be set up of transforming the expression in question into one of the expressions to which the operator *can* be applied. In terms of our analysis so far this goal of applying an operator is a sub-sub-goal. It should be noted that this sub-sub-goal is identical in form to the overall goal of transforming one expression into another, and the interesting situation arises that this sub-sub-goal can in turn give rise to a further hierarchy of goals—reducing differences and applying operators—and the same methods may be used by the program at these lower levels. Situations of this kind in which methods may be employed during the course of using these very same methods are called 'recursive' in computer terminology. To summarize so far, GPS deals with three kinds of goals that are related hierarchically: (i) to transform one object into another, (ii) to reduce a difference between one object and another, and (iii) to apply a given operator to an object. In the kind of problem being described here objects are expressions in symbolic logic and operators are the rules of logic.

GPS starts by listing the differences between the first and terminal expressions and then chooses the most difficult of these differences to reduce. (The order of difficulty of the various kinds of differences, like 'different connectives' and 'different position of terms', has previously been decided by the programmers.) The expression that it derives if it has succeeded in reducing the difference is then tested to see if, overall, it is more similar to the terminal expression than the original expression was. (This is not a foregone conclusion because in reducing one difference a number of new differences may have been generated concurrently.) If it is, the most difficult difference on the new list is attempted, and the same procedure followed. If not, another operator may be chosen to apply to the first expression (if some operators make a number of changes concurrently, any given change may be made by a number of operators). If none of these succeed, a new difference is chosen to be reduced. A further complication, as we have seen, is that to apply a given operator the current expression may have to be transformed and this may lead to further operations. Without going into any more detail it can be seen that GPS continually makes decisions about which path to follow, the various decision points being generated in what can be visualized as a branching tree-like structure. GPS continually monitors its own progress, and if a given path turns out to be unsuccessful it returns to an earlier point (which may be a higher-level goal) and chooses a new path. Lack of success includes, as we have seen, an expression being produced that is more dissimilar than the original expression from the required expression, and also a problem being met which is the same as a higher-level problem: in this case unless the program returned to an earlier point and took a new direction it would recursively go through the same sequence over and over again —like Scheherazade in the 'Thousand and One Nights' when she tells the King his own story which includes hearing the beginning of this story which in turn gets as far as the beginning of this story once more, and so on.

When human subjects are presented with the same problems as GPS they appear, from their verbal protocols and overt decisions, to use similar strategies—it was of course the intention of Newell, Simon and Shaw that this should be so. Such similar strategies include the generation of intermediate goals, the transformation of expressions so that the appropriate logical rules can be applied to them, and the monitoring of progress and return to an earlier stage if a line of thought appears to become too complicated or too far removed from the main line of thought. But having derived this theory in the form of a computer program its authors were able, by comparing its performance in detail under a range of different conditions to that of human subjects under the same conditions, to see whether it should be modified and to examine how it could be improved. They have already noted a number of ways in which humans seem to differ in their problem-solving behaviour from GPS in its form as described here (Newell and Simon, 1963).

Criticisms of the technique

An objection sometimes made to computer simulation as a technique is that a computer will only do what it is told to do and that therefore it is not possible to learn anything new from it. The premise here is true: a computer acts in accordance with its program. But the conclusion does not follow, any more than it follows that if we know the axioms and rules of deduction of arithmetic then we cannot learn anything new about arithmetic. A computer may display behaviour implicit in, but not apparent from, a program. Thus a few rules can, in interaction, quickly generate comparatively complex results. Of course it *is* true that one could sit down and work out on paper what the computer would do, provided no random processes were involved. In this sense one can learn nothing from a computer that one could not learn *without it*; but it would also be highly inconvenient and time-consuming to do without it in this way except in the case of the very simplest programs. A certain minimum complexity is required before it is worth using the computer, but given this requirement the computer can work out the implications of the ideas programmed into it with less chance of error and in a considerably shorter time than it would take for the programmer to work them out for himself. And these implications may be unexpected ones. It remains true that a computer model is no better than the assumptions programmed into it, but this is a rather different point and one with which surely no one would wish to disagree.

There are of course some elements of inconvenience in using a computer. In particular, as many researchers will point out with feeling, programs do not always work. There are two kinds of mistakes: coding mistakes, where a mistake is made in converting the program into

6—TCIP * *

computer input; and programming mistakes. The former small mistakes can indeed be highly frustrating; but as far as the latter are concerned, computer programming can be advantageous in that it helps to ensure that one's ideas are precise and effective.

A further difficulty is that one may have to learn how to write programs, or how to write them in particular languages. Many psychologists today have not learned this. But this is a fact of life, not a criticism of the method—any more than it would have been a criticism of the principle of using statistics in psychology to say at the turn of the century that not many psychologists knew how to carry out statistical computations. The situation has changed for statistics and is in the process of changing for computer programming.

A criticism which requires more serious attention at present is this: it may be difficult to decide whether the behaviour of a model is sufficiently similar to the behaviour being modelled to count in fact as a model and to be worth drawing inferences from about mechanisms underlying the behaviour.

One method of evaluation arises from Turing's (1950) suggestion for a test to decide if a computer is thinking or not. This test was based on a party game in which someone has to guess which of two people, who are hidden from view, is the woman and which is the man. He is allowed to ask them any questions he may choose and the responses are given him in written (preferably typewritten) form. When he feels he has sufficient evidence of their styles of thinking, he may guess which is which. Suppose now that the same kind of game is played with a computer and a human being (of either sex) instead of a man and a woman; the 'observer' still has to guess which is which. Turing argued that if, after a reasonable period of time, the observer has no better chance of guessing correctly which is which than he had in guessing between the man and the woman, then we would be justified in saying that the computer was thinking. If he had a *better* chance of guessing which was which, this would imply that the computer was not 'playing the game' of imitating human thinking well enough. Suppose the observer was right 60 per cent of the time in the man-woman situation. Then if the observer was right 70 per cent of the time with the computer we would have to admit that the simulation was not adequate; if the observer was right only 55 per cent of the time, we could say that the computer was being successful. It should be noted that if the computer were completely successful, so that the observer had no idea which was the computer and which the human being, he would still expect to be right by chance 50 per cent of the time. Total

lack of success by the computer would of course be represented by
100 per cent correct guesses by the observer.

'Turing's test', as it has become known, could in principle be applied
to the computer simulation of any kind of human behaviour, not just
thinking—and in any case in Turing's terms, since no questions are
barred, 'thinking' can cover may different processes including decision-
making, mental arithmetic, evaluation of works of art, etc. An advantage
of this test for simulation in general is that it makes some allowance
for the type of task concerned. Different tasks may afford the observer
different amounts of useful information. The less the observer has to
go on, the less his chance of guessing correctly and the easier it would
be to produce an adequate simulation if a once-and-for-all chance level
were chosen; but the level in Turing's test would be reduced because
the observer would have a smaller chance of guessing correctly in the
man-woman situation too. For example, if the computer was modelling
human behaviour in a binary-choice experiment (where at each trial the
subject has to guess which of two equiprobable events will occur), all he
has to go on are sequences of choices. These may give him little clue
as to which was produced by man and which by machine—but he
would also have little chance of guessing which had been produced by
a man and which by a woman.

It might appear that it would be preferable where possible, as it
would be if the computer were modelling behaviour in some experimental situation like the binary-choice situation, to use standard
statistical tests. In such cases one might ask whether the computer's
responses were significantly different in some respect from the responses
of the human subject. One difficulty here is that if the behaviour were
actually found to be significantly different in the chosen respect, it
might still not be possible to decide which behaviour was produced by
the human and which by the computer. Perhaps this would not matter:
provided a difference was demonstrated the computer model could not
be considered to be sufficiently similar to the organism for inferences
to be drawn from the model. However, there is still a difficulty. Two
systems may be operating in accordance with the same general principles
but produce behaviour which in detail is different according to statistical
tests; after all, two human beings might produce samples of behaviour
in a particular experimental situation which are significantly different
for some reason, but they are both systems of the same general kind and
may both be following the same general rules. For example, one subject
might be good and one bad at solving problems of the kind that Newell,
Simon and Shaw have been interested in; but they might still be trying
to solve the problems in the same way by setting up hierarchies of goals,

monitoring their own progress, etc. So statistical tests may be *too* stringent: they may disqualify models which do not need to be disqualified. From this point of view, then, Turing's naive observer may do a better job.

Nevertheless, even if we use Turing's test, a problem remains. Not only may different behaviour be produced by the same kinds of means, as has just been argued, but the same behaviour may be produced by quite different means. So it may be dangerous to infer a similarity of means from a similarity of ends as Turing does. For example, a move in chess may be the result of calculation of some kind or may be the result of information-retrieval (i.e. what is termed 'memory' in the human case). If we tested the two systems (human and computer) under many different circumstances, presumably some overt difference in behaviour at some stage would indicate that the means used to generate it were different if they really were different. But this shows the danger of making inferences about the similarity of two systems on the basis of a limited sample of the behaviour of each and in the absence of any information about the mechanisms used other than the evidence of the resulting behaviour. It also raises an interesting philosophical question: if two systems behave identically under *all* circumstances, does it follow that they *must* use the same means to generate this behaviour?

Methodological difficulties, therefore, do exist in attempting to evaluate computer models. However, it can be argued that these are not specific to computer modelling but apply to any kind of theorizing in psychology, especially theorizing of a structuralist rather than a functionalist kind.

Further Reading

Apter, Michael J. (1970) *The Computer Simulation of Behaviour.* Hutchinson, London. Harper and Row, New York. A more detailed introduction to the subject-matter of this chapter and to related philosophical problems.

Deutsch, J. A. (1960) *The Structural Basis of Behaviour.* The University Press, Cambridge, England. Contains arguments for, and original examples of, structural explanations in psychology.

Dutton, John M., and William H. Starbuck (Eds.) (1971) *Computer Simulation of Human Behavior.* Wiley, New York. This contains a large collection of reprinted papers from a variety of areas including sociology, economics and management studies as well as psychology.

Feigenbaum, Edward A. and Julian Feldman (Eds.) (1963) *Computers and Thought.* McGraw-Hill, New York. This is a classic collection of papers on computer research in artificial intelligence and the simulation of cognitive processes.

George, Frank (1970) *Models of Thinking.* George Allen and Unwin, London.

An examination of certain aspects of thinking especially from the standpoint of computer studies.

Loehlin, John C. (1968) *Computer Models of Personality*. Random House, New York. A lucid and readable introduction to computer modelling with detailed descriptions of four computer models of personality.

Tomkins, Silvan S. and Samuel Messik (Eds.) (1963) *Computer Simulation of Personality*. Wiley, New York. An entertaining and thought-provoking collection of papers and discussions presented at a conference, including contributions from such well-known figures as Ernest R. Hilgard, George A. Kelly and Jerome Kagan.

Part 2
Areas of Application

CHAPTER 6

The Computer in the Psychology of Perception

John A. Wilson

Experiments on perception often require the preparation of drawings and displays to be used as stimuli. For drawing static displays—curves, dot displays, histogram-type figures—the computer has become an important tool; it is most useful here when we want to draw complex diagrams in accordance with simple rules. And if we require moving stimuli, then the computer can produce diagrams in motion, drawn accurately and controlled with precise timing.

These uses can be extended, in perception as in other topics of psychological experiment, into the use of the computer for on-line control of experiments. The computer can time the responses of the subject and record them as data for later analysis; or it can choose the path which the experiment is to follow, by analysing the data immediately and using the results of the analysis to determine the properties and order of succession of the stimuli. In these uses the computer is a tool, or perhaps a laboratory assistant. But it is too versatile to remain always in these humble roles: we use it to simulate the human or animal subject of our experiments, to imitate his perceptual processes. In this way the computer becomes an embodiment of our theories, and enables us to test them by seeing if the computer acts in the same way as the subject would under the same circumstances.

We can even leave the living subject aside altogether. Instead of asking how the subject perceives, we can ask how to make a machine perceive. In doing this we hope that our work, inventing machines to perform this function, will help us to understand how the human brain can perform it. For the present, however, this task of designing a machine which can perceive is far too difficult and work in this field has come to centre round the problem of pattern recognition: how can patterns be recognized by a machine, and how can a machine be made to 'learn' to recognize patterns? We have not yet any clear answer to these questions, but certain general principles are emerging and, while

153

these principles cannot be indiscriminately applied to perception, it is nevertheless true that pattern recognition is an important function of the perceptual mechanisms and its principles must ultimately become important to psychology.

The computer in perceptual experiments

Drawing displays by computer

Many perceptual experiments depend on getting the subject's response to a diagram and sometimes the diagram is easy to specify but laborious to prepare. When this is so, we can often use a computer to generate the diagram for us.

A simple diagram of this kind is the spiral, used for studying movement after-effects. If one looks at a spiral which is rotating, it seems to expand or to contract, depending on the direction of rotation with respect to the sense of the spiral. When the rotation is stopped the after-effect appears, in the opposite sense to the original motion: if the spiral had been seen as expanding, it is now seen as contracting; if it had been seen as contracting, it is now seen to expand. The effect is usually slow but powerful. The spirals which are needed for this work are difficult to draw accurately, since they constantly change in curvature, but it is easy to write down an equation which represents a spiral, indeed a variety of spirals: e.g. an Archimedean spiral is given by $r = a\theta$, a logarithmic spiral by $r = a^\theta$. It is easy to set up the equation on a computer, and have the computer draw the spiral for us. At first analog computers were used; Holland (1965) has published a fine collection of such spirals drawn by an analog computer. But digital computers are more generally available and with a graph-plotter as output they can be made to draw out the spirals. Some examples of spirals drawn by a digital computer are shown in Figure 6.1.

Rotating figures are also useful for studying the relation between real and apparent brightness of a surface. The difference between real and apparent is surprisingly great, even in simple situations. To study this we need surfaces which vary from black through grey to white, with a careful control of the shade of grey. To control the greyness of a surface is not easy: we might try, for example, to mix a graded series of pigments, and with careful measurement of quantities and careful mixing we could produce an accurate series of greys. There is, however, a much easier way to get an accurate grey: instead of mixing black and white pigments, we use a disc with black and white sectors; we then spin the disc rapidly, relying on persistence of vision to mix the

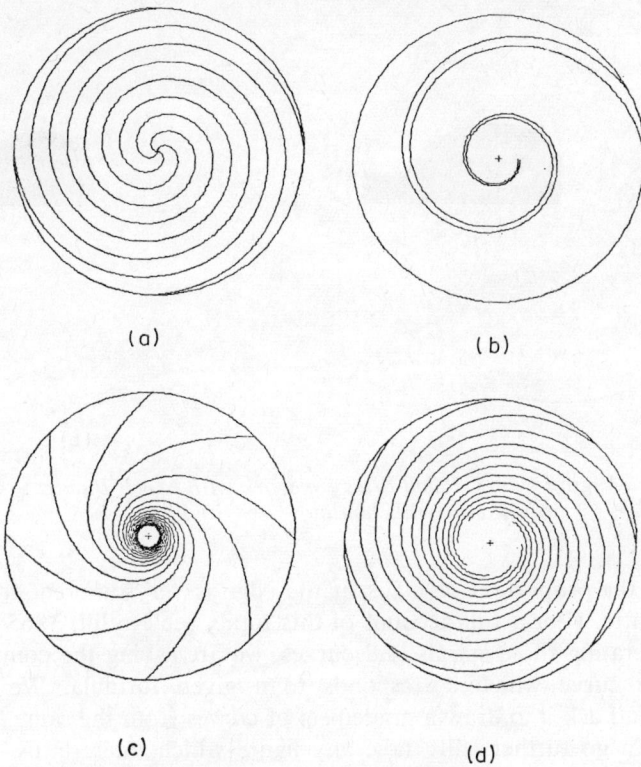

Figure 6.1—*Four spirals drawn by a digital computer.*
(a) Archimedes spiral, 4–start
(b) Logarithmic spiral sector
(c) Hyperbolic spiral, 8–start
(d) Logarithmic spiral, 8–start

colours in the eye. It is easy to control the width of the black and white sectors and so to get an accurate grey of the required proportions. If we change the proportion of black to white as we go from the edge to the centre of the disc, say 10° of black around the edge grading to 90° of black as we approach the centre, then we will have a disc with a graded grey (see Figure 6.2a).

This grading can be done by hand, but it is often convenient to use a computer, especially when the desired grading follows a simple formula. For example, the disc in Figure 6.2b was calculated and drawn by a computer, to grade from dark grey to white according to a sigmoid law. When the disc is spun rapidly, it appears as a uniform grey,

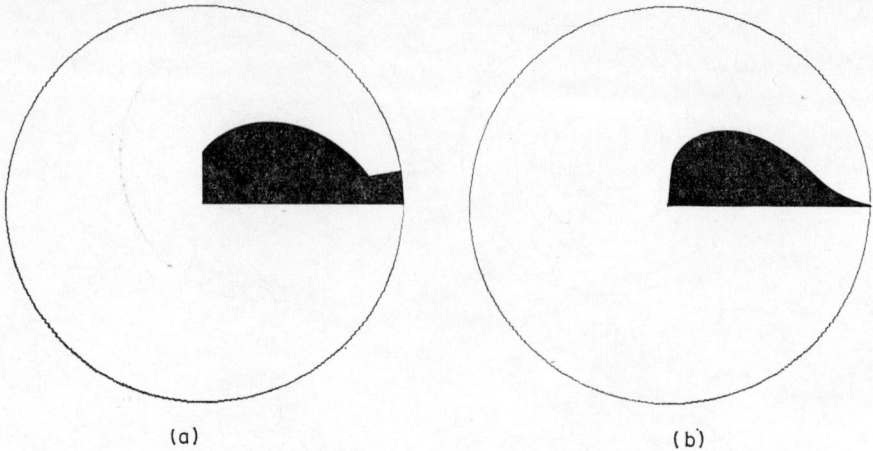

(a)   (b)

Figure 6.2—*Graded discs for work with Mach Bands.*
(a) Ramp with landings   (b) Sigmoid

although the proportion of black at the edge is very different from that
at the centre. (For a full account of this topic, see Ratliff, 1965.)

In generating these spirals and curves, we are asking the computer to
draw the curve which corresponds to a given formula. We can go
further, and ask it to draw a graded set of curves from the same formula.
Or we can go further still: take any figure which interests us, and use
the computer to generate a graded set of variations on that figure.
Green (1967, p. 60) gives an example in which he starts from a set of
numerals, and generates several sets in which the numeral is progressively more blurred. These figures are then used for experiments on the
perception of characters which are partially degraded.

A fine example of the use of graded sets of figures is that of Shepard
and Metzler (1971) who studied the mental rotation of three-dimensional
objects. They used perspective drawings of objects built from cubes by
placing the cubes face to face (see Figure 6.3). Each object was made of
ten cubes, to form a rigid arm-like structure with three right-angled
'elbows'. The drawings were shown in pairs, some pairs showing the
'same' object, some pairs showing 'different' objects. The two drawings
of a 'same' pair showed the same object, but rotated about one axis
or another; the rotation from one member of the pair to the other
varied in 20° steps from 20° to 180°. The drawings of the 'different'
pair showed different objects, which could not be transformed into one
another by rotation. All these drawings were produced by computer,
then photographically reproduced and mounted for the experiment.

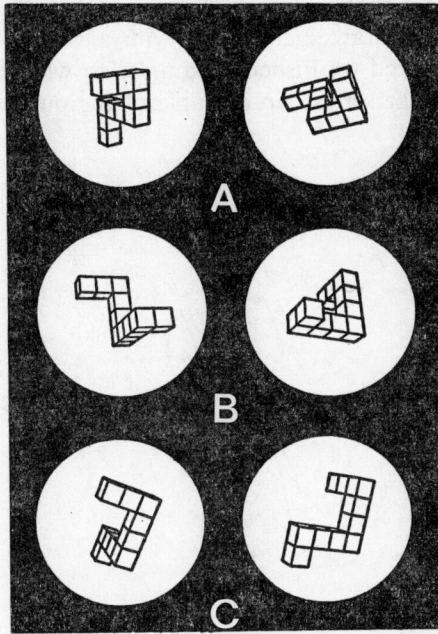

Figure 6.3—*Perspective drawings of objects built from cubes.*
(a) 'Same' pair, differing by an 80° rotation in the picture plane
(b) 'Same' pair, differing by an 80° rotation in depth
(c) 'Different pair, which cannot be brought into congruence by any rotation
(From Shepard and Metzler, 1971)

In the experiment, recognition time was measured. The pair of draw-ings was exposed to the subject and he was required to respond as quickly as possible by pressing a lever to indicate 'same' or 'different'. The lever shut off the picture and stopped the timer. The result of the experiment was intriguing: the time taken to recognize a pair as 'same' was proportional to the angle of rotation between the pictures of the pair. (For pairs which are 'different', the angle of rotation has no clear meaning, and the time taken was more variable.) It seems that the determination of identity of shape depends on a 'mental rotation in three-dimensional space', which proceeds at about 60° per second.

Graded stimuli are sometimes required for work with ambiguous figures. Fisher (1968) for example, produced graded series of a number of ambiguous figures, to be used in finding which figure would be equally likely to be seen in either aspect. In one series, an unambiguous face of a colonel was graded to become a fancifully dressed mannequin; in another, a man's face was graded to become a seated nude. Intermediate figures were ambiguous, with varying degrees of bias. A computer can be used to draw such figures with a variety of gradings, and the author was inspired by Fisher's examples to write a program which would produce similar series. An example of the output of this program is shown in Figure 6.4.

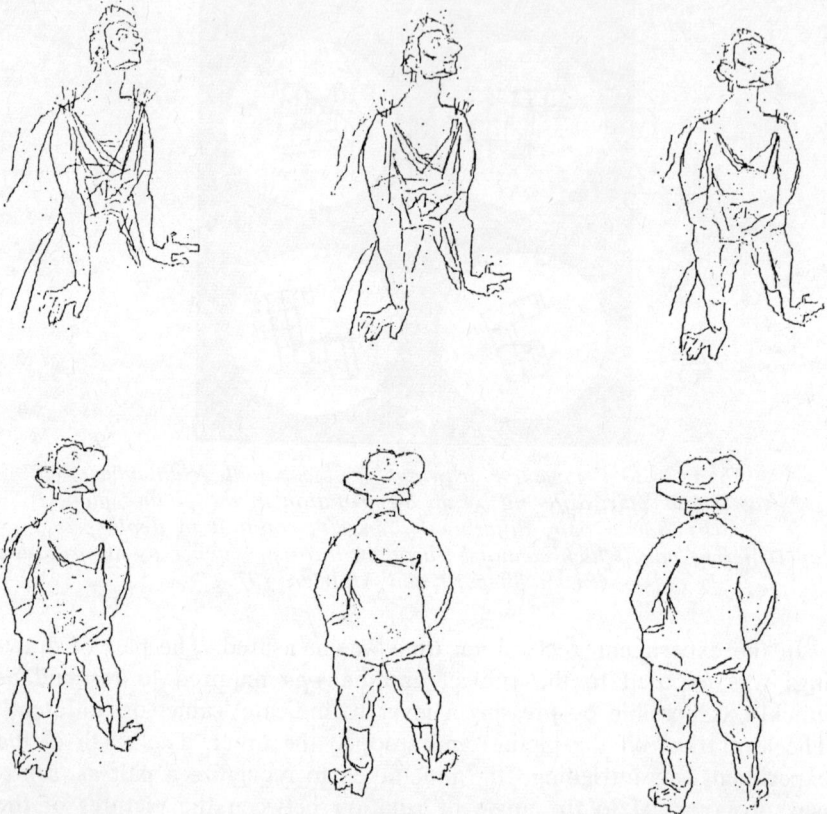

Figure 6.4—*Graded ambiguous figures drawn by a digital computer (two posters by Toulouse-Lautrec). If one stares at the third figure for several minutes, it can be seen as either the woman or the man. Other interpretations can also appear*

Stereoscopic figures drawn by computer

We can, of course, use the computer to produce stereoscopic pictures. Figure 6.5 shows an example drawn by a program written by the author of this chapter; by feeding in new sets of data, the program can be made to draw other variations of the same basic figure.

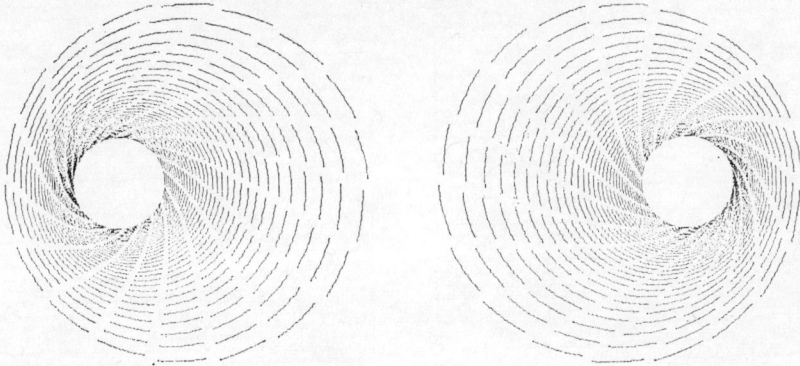

Figure 6.5—*A stereoscopic pair drawn by a computer. Great depth appears in this figure when it is examined in a stereoscope. It may be necessary to continue the inspection for some minutes before the figure is seen clearly and in depth*

The use of the computer for drawing stereoscopic pictures was developed in a subtle and important method invented by Bela Julesz, of the Bell Telephone Laboratories. Julesz (1960) wanted to study depth perception using a stereoscope, and he wanted to do this in such a manner that there were no cues to depth other than the stereoscopic cues of disparity between the images presented to the two eyes. He would use stereoscopic pairs of figures, but whatever figures he used were to be such that each separately held no cues to depth. This would not be true, for example, of a pair which showed a landscape; each of that pair would have many cues, in the perspective, in the placing of figures on the ground, in texture, in the overlap of one object on another.

Julesz chose to use picture pairs made up of squares in a random pattern. Each picture was like a chessboard, but with thousands of small squares rather than 64 large ones; and instead of a regular alteration of black and white, he used varying shades of grey chosen at random for each square. The computer generated the random numbers and displayed the pattern, which could then be photographed (see Figure 6.6).

Basically, the left-hand picture is the same as the right-hand picture, with the same random pattern; so that when the pictures are presented to each eye, the images coincide and a single pattern is seen. With these identical pictures, the pattern which is seen is flat; to get stereoscopic depth, part of the pattern of one picture is shifted sideways and the gap is filled in with more of the random pattern. When the two pictures are now fused, the part which has been shifted fuses with the corresponding part which has not been shifted; a single pattern is again seen,

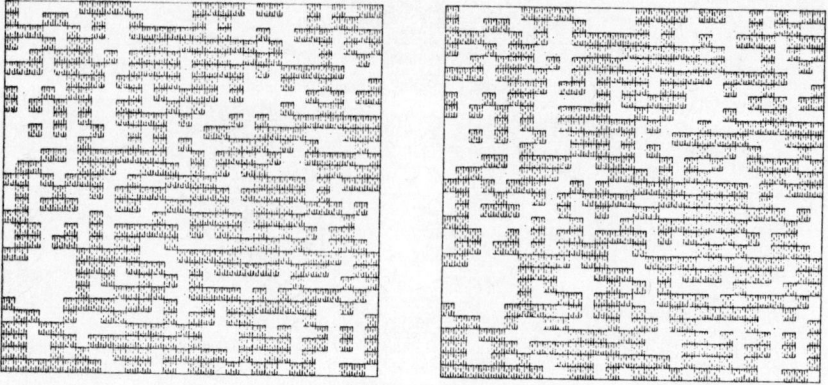

Figure 6.6—*A Julesz pair. When the figure is viewed through a stereo-scope, the central area appears to recede behind the rest of the figure. It may be necessary to wait several minutes before the effect is seen with perfect clarity. To show the technique, the cells in the figure have been made larger than those used by Julesz*

but it is seen at a different depth from that of the surrounding part of the picture.

It can be seen that Julesz has succeeded in having no depth cues other than the binocular ones. Each picture is merely a flat random pattern of light and dark squares. No depth exists, except as a difference between the two random patterns, and that difference is only a sideways displacement. Yet when the pair is presented in a stereoscope, the displaced area is seen to lift up clearly, with well-defined edges.

Julesz used a computer to prepare these figures, but later workers have found simpler ways of producing them, using available forms of random texture—photographs of sandpaper, or the textured patterns made commercially for draughtsmen (e.g. Letraset). This is an interesting example of the way in which work with computers has opened up the way for further work in which no computer is needed. Nevertheless, a computer is still needed for some figures, as for example when we want to obtain a complex variation in the depth effect (Julesz, 1965).

These Julesz figures have become an important tool for work on perception. They provide a means of hiding a meaningful design in a random pattern, to emerge only as the subject achieves stereoscopic perception of the figure. Since the design is not present in the figure presented to each eye, indeed does not exist for that eye separately, we have strong grounds for localizing any effects which we find to be produced by the design: we can say that these effects are produced after stereoscopic fusion, since they could not have been produced by the eyes separately.

Papert (1964) used Julesz figures in this way to investigate the motion after-effect. He made stereo movies from a succession of different Julesz pairs. Each eye separately, saw only a succession of random-square pictures; since each was different, this appeared as a randomly moving pattern of visual noise. When the pictures were seen in a stereoscope a set of squares appeared, standing out in depth and moving downward. The subject inspected these for some time, and when the film was stopped he saw an upward movement. Thus it seems that the motion after-effect is produced at least partly after stereoscopic fusion. Anstis and Moulden (1970) followed up this work with an experiment not using computer-generated figures, showing that the effect has components before and after stereoscopic fusion.

A related question arises for the figural after-effect in which, for example, a person who has been looking at a curved line then sees a straight line as curved. This after-effect occurs in depth too, but it has not been clear whether the depth after-effect is independent of the two-dimensional effect; it might be a secondary effect of the separate after-effects in the two eyes. But Blakemore and Julesz (1971) have now settled the matter, by showing depth after-effects on Julesz figures, which therefore could not be the secondary effects of separate-eye effects which in this experiment could not occur.

A number of workers have used computers for drawing other kinds of random patterns. Evans (1967), for example, computed sets of histogram-like patterns with controlled information content and redundancy. (These are measures used in the mathematical theory of information: information content can be characterized briefly as a measure of the complexity of the stimulus, and redundancy as a measure of the degree of regularity in the stimulus—the degree of interdependence between its parts. A regular staircase, for example, has a high degree of redundancy, an irregular rise has very little.) The figures were printed out by the computer in the form shown below:

```
                        @
@                     @ @    @
@    @    @    @ @    @ @
@    @    @ @ @ @    @ @ @
@ @ @ @ @ @ @ @ @ @ @
@ @ @ @ @ @ @ @ @ @ @
```

Evans used these figures as a set of stimuli in experiments on perceptual categorization.

Attneave and Arnoult (1956) have described a number of methods of generating figures with controlled complexity; several of these methods lend themselves naturally to mechanization by computer.

The perception of space and movement

An example of perceptual work which does not itself use a computer but has been applied with the help of computers is seen in the work of Gibson (1952) on the perception of space and movement. This work is well known and shows the importance of the continuing existence of the pattern of light which our eyes explore; and within this pattern the importance of gradients of texture, spacing and size in determining our perception of the position and orientation of the objects and surfaces in the space around us. Underlying all these gradients are the laws of perspective, and Gibson pays a great deal of attention to these laws.

Gibson himself uses very little formal mathematics in his work, but some of the ideas which he uses, for example that of the invariants which underlie transformations of perspective, are clear-cut mathematical ideas which can easily be put into symbolic form. Gibson's experimental work depends largely on photographs and diagrams, and on the use of shadow-casting point-source projectors, not on computers. The use of computers comes later, in the application of these ideas to situations in which the accurate perception of space is essential, such as the piloting of an aircraft. Yet we can regard the point-source projector as an analog computer which operates according to the laws of perspective. If the projector is placed so as to cast the shadow of an object on a screen, then the shadow will be a representation in perspective of the object. This can be seen by drawing an outline around the shadow, then removing the projector and looking at the screen from the same position. The outline of the shadow will fall exactly into place, to outline the object as well. And since the object itself is seen in accurate perspective, the outline and the shadow are also perspective representations of the object. Gibson did not draw outlines, but used the shadow direct by placing the projector and the observer on opposite sides of a translucent screen. The observer sees the shadow which is a perspective representation of the object; and as the object moves the observer sees its movement, not as changes in the shape of a shadow on a flat screen, but as an object which preserves its shape as it moves in space.

Here we can see clearly the idea of the perspective transformation. The shadow changes its shape as the object moves, but all of these shapes belong to a single set, in the sense that any one of them can be changed into any other by transforming the perspective—in effect, by moving either object or projector or screen. The shadows of a different object will belong to another set, the members of which can again be transformed into one another. Some shapes may be common to the two sets, as when a disc casts the same shadow as a ball, but each set of shapes is a complete and consistent whole which is different from any other. (We are discussing only the situation in which the screen is flat. When the screen is not flat a more complicated argument is needed, but the principle still holds.) We can sum this up by saying that an object has its own characteristic set of perspective transformations. Moreover, and this is the point which Gibson emphasizes, our perceptual systems are sensitive to these transformations in such a manner that they are able

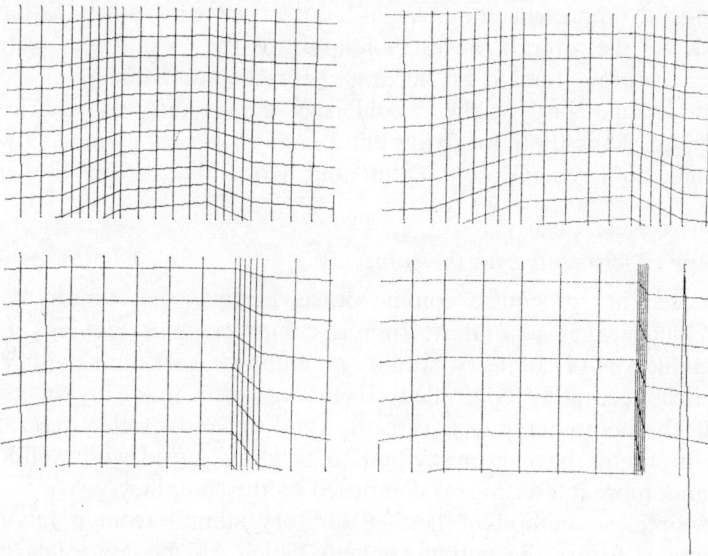

Figure 6.7—*Perspective views of a set of vertical surfaces as they are approached*

to retrieve the shape of the object from the perspective representations of it. Gibson's experiments have shown that our perception of space and movement depends strongly on this ability of our perceptual systems.

These perspective transformations can readily be produced by a computer. An example is shown in Figure 6.7. Another example, not attributable to Gibson, is the set of figures used by Shepard and Metzler in the experiment on mental rotation described earlier in this chapter. (See Figure 6.3.) Derived directly from Gibson's work, however, is an important practical application in which computer-controlled displays in

perspective are used as an aid to the flying of an aircraft in poor
visibility. A pilot cannot rely on his organs of balance, which evolved
on the ground; without his eyes, he can lose control completely. Ordinarily, several instruments indicate to the pilot the attitude of his aircraft;
to interpret these, he must have had a great deal of training and even
then the set of instruments make a considerable demand on his attention.
The computer-controlled display developed by the General Electric
Company, removes this demand. Information from the instruments is
used to generate a picture of the environment in correct perspective,
and this picture is displayed on a screen in front of the pilot. The
display shows a grid marked out to represent the ground below, with
markings to represent the present course and any other features of
interest. As the aircraft moves in relation to the ground, the picture is
changed so as to remain an accurate representation; the pilot sees the
picture change just as he would see the ground change in that
manoeuvre. Thus the pilot flying blind is given almost as much freedom
as if he could see (Gibson, Olum and Rosenblatt, 1955; Sutherland,
1970).

Auditory experiments with the computer

We need not of course confine ourselves to visual stimuli. We can
use a loudspeaker as output from a computer, thus making possible
the production of auditory stimuli in complex sequences with timing
and pitch accurately controlled. Even the overtones can be inserted,
making the computer into a versatile (and expensive) electronic organ.
Many programs have been written to produce music with well-known
tunes and, more interesting, as composed by the computer.

The simplest method of getting auditory stimuli from a laboratory
computer is to use the output contacts which can be controlled by the
program. A standard oscillator is used to feed an audio signal to a
loudspeaker. The computer contacts are used to switch the signal on
and off, so that the sequence of stimuli can be controlled by the program. More complex stimuli can be obtained by using a set of tone
generators, or a tone generator which can be varied in pitch. The intensity of the tones can be varied by a controllable attenuator or, if this is
not available, pre-set attenuators can be used and the program can
switch between them.

Auditory stimuli can also be generated directly by the computer,
without the use of a peripheral tone generator. This allows more accurate
control of the waveform, but requires more sophisticated programs and
more space in the computer store. The reason is that the program must
calculate and store every part of the waveform, in detail. This complete

control is not necessary when using tone generators; in that case the generators provide the waveform, and the computer with its program need only specify the times for switching the generators on and off.

To generate the waveform directly, the simplest method is to take a signal from the computer through an amplifier to a loudspeaker. If the computer is slow enough, the sequence of signals which come naturally from the computer will produce a pattern of sound; sometimes a loudspeaker is used in this way as a monitor, to keep the operator aware that the machine is working normally. When a particular sequence of sounds is required, a program is written to pass the appropriate sequence of numbers to the output from which the loudspeaker connexion has been taken.

The signals produced by the computer are in the form of pulses representing digits, whereas the signal required by the loudspeaker is a continuously varying waveform; thus the above method does not give as complete a control of waveform as is desirable. A conversion stage must be used, the best form of which is a digital-to-analog converter. This produces an output voltage which is proportional to the number given out by the computer in digital form. Thus to get an accurate waveform, the computer must produce a sequence of numbers which specify the amplitude of the wave at each successive time, and the converter will produce from this sequence of numbers the varying signal which feeds the loudspeaker.

The main advantage of this method of direct generation is the accuracy which can be obtained over the whole of the waveform. Tone generators can be accurate enough for simple sine waves or for continuous waves, but the transients at switch-on and switch-off are not controllable. Yet, in some kinds of work, it is the transients which are most important. Such is the case, for example, in studying the action of the cochlea of the ear. In some laboratories a computer is dedicated entirely to this kind of work. The waveform may be generated by a program, or it may be merely stored in the computer as a sequence of numbers with a simple program to read it out.

For studying the perception of speech we do not require quite this degree of accuracy: we, as listeners, are relatively insensitive to changes in the shape and amplitude of speech waveforms. It is the frequencies of the speech sounds and their durations which are most important for intelligibility. But there again the computer can serve us well; as we have seen we can program it to produce the required frequencies for the required short durations in whatever complex patterns are required, or we can store the complex waveforms and produce them when they are needed.

There is another feature of speech and speech perception which makes the computer indispensable for this kind of work. The speech sounds which people produce are not invariable, not produced by simple rules. The same phoneme is pronounced differently according to the context in which it occurs. This influence of context on pronunciation sometimes extends over a sentence or more. Associated with this effect of context is a difficulty in the artificial generation of speech sounds. If an attempt is made to generate synthetic speech by rules which are too simple, the same sound placed in different contexts will often be heard as different phonemes; it might for example be heard as an *a* in one word and as an *e* in another. We can begin to meet this difficulty by programming the computer to take account of context when synthesizing the sound. But the rules which govern speech are not simple and, although a great deal of progress has been made, this work still has far to go. For an example of this kind of work, see Denes (1970).

As a last example of the use of computers with auditory perception, we consider the use of the computer for producing a signal which is recorded on tape for later use. With this technique we can produce complex combinations of tones. An interesting recording of this kind was prepared by Shepard (1964) to investigate circularity in judgements of relative pitch. When the tape is played, listeners hear a sequence of tones each higher in pitch than the preceding one; the rise in pitch continues for as long as the tape is played. The effect resembles the ever-rising staircase described by Penrose and Penrose (1958). Some listeners became puzzled that the tones did not really seem to get higher, in spite of the rise from each tone to the next; other listeners did not notice the paradox. With this tape, Shepard showed that perceived pitch cannot be adequately represented by a purely rectilinear scale.

Live displays

Instead of drawing out the display on paper, we can use a computer-controlled cathode-ray tube (CRT) to present the display directly to the subject. The displays can be made to change rapidly, with accurate timing and in elaborate sequences which would be difficult to achieve by other means; and as with other kinds of computer-controlled experiments we can arrange for the computer to determine the course of the experiment according to the responses which the subject makes.

Mayzner *et al.* (1967) used a CRT display to present sequences of letters to the subject, in various locations on the screen and at various rates. The computer could light up any one of 1024×1024 points on the face of the display tube, and since all points were separately programmable they could show any figure they chose. In these experiments Mayzner and his colleagues use the points to make alphanumeric characters each within a rectangle of 5×7 points.

Their program was written so as to allow a certain control by the experimenter. He could type into the machine the required number of characters and what they were; then, again by typing, he could specify the order in which the characters were to be displayed, the duration of display for each character and the time-lapse between characters. He might choose for example to show the letters of a word in their correct positions, but timed in reverse order so that the final letter of the word is seen first and the initial letter is seen last.

In the experiments, several masking effects were found. When they showed the word 'SOMERSAULT' in an irregular order, at about ten to twenty milliseconds per letter and per interval between letters, approximately the first half of the letters shown were not seen; the subject saw only the letters which appeared later in the sequence so that the display appeared to him as 'S M   S   LT'. If on the other hand the letters were presented in the correct sequence 1–10, none of them were blanked out. In another condition the letters were presented still in their proper places in the word but with the time sequence S S O A M U E L R T (i.e. interlacing the letters from the first and second halves of the word, SOMER and SAULT). The subjects saw all the letters, none being blanked out; but there was a marked appearance of spatial displacement of the second S away from the R.

In this work we can regard the computer as a tachistoscope: a device which will flash a picture on to the screen for a controlled time. But the computer can display any of a large number of pictures, whereas the most commonly used tachistoscopes are limited to two channels, supplemented by a rather slow change of pictures by hand. The computer display is obviously more useful although it is also very much more expensive. Eriksen et al. (1969) tried to meet the challenge by designing 'N-channel tachistoscopes' which would be cheaper to make. These used fibre optic light guides to illuminate the display and the timing of the lights was controlled by electronic circuits. These machines are certainly useful and relatively cheap; but when the tachistoscope was actually constructed the N which gives the impression of being any desired number, took on the value of ten. This is still a small number of channels; the computer can provide the equivalent of thousands of channels together with precise sequence and time control. It is true that ten channels would be enough to perform the blanking experiments described above, but the computer can easily be extended to perform more complex experiments when required to do so.

Since we have so large a number of channels we can speed up their presentation until we have a moving picture. Uttal (1969) did this to produce a pattern of dancing dots which can be regarded as dynamic visual noise. He displayed letters with the dancing dots painted over them; few dots or many, at fast rates or slow rates. By using this technique, Uttal claimed he was able to separate out masking due to pattern confusions, and masking due to peripheral stimulus mixing: if enough dynamic noise was shown with the letter, it was completely obliterated; the peripheral mixing of the noise with the letter had masked it. But if the letter was shown with the same amount of noise occurring a fraction of a millisecond before or after it, the subject could see it; thus no masking occurred, and Uttal concluded that there was no confusion between the pattern of the letter and the pattern of the noise.

Experiments using interactive control

The next step in the on-line use of computers is to control the display in accordance with the subject's responses. The procedure may be a simple one, as for example in the control of a psychophysical measurement. To measure a threshold, say, of brightness, an old-established and effective method is to give the subject a control knob which he can adjust. A light is flashed at regular intervals. If the subject sees the light, he adjusts the control to make the light dimmer; if he does not see it at the expected time, he adjusts the control to make the light brighter. The subject's settings are recorded, and a typical result is that the record goes rapidly towards the threshold, then wavers about it. For an example of this method see Blough (1957), who measured the colour sensitivity curve of a pigeon; another example, showing the decay of a figural after-effect, is shown in Figure 6.8 (Wilson, 1962).

Kappauf (1969) used a computer to control the measurement, by this method, of visual latency; this is a delay which occurs in the eye or the visual system, greater delay occurring if the light is dim or coloured. In this experiment, he compared the delays of two stimuli which differed in intensity, in colour and in their distance from the centre of the retina. The two stimuli were presented as a pair. One was regarded as the standard, and its intensity, colour, etc, were kept fixed. The other was regarded as a test stimulus and its properties were varied from trial to trial. Varying the properties in this way leads to a variation in latency, so that one stimulus appears to the subject to come later than the other; this apparent delay can be compensated by introducing a time interval between the stimuli. If the subject reports, by pressing a key connected to the computer, that the test stimulus comes later than the standard, then the computer advances the timing of the test stimulus relative to the

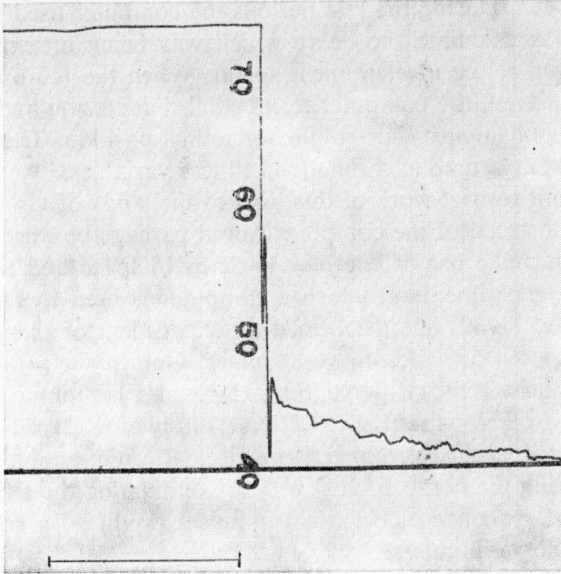

Figure 6.8—*Recording of a figural after-effect. For 90 seconds, the subject inspected a cross with the vertical bar tilted at 10° from the vertical. He then attempted to set the bar at vertical, trying continually to improve his setting. The curve shows his error in setting; the error decreases as the after-effect fades away. The bar shows 60 sec.*

standard; if the subject reports that the test stimulus comes earlier than the standard, then the computer retards the timing of the test stimulus relative to the standard. Thus adjustments are made until the two stimuli are subjectively simultaneous and when that state has been reached the objective time interval between the stimuli will be equal and opposite to the difference between them in visual latency. Thus, for example, the test stimulus may be brighter than the standard; this gives it a shorter latency than the standard, so that it appears to come before the standard in time. The subject indicates this apparent delay, and the computer responds by delaying the test stimulus until it appears to be simultaneous with the standard. The delay is then equal to the difference in latency between the test and standard stimuli.

Once the point of subjective simultaneity is reached there is a tendency for the adjustment to alternate in direction, one way and then the other. To prevent the subject getting into a routine two series of steps were interlaced. Refinements of this kind can readily be incorporated into a computer program and thus into a computer-controlled experiment.

The computer presented trials to the subject in blocks of ten, with rest periods between. During the rest periods the computer used the accumulated tallies to calculate the delay which was being measured and the standard error of the measurement so far. When the required accuracy had been achieved, the computer terminated that session and went on to other settings of intensity, or colour, or retinal position. Thus delay was automatically measured as a function of these variables.

We need not restrict work of this kind to the study of vision. For taste and smell, the speed of the computer would perhaps be wasted; the skin, however, can make use of complex patterns in space and time, and we can perform experiments in which a computer is used to generate these patterns. Uttal (1969) has performed an experiment of this sort, but he by-passed the sensory receptors altogether. One might say that he was working on 'infra-sensory' perception. He used a computer to provide a precisely-controlled pattern of electrical stimulation to the skin. Each "brief electrical impulse produced a precise pattern of action potential on the nerve, firing the nerve directly without stimulating the sensory ending and the short sequence of electrical impulses produced a corresponding sequence of nerve impulses.

In one experiment Uttal used two bursts of ten impulses each. One of the bursts had the pulses evenly spaced in time, the other had a jitter (i.e. the ten impulses were unevenly spaced). The subject was required to judge whether the jitter was on the first or the second burst of the pair. The program was made to reduce the amount of jitter if the subject perceived it, and increase the amount if he did not. Thus the system arrived at the threshold for jitter by the adjustment method described above. In this way Uttal was able to measure the sensitivity of subjects to the variability of interval within bursts of nervous impulses.

This procedure could perhaps have been performed by a simpler device than a general-purpose computer and some workers have preferred to construct a special-purpose logical circuit to control the experiment. This is easily done, since many digital switches and counters are on the market, and these need only be wired together to make up a small computer-type control system. Kelley (1969) used simple circuits of this kind to measure visual acuity. He used an arrangement in which targets on a cathode-ray tube were made smaller when the subject discriminated correctly and larger when he made an error; eventually a target size was reached at which a pre-established proportion were discriminated correctly. The proportion correct was not necessarily 50 per cent, as is conventional in psychological measurements of thresholds; he could set the proportion in advance to any desired value.

Kelley also put this technique to practical use: he was developing a 'head-up' or 'through-the-screen' display for an aircraft. A display of this kind is projected in front of the pilot so that he sees it superimposed on his view through the windscreen and can read it without moving his eyes away. Kelley set a criterion that approximately 90 per cent of the symbols should be correctly identified against the background of outside light. The 'adaptive measurement system' was then used to find the brightness at which the symbols must be set to meet this criterion.

This adaptive technique as applied by Kelley is capable of very general application; in the work described above it was used as a measuring device. It can also be used as a training device and it can be used as a test of the student's skill.

These uses are explained by Kelley. He points out that for experimental measurement it is only the stimuli or problems which are near the performance threshold that are useful. Those which are too easy or too difficult are of little value, since if a test problem is always solved it tells us only that the subject can do better than that; and if the test problem is never solved, it tells us only that he cannot do so well. The adaptive measurement system adjusts the problem until it reaches the desired level of difficulty and thereby achieves an efficient measurement of just how well the subject can do.

When we use the method in an adaptive training device, we find that this is exactly what is needed: an adaptive training device should automatically maintain the difficulty of the training task at the level appropriate to the skill of the student, since this is the level of difficulty at which he will learn best.

The use of the adaptive technique for the testing of the student's skill also derives from this adjustment of difficulty. To measure performance, the usual method is to test the student and get from the test a score which represents the skill of the performance. With the adaptive techniques, however, we increase the difficulty until the performance is degraded to a standard level, then use the level of difficulty as our measure of performance. Thus we have a new set of measurement tools, the scales of which are any of the variables that affect task difficulty.

Computer simulation of pattern recognition

Until now, we have been dealing with work in which the computer is used as an aid to psychological experiment. We now come to work in which the computer takes the place of the experimental subject. Instead of experimenting with perception as it occurs in a human brain, we use a computer to simulate perception. By far the greatest part of this work has been in pattern recognition; this requires explanation, since pattern recognition is only a small part of perception.

The answer seems to be that study by experiment and study by simulation require quite different approaches. An experimenter seizes on some phenomenon which he can get at by experiment and which he suspects to have theoretical importance. He then explores, to find the laws which that phenomenon obeys and to place the phenomenon in its precise position in a theoretical framework. From this approach have come all the usual topics of the psychology of perception: figure-ground effects, the perception of brightness and colour, of shape and position, the apparently constant shape and size of objects in spite of the changing image on the retina, illusions, etc.

The designer of a perceptual simulation, on the other hand, is forced away from phenomena in the direction of a functional problem. He starts from the computers which he has available and attempts to define a behavioural function which is within the capacity of the computers. He must then design the programs which will enable the computer effectively to perform that function. We do not immediately learn from this work anything about the phenomena of perception; what we learn is indirect. Our ideas about function become clearer and we come to know and understand the kind of mechanisms which can perform those functions. We develop a technology within which perceptual functions and mechanisms will find their place. Eventually, this research should help us to understand the phenomena of perception, but it is focussed first of all on mechanisms and on the functions which they must perform.

The most important functional problem that has emerged from this research is that of pattern recognition. Most situations present to us—or to the program which is simulating perception—a mass of data, and hidden in that mass are the patterns which are relevant for the task in hand. How is the perceiver to take in the information, how isolate the patterns from the background, how recognize them and classify them so that they can be used?

There is already a vast literature on pattern recognition, describing work on a variety of problems by a variety of techniques. In the following, we shall first deal briefly with several topics which are interesting though not central to our theme. We shall then trace a thread through the literature, dealing in some detail with important studies which have used computers and which are of psychological interest.

A great deal of work has been done on the design of pattern recognizers for practical applications such as the reading of characters for input to a computer. We might solve this problem by using specially designed characters which can be recognized by techniques which are already available. Thus, for example, banks have adopted for their cheques a system which uses characters printed in magnetic ink which are so shaped as to give distinctive signals when read by a magnetic pick-up head of the type used in tape-recorders.

Another approach, which requires more elaborate engineering but is nevertheless practical, is to read ordinary printed characters by photocell and to recognize them by a system of matching against templates. One template is used for each different character which might occur and if different fonts of type are to be used then a set of templates must be provided for each font. Machines of this kind are available commercially. The makers of one of them claim that it can read from print at a speed of 14,000 characters per second (Control Data Corporation, 1970).

These are however practical problems which are solved by practical methods without regard to the theoretical implications of those methods. It is clear that the mechanisms of perception are much more subtle than the matching of templates; in itself, this would be reason enough for the theoretical work to become separated from the practical. There is however a more potent lure, the same as that which has attracted workers in other fields of artificial intelligence: our perceptual mechanisms are so much more powerful, in their ability to attend to and recognize patterns than present-day machines, that they present at the same time a challenge and a promise to the designers of machines and of computer simulations. Thus it comes about that the work on computer simulation which we shall discuss is almost completely separate from the work on pattern recognition for practical applications.

An aspect of the work which is connected with practical application is that of input and the processing of input. Before recognition can start, it is necessary to get a representation of the pattern into the pattern-recognizing machine (or its equivalent computer program). For practical applications this is done, for example, by giving the machine an array of photocells to serve as eyes (Figures 6.9a) or a scanning device like that of a television camera. For theoretical work, there are more interesting problems to be solved and most researchers by-pass this step by using a more readily available form of input, for example the conventional punched cards (Figure 6.9b).

This input from cards is of course highly stylized. When input must be obtained from the real world, as for example from a radar screen, it is necessary to take the raw input and shape it up to the required standard. Out of this need has arisen a whole field of work, that of computer operations on pictures. These operations are designed to correct known distortions to clarify the picture by removing noise, to sharpen it by operations which increase contrast or compensate for blurr and which isolate features from their background. Such operations are amenable to mathematical treatment and some very general principles have

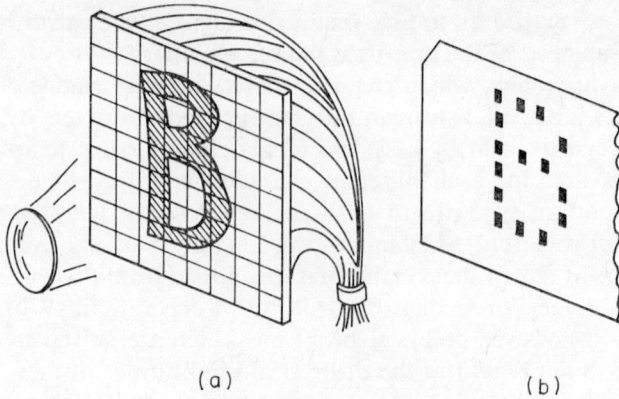

(a)   (b)

Figure 6.9—*Input of pattern to the computer.*
(a) *Photocell array, with lens to form an image and wires to carry the signals to the computer*
(b) *Card punched with holes to represent the pattern*

emerged. These principles are probably important for an understanding of visual sensation, but they are perhaps less important at the higher levels of perception. (See for example Lipkin and Rosenfeld 1970.)

A field of work which we shall not discuss in the following, but which we must mention briefly, is that of pattern recognition applied to speech. The work on this subject tends to be separate from the main body of pattern recognition work, which is concerned primarily with vision. We cite, for example, Liebman (1971) for a voice recognition system, in which a voice-signature is used for indentification; and Reddy (1967) for the computer recognition of connected speech. There are some possible applications of this work, as for instance in enabling us to control a computer by verbal instructions, but a great part of the interest is in showing which features of speech are important for recognition and in giving some hints about the mechanisms by which we perceive speech.

Pattern recognition as a classification

One way to characterize the method by which we recognise patterns is as a categorization or classification. No doubt this is a simplification, but it is nevertheless an idea worth developing as a description of a process which occurs at a number of levels in sensation, perception and thought. Bruner (1957), for example, developed the idea of recognition as a categorization, first into general classes and then into more specific classes. Recognition would be complete when the stimulus had been put into the appropriate categories; false recognition or delayed recognition can occur depending on the 'perceptual readiness' of the subject to put stimuli into this or that category.

Ideas of this sort were also applied to thinking about the connexions in the nervous system. They received a boost when, in the late 1950s, at about the same time that work was beginning on pattern recognition by machine, cells were discovered in the cat's brain which seem to perform a simple categorization of stimuli reaching the eye. These cells appear to be neural mechanisms which can recognize patterns. The cells were discovered by Hubel and Wiesel (1959) in the striate cortex of the cat. A micro-electrode was inserted into the striate cortex, to pick up impulses from one of these cells. The cell could then be made to fire by a light shone into the eye of the cat. Using small spots or bars of light, Hubel and Wiesel explored the eye to plot out the region of the retina to which the striate cell was sensitive. They found cells with retinal fields which were elongated vertically or horizontally, or at some other inclination. To a large patch of light, or to a line *across* the field, such a cell was insensitive; but to a line *along* the field; it responded vigorously. They found many cells of this and similar kinds (see Figure 6.10a). Particularly interesting were the cells which would not respond to a spot of light, but required a properly oriented bar or edge of light—and which would respond to that stimulus wherever it occurred, over a large area of the retina. It seems that these cells are generalizing the shape, irrespective of its retinal position.

When one tries to design a pattern recognizer as a network like the nervous system, of interconnected units, one readily arrives at something very like the Hubel and Wiesel cells. An input array is provided, the cells of which will be stimulated by the pattern which is to be recognized. This is like the retina of the eye. To recognize the patterns, another set of units is provided. These recognition units correspond to the Hubel and Wiesel cells, and each unit is connected to the cells of the input array (Figure 10b). Usually, each recognition unit has a threshold setting: it will respond if the stimulation reaching it exceeds the threshold. By adjusting the sensitivity, or weight, of the connexions to the various cells of the input array, the unit can be made to respond to one pattern of input rather than another; and by making some of the connexions negative, stimulation at one point can inhibit response to stimulation at another point of the array. Thus if we can set the weights properly, we can make the units discriminate between patterns, each responding only when its own pattern is received at the input (Uttley, 1956; Rosenblatt, 1958; Taylor, 1956).

(a)

(b)

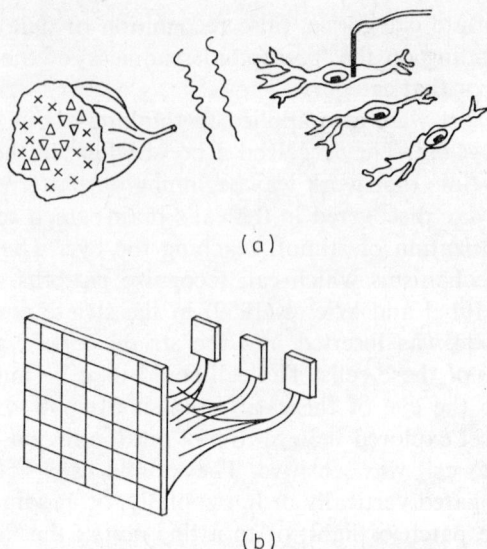

Figure 6.10—*A pattern recognizer compared with the Hubel and Wiesel cells (simplified)*
(a) *A receptive field on the retina, and three cells in the striate cortex, with a micro-electrode. Each cell has its characteristic receptive field, different from the others*
(b) *A photocell array and three pattern-recogniser cells. By adjusting the sensitivity of each connexion, the pattern-recognizer can be made to respond to one pattern rather than another*

Linear separation

But how effective is this kind of machine as a classifier of patterns? We can represent the situation diagrammatically. Suppose that we use dots to represent patterns, round and square dots to represent two kinds of pattern. We could try to separate the round dots from the square dots by drawing a straight line across the paper. We would succeed more or less, according to the degree to which the dots were mixed up and according to our skill in choosing the position of the line (see Figure 6.11). It turns out that the pattern recognizer described above is closely analogous to this, the *position* of each dot depends on the pattern which it represents and our action in setting the weights is equivalent to choosing a position for drawing the line. Setting the weights serves to discriminate between patterns; drawing the line serves to separate dots.

The question has been studied mathematically, as the problem of linear separation (see for example Griffin *et al.*, 1964; and Casey and Nagy, 1971). We can specify any input pattern by showing in a list the

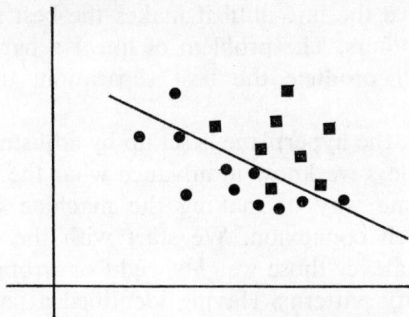

Figure 6.11—*Linear separation of round dots from square dots. Success or failure depends on finding a suitable position for the line and on the degree to which the two kinds of dot are mixed together*

intensity with which the pattern stimulates each of the cells of the input array (as, for example, the light value for that pattern at each receptor cell on the retina). Then the list of values represents the pattern and a different pattern would be represented by a different list. But any list of numbers can be regarded as the coordinates of a point in space. For instance, the numbers (2,3) could represent a point two centimetres from the left of the paper and three centimetres up. Thus a given pattern can be represented by a point in the space and each different pattern is a different point.

The space would have as many dimensions as there are numbers; since there is one number for each receptor cell, there would be as many dimensions as there are receptor cells. For two cells, the values of x and y would fix the position of the point on a two-dimensional plane, the sheet of paper; (x, y, z) would fix it in a three-dimensional space, and so on, into hundreds or thousands of dimensions. These multi-dimensional spaces are not easily visualized, but the mathematics is straightforward.

Now consider the set of input patterns which are to be used. These are represented by points in the space. Suppose some of these belong to the same class, all being different versions of the letter a, for instance. Then to recognize the letter a, the machine should give the appropriate a response for each of these points, and for none of the others. In effect, it should draw a surface around the a points to separate them from the others.

To set the strengths of connexions, as described above, is in effect to draw a surface in the space. But the surface is a flat one: in two dimensions, a straight line; in three dimensions, a plane; in four or more dimensions, a *hyperplane*. In two dimensions, the straight line is represented by the equation $y = mx + c$. By adjusting the coefficients m

and *c,* we can move the line until it makes the best separation between the *a* set and the others. The problem of linear separation is to find the settings which will produce the best separation, using one or more hyperplanes.

As we have seen, the hyperplane is set up by adjustment of the strength of connexions. Unless we know in advance what the settings should be, we must have some way of making the machine choose the correct adjustment for each connexion. We start with the weights which are already set up; whatever those weights, right or wrong, the machine will use them to identify patterns. Having identified a pattern, it must produce a response of some sort, perhaps merely to name the pattern. We arrange to indicate to the machine whether it is successful or not. We might have a 'teacher' for example, who indicates whether the pattern has been correctly recognized. The machine then follows rules which determine which connexions are to be strengthened after a success, which weakened, and similarly after a failure.

Rosenblatt's Perceptron incorporated a training system like this. Another example is the ADALINE system developed by Widrow and Smith (1964). Each ADALINE element had a number of inputs linearly combined with adjustable weights, as discussed above. If the inputs combined to give a signal above the threshold the element indicated by a positive signal that it recognised the pattern; otherwise it gave a negative signal, indicating that it had not recognized any pattern. For adjustment of the weights, a teacher indicated to the machine whether it had been right or wrong. The settings were then automatically adjusted; each setting was made more sensitive or less sensitive, whichever would have given a smaller error for that particular input pattern.

A number of ADALINES could be connected together into a network, to recognize more complex patterns. The system was not actually constructed, but was simulated on a computer. In one test, the network was fed with the barometric pressures for a number of points around San Francisco, for successive days, and differences day to day. The desired output was whether it rained at San Francisco during the next 12, 24, 36 hours. In the various parts of this test the network achieved a score of between 67 per cent and 89 per cent correct.

The method of clustering

Casey and Nagy (1971) have described a computer method of pattern recognition which replaced linear separation by a method of clustering and which makes its adjustments without the help of a teacher. Each pattern is represented by a point in multi-dimensional space as described above. It is to be expected that patterns which are similar will be represented by points which are not far apart. If the patterns were the letters of the alphabet, for example, we would have clusters of points, one cluster for each letter. A badly printed letter might be far from the centre of its cluster, but it would usually be nearer to its own cluster than to the clusters belonging to other letters. Thus the problem for the machine is to discover, from the sample of patterns which it has been given, where the clusters are and which points belong to which cluster.

The procedure is simple: to fix the cluster centres arbitrarily, then to group the points and adjust the positions of the centres in just two steps which are repeated again and again. 1. Calculate for each point in turn its distance from every cluster centre, and allocate it to the nearest centre; this separates the points into groups. 2. Calculate new cluster centres by averaging the positions of the points of each group. The first step forms the groups, the second shifts the centre to the centroid of the group. On repeating the two steps, the groups are reformed and the centres again shifted. Eventually the process converges, and the groups no longer change from one iteration to the next. When this occurs the final groupings are accepted as being the desired clusters.

Casey and Nagy used this system to decipher type-written text. The material was read into the computer by a photo-electric scanning system. The computer analysis was performed on about 1,000 characters, but about 20,000 characters of connected text could be read in for one experiment and the computer could then print out its interpretation of the whole of this text. The first stage of the analysis was as described above, and succeeded in separating the letters into clusters. There were some failures with infrequent letters, as for example most of the *z*s were assigned to the same cluster as the *x*s.

At this stage, the program has placed the *a*s together, the *b*s together, and so on, but without a teacher it has no way of discovering which is which. Casey and Nagy completed their program by using one of the oldest tricks of the cryptographer when confronted with a message in code: the program counts the frequency with which each symbol occurs in the text. The most frequent symbol is then taken to be the letter *e*, which is the letter occurring most frequently in English; the next most frequent symbol is taken to be *t*, and so on. This procedure soon fails, but when the frequency of pairs of letters is taken into account, the text which emerges is easily readable, with only a few errors. Thus they have succeeded in producing a program which reads a text into the computer by a photocell device, which recognises the characters in the sense that it sorts them into clusters and which then uses its store of information about the statistical structure of English to choose a tele-typewriter character for each cluster of symbols. The computer thus *recognizes* the symbols which are presented to its photocell scanner and prints them out on its teletypewriter as connected English text.

Finding the features

In most sets of patterns, certain features are more useful than others for discriminating between the members of the set. In ordinary printed letters, for example, the upper halves of the letters are more useful than the lower halves. Probably the kind of adjustment described above would isolate useful features and use them, but we can work more directly towards the isolation. The importance of this is that the number of features is usually much smaller than the number of patterns which can be made up from them. An obvious example of this is our use of a small alphabet for writing a great number of words. Given this possibility of a small 'alphabet' of useful features, we can usually effect a worthwhile economy by looking first for the features and only then for the patterns which they form.

Two methods of finding the features, to be used in Perceptron-type machines, are described by Block, Nilsson and Duda (1964). For example, to isolate a feature which is present in both patterns P1 and P2: Pattern P1 is presented to the pattern recognizer, and the weights are adjusted to match the recognizer to that pattern. Then P2 is presented. If the recognizer becomes active (i.e. accepts P2 as similar to P1), then match to the pattern which is made by the overlap between P1 and P2 (i.e. set those points to zero which were set to P1 but are not in P2, leaving only those points which are in both P1 and P2). If the recognizer does not become active, no change. This isolates the feature common to the two patterns and which can therefore be used to classify them together.

To isolate a feature which can be used to *discriminate* between the patterns, a similar procedure is used but the common elements are neutralized. It is interesting to note that this is the procedure suggested by Restle (1962) for a statistical learning theory. This kind of procedure is systematic and logical, but it works only when the patterns which have the same meaning also have features in common by which they can be recognized. This is not always so; compare for example, the upper and lower case versions of the letter G, g. Hand-written characters are another example. They are easily identified by humans but present a difficult problem for computer pattern recognition. The programmer must use his judgement to find features which can be used for discrimination and very often the features which he selects do not live up to their promise, and turn out to be poor discriminators.

Many workers have tried to overcome this difficulty by getting the machine to find the features, not by comparison of patterns, but by the success or failure of the feature as an aid to recognition. It could be supposed that useful features will emerge from the adjustment of weights in a network, but the performance of these network machines has been weak. It is necessary to discover more powerful methods by which the computer can find the features which will enable it to discriminate between patterns.

Let us look closely at an excellent example of these more powerful methods, the program written by Uhr and Vossler (1963) to generate its own feature selectors (which they called *operators*) and to select the best of these by an evolutionary method. They tested the program on a variety of hand-written letters, line drawings of faces and other objects, segmented handwriting and spoken numbers. On sets of five or ten letters, identification was often perfect after three passes through the set, each pass providing a 'practice trial' for the program. With a full alphabet of handwritten letters, identification reached better than 90 per cent. For the line drawings and spoken numbers the score was better than 50 per cent. When the program was compared with human subjects on small sets of meaningless patterns, the computer performed better than the human subjects.

The unknown pattern is broken up into a matrix (or rectangular grid) of 20 $\times$ 20 squares each with a value of 1 or 0. A matrix of this sort can be represented in a punched card by punching a hole for a 1, not punching for a 0. The card can then be read into the computer as a set of numbers which will then represent the pattern. Once in the computer, the 'margins' are cut away in a calculation which leaves only a 'rectangle' big enough to hold the pattern. To recognize the pattern, it is scanned by a set of operators (feature selectors), to test whether the pattern has the features represented by each operator; the features of the pattern are then compared with the record of features belonging to previous patterns, and the identification is made. Success or failure would be noted and the program would then go back to adjust the operators in accord with the degree to which they helped or hindered the recognition.

The *operators* are 5 $\times$ 5 matrices, with each square 0, 1, or blank; a 0 or a 1 is for matching with the input pattern, a blank allows for variability in the pattern (see Figure 6.12). There are three basic ways in which operators can be generated: they can be designed by the programmer and put into the program; they can be generated by filling the squares with 0s, 1s, and blanks at random; or thirdly, the 5 $\times$ 5 matrix can be taken from the input pattern at random, in effect extracting a sample of the input at random; some blanks are then added to allow

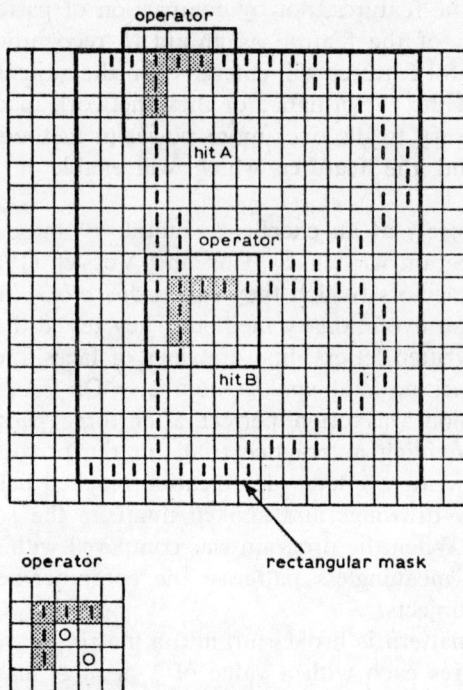

Figure 6.12—*A Uhr and Vossler 'Operator'. The diagram shows how two hits are scored when matching the operator against a pattern representing the letter B. (From Apter, 1969, as adapted from Feigenbaum and Feldman, 1963)*

for minor distortions in the pattern. A fourth and more complicated method is to make a new operator by combining two of the existing operators, using one of several arithmetical or logical formulæ. This method is brought into effect by the program randomly choosing a pair of operators and a method for combining them. The operators which are produced by this method may be quite complex, since they are built up from previous operators of the same type.

With a set of matrix operators in store, the program can search the input pattern for features. Taking each operator in turn, it scans the pattern and records the position of every hit, (i.e. match between operator and pattern). The record can be summarized in four numbers for each operator: the number of hits, the average vertical and horizontal positions of the hits, and the mean square scatter of the hits about the centre of the pattern.

In the computer memory, the program has stored similar lists of characteristics for previous patterns, one *list* for each *type* of pattern which is to be distinguished. These lists show the applicability of each operator to each of those previous patterns and carry also a record of the current weight for each characteristic in the list. Recognition then proceeds by taking the differences between the input pattern and each pattern in memory, weighting them appropriately and adding them for each list of characteristics. The input pattern is taken to be of the same type as the list from which it is least different and it is given the name of that list. Thus the pattern has been recognized.

When recognition has been achieved and success or failure has been noted, the program goes back to the adjustment of weights and the selection of operators. It concentrates on the difficult discriminations by adjusting weights only for those patterns which have difference scores less than or close to that of the correct pattern. For each characteristic, the weight is turned up if that characteristic by itself would have identified the input pattern correctly; it is turned down if it would by itself have been wrong. If the characteristic was the same for both patterns, and thus gave no information, it is turned down. This adjustment improves the ability of the program to recognize patterns, with the set of operators which it has then in store.

The value of the operators is assessed by averaging the weight for each operator across all patterns. To give credit for usefulness in recognizing patterns and also for the importance of the characteristic in combining to form other operators, the calculation is slightly more complicated than a simple average and the result is called a success count. When the success count falls below three the operator is rejected and a new operator is generated to take its place. At first this new operator is set so that it will have little effect on decisions. If it is useful its effect will be increased by the procedures which adjust weights; if it is not its success count will fall and it will be eliminated.

As mentioned above, this program was successful in recognizing a variety of quite subtle patterns, including handwritten characters, spoken numerals and pictures of faces. The operators which it uses are a plausible representation of neural networks in the eye or in the brain. It is at least possible, for example, that several sensory cells in the retina are connected to a single output in the way that the 5×5 matrix forms a single operator. The Hubel and Wiesel cells, too, seem to form operators of a similar kind. The resemblance here is even closer, since the operators in Uhr and Vossler's program were scanned over the pattern, abstracting the feature in every place that it occurred and many Hubel and Wiesel cells seem to have this same property of responding to a feature whatever its position over a large area of the retina. Moreover, there has been evidence to show that the Hubel and Wiesel cells are not fixed, but develop and change; their mode of change is hardly likely to resemble the methods used in the program, but the capacity for change certainly adds to the interest of the program.

Scanning and exploration

In this program the input pattern was scanned by the operators, to locate the places at which the operator fitted the pattern. Scanning of one kind or another seems to be important for vision. For example Hebb (1949) has argued that our ability to see form develops in conjunction with the development of patterns of eye movement and there are many experiments showing the way in which our eyes explore the scene in front of them (e.g. Noton and Stark, 1971). Gibson (1966), in a development of the work which was described earlier in this chapter, has presented an important theory of perception in which exploration becomes paramount and the pattern on the retina is relegated to a secondary function. According to Gibson the perceptual system builds up a stable representation of the world, using the senses to obtain the information which it needs. The eyes and the other senses explore the world under control of the perceptual system and if the movement of eyes and hands does not bring in the information which is required, the person may move bodily and so extend the exploration into new places.

This active exploration has not yet been incorporated into pattern-recognizing programs, though some approaches have been made. One of the most active is the FREDDIE system designed by Popplestone and others, in the Department of Machine Intelligence at Edinburgh University (Brata, 1970). In this system, a movable television camera is controlled by a computer program. The camera scans the object and the program builds up a description of the object and compares it with a set of descriptions in store. The FREDDIE system recognizes real objects, such as a cup. It goes further still: having identified a given object as a cup, it can use its mechanical 'hand' to pick the cup up by the handle.

A further step in the direction of our own perception would be to make the pattern recognition system select features of interest according to the purposes for which they are needed. It might even be desirable that the system should choose to recognize only those patterns which are relevant to the attainment of its goals. This possibility is discussed by Holland (1969), who points out that the checker-playing program written by Samuel is a system of this sort; it must recognize the situations which lead to more highly valued configurations. More generally, such a system must discover the situations in which a given response produces the same desirable outcome reliably on different occasions.

The hologram

Finally, a brief reference to some work which does not often use computers, but which is relevant to the problem of pattern recognition, and which has some interesting features as an analogy to the brain. This work concerns the hologram, invented by Gabor (1948), and developed greatly in recent years. (Pennington, 1968; Metherell, 1969; for a recent review see Gabor, Kock, and Stroke, 1971. Gabor was awarded a Nobel Prize for this work in 1971.)

A hologram is a photograph, but instead of being made from an image of the object, it is made from interference patterns in the light scattered by an object. The significance for psychology is that the hologram can be used as a pattern recognizer and that it presents us with an example of distributed storage—a hologram when broken in two can still reconstruct an image of the whole object, though the quality of the reconstruction is degraded. This reminds us of the work of Lashley (1929), in which he showed that the storage of memories and skills is distributed widely over the brain. He trained rats to run a maze and then made cuts in various parts of the cerebral cortex of the rats' brains. The results may be summarized briefly by saying that the degradation in performance did not depend on the place at which the cut was made. Performance deteriorated in proportion to the size of the cut.

The obvious usefulness of the hologram and these similarities to the action of the brain have led to a number of suggestions for mechanisms in the brain analogous to the hologram (Gabor, 1968; a related approach is seen in Pollen, Lee and Taylor, 1971). It is perhaps too early to expect that any of these suggestions will prove fruitful, but it does seem that the hologram is of extraordinary interest for those who are studying the mechanisms of pattern recognition and perception. And since holograms can be generated by computers, may even perhaps be used as the storage element in computers, it is quite possible that this work might lead to computer simulations involving holographic models of perception.

Further Reading

Bongard, M. (1970) *Pattern Recognition.* Spartan Books, Washington. Macmillan, London. A textbook with consideration of theory and of computer simulation. Translated from the Russian.

Corcoran, D. W. J. (1971) *Pattern Recognition.* Penguin Science of Behaviour, London. Treats pattern recognition with an emphasis on experimental psychology leading on to the use of computers for testing theories of the perception of form and speech.

Mendel, J. M. and K. S. Fu (Eds.) (1970) *Adaptive, Learning and Pattern Recognition Systems.* Academic Press, London. A collection of papers.

Pattern Recognition (1971—) The Journal of the Pattern Recognition Society. Pergamon, Oxford.

Tou, J. T. and R. H. Wilcox, (1964) *Computer and Information Sciences. Collected Papers on Learning, Adaptation and Control in Information Systems.* Spartan Books, Washington. Research papers, many of them on pattern recognition.

Uhr, L. (1966) *Pattern Recognition. Theory, Experiment, Computer Simulation and Dynamic Models of Form Perception and Discovery.* Wiley, New York. A comprehensive collection of papers.

Watanabe, Satosi (Ed.) (1969) *Methodologies of Pattern Recognition.* Academic Press, London. A collection of theoretical papers and reports of simulations. See especially the article by Gose: 'Introduction to Biological and Mechanical Pattern Recognition.'

CHAPTER 7

The Computer in the Psychology of Language

Godfrey Harrison

Introduction

Most chapters in Part II of this book review work done in particular areas of psychology influenced by the development and use of computers. Computer operation does not depend on topics like, say, clinical psychology. However, clinical psychology may come to depend on computers. By contrast, using computers depends on languages whereas languages have existed for millennia and are in small need of computers. All languages used on computers have limited scope. Limitations hold both for artificial languages that are intellectually contrived and for natural languages which have been acquired as first languages. The limitations in computer versions of natural language arise from our everyday language performance exceeding our understanding of language. These inadequacies have encouraged the development of theories of language. Language theorists have not always been interested in human language capacity. Bar-Hillel (1964, p. 180) interested briefly in the psychology of translation wrote '... in 1952 ... I tried at first to find out what psychologists knew about human translation, only to discover to my dismay that very little was known that was not purely anecdotal or speculative.' There are other examples but most of those interested in computers and language have been little concerned with computers and psychology. Complementing this there has been little interest shown in computers by other workers, Noam Chomsky and Fodor amongst them, who have however contributed much on language and psychology.

The outcome of efforts in three active fields has been more often merely relevant than central. This chapter mainly gives a general view of major themes and principal directions which are of psychological interest in work on language and computers, but it is not concerned with numerical solutions. Computer work on language relevant to psychology

and numerical in character is exemplified in a shorter section which now
follows.

Psychology and the calculative processing of language by computer

Biblical concordances illustrate the centuries old history of compiling
data on language. Analyses of style have used frequency counts of
grammatical constructions to establish, or exclude, claims to authorship;
their history is shorter than the biblical concordances but they resemble
more the psychologist's frequency counts. In both of the newer fields a
principal interest is establishing a particular characteristic of a set of
words, for example average word length or the frequency of use of
nouns. This statistical interest may precede or follow obtaining the set
and can be in sets from continuous language or in separate items.
Acceptable experimental material may have to conform to specified
statistical criteria as we saw earlier. Obtaining representative language
counts required considerable application and was undertaken infrequently. Consequently, word counts have often lacked recent revision
and so ceased to be representative as usage changed. For example, the
Kent/Rosanoff data on word association of 1910 was superseded by the
Russell/Jenkins norms of 1954, and the Dewey data on word frequencies
of 1923 was superseded by the Thorndike/Lorge count of 1944, among
others.

Changes through time are one aspect of the problem of selecting
counts for particular purposes. The importance of this problem appears
in Denes' (1963) comparison of his results and methods with those of
Dewey and of French, Carter, and Koenig (1930). For example, Dewey
found 'I' to be the tenth most common English word, the other two
counts agree it is the most common. In contrast, Dewey gave 69 words
and Denes 67 as accounting for half of all the words counted but
French, Carter, and Koenig gave 31. Some disparities are attributable to
different definitions and one can select a count whose authors'
definitions are most appropriate to one's problem. Other disparities are
not open to choice: they depend on different language uses. Dewey
worked, like Thorndike and Lorge, with conventionally printed texts in
English. Denes, like French, Carter, and Koenig, and Voelker (1935),
was concerned with speech sounds but he took his corpus from phonetic
'readers' (these are books printed in an extended alphabet used for
phonetic transcriptions); French, Carter and Koenig used a corpus of
speech from telephone conversations and Voelker applied his techniques
to 'Formal American Speech'. Another main distinction of a corpus is
its locality of origin. Fry (1947), like Denes, studied the English spoken

in southern England. Most counts of English have studied one or another variety of American English. Some of the differences mentioned may be unimportant in psychological studies but one anthology of sociolinguistics (Fishman, 1968) shows the diversity of possibly relevant attributes of language.

New tabulations do help in determining relevant attributes, given a framework for their data and computers have hugely facilitated preparing new counts. This is clear on noting that Howes' (1966) corpus of 250,000 spoken words in over three times the size of that used by French, Carter, and Koenig and over eight times the size of that used by Fairbanks (1944) in her spoken word count. Another demonstration of computer assistance is the large number of counts made in the last decade. Perhaps the currently most impressive computer-aided compilation on language statistics is the count undertaken by Carroll, Davies, and Richman (1971). This uses a corpus of over five million words and parts of their book are computer-printed.

Other numerical uses of computers germane to the psychology of language involve more calculation than counting. Word frequency data present problems in distributional statistics often best examined using computers and sometimes fruitfully approached using concepts evolved in the climate which following pages describe as marking the advent of computers. Zipf (1935) collated evidence that suggested, over a wide range of utterances including the babbling of babies and Chinese idiographs as well as American English, the following relationship:

the logarithm of the frequency of use of items bears an inverse linear relationship to the logarithm of the rank order of those frequencies.

Zipf, energetic in marshalling evidence for this relationship ascribed it, as it may seem ironically, to a principle of least effort. Mandelbrot (1954), working on theoretical problems in information transmission showed that the regularities summarized by Zipf derived from random processes. Consequently the adduced psychological or linguistic pertinence of the principle of least effort was lost.

There are however empirical relationships in psychology that not only survive mathematical analysis but also gain from it: recent psychophysics affords a major example. The usefulness of the lognormal distribution provides another; the details of this distribution need not be discussed here. In his work with this distribution Carroll (1967, 1968, 1969) has attempted to show why it should fit the frequencies with which subjects give particular response to stimuli in word association tasks. He conceives of the process by which particular response words are chosen as being represented by a tree structure. That is, the subject is thought of as making a series of decisions between alternate possibilities in which the paths for present choice are dominated by earlier choices and will, in turn, dominate subsequent possibilities. Carroll argues that it is irrelevant what particular classifications and tree structures are involved in associations, the final form of the frequency distributions of selected items is independent of these. What is relevant is that choice probabilities at choice points will tend to be randomly distributed. In order to formulate a fully satisfactory quantitative model Carroll had to do more than fit parameters to a theoretical distribution. He showed how the particular form of bias arising from using samples lay about the theoretical form of the lognormal distribution for the population; and he also established the relation of such biases to sample size. These points improve the precision of investigations into the goodness of fit of the theoretical distribution. The practical necessity of a computer in work like Carroll's is obvious on considering a few details. For example, one of the samples investigated contained over one million words. While smaller samples were also used, with the greater range of sample sizes more clear-cut evidence became available on the relation of bias to sample size. Again, even given the distributions of words in numerical form, some of the subsequent theoretical calculations on the distribution were taking *seconds of computing time* on an **IBM** 360 series machine. For human performance such calculations would take hours and, being repetitive, would involve tedium and be prone to error.

The computer and non-numerical studies of language

In 1948 Wiener published his *Cybernetics* and Shannon completed his *Mathematical Theory of Communication*. Nine years later Chomsky's slender volume *Syntactic Structures* appeared. The psychology of language and the intellectual climate in which it developed after the end of World War II are inextricably related. In general terms these works were contributions to the post-war increase in psychological knowledge that provided alternatives to associationist theories. That is not to pretend that stimulus-response formulations or re-formulations about language, and other cognitive processes, have been unimportant.

The efforts of Skinner, Mowrer, and Osgood were subjected to sometimes savage criticism by adherents of newer theoretical frameworks. Their conceptions of language as a form of behaviour, even if not altogether resting in peace, remain in the tradition of Watson, Max, Hull and Spence and many critics see them as comparably ill-formed. Each of these psychologists attempts to improve the theoretical accounts derived from the investigators preceding him and to argue the strengths of his own approach over those of contemporary associationists. All of which is to say that the basic terms of any satisfactory account are not in dispute for S-R theorists. For them the problem is how best to extend their paradigm to embrace language behaviour. That their problem is necessarily insoluble given their means is the comment of other workers made implicitly by Wiener, explicitly by Chomsky.

Wiener brought together in his theory of control and communication the concepts of feedback, noise, and information. The open-ended chains of association theory, however parsimonious, were in comparison with the cybernetic concepts impoverished in theoretical power. Shannon's metric for information gave to the new approach qualitative formulæ involving probabilities and having formal similarity to successfully predictive formulations of thermodynamics. With the advent of computers which embodied the terms of cybernetics and for which information measures were in some ways appropriate, the escape from S-R conceptions gave hints of imminent explanation of the long recognized, if less considered, problems of higher mental processes. There was apparently an encouraging, if far from accidental, coincidence: computers would allow *direct* demonstration of the refutability of new accounts of language. What is meant by 'direct' in this context can be better appreciated on noting that evidence in many disciplines is obtained by reading instruments; and, after expressing the readings symbolically, analysing their significance. The effects of penicillin, for example, are demonstrated by analysing the observed numbers of bacteria in the region of the anti-biotic; the demonstration involves specialized knowledge. As Turing (1950) implied (*vide* Chapter 5 above) a successful computer account of natural languages would partly lie in producing utterances indistinguishable from those of the people whose language capability was being studied. Obviously these people are well able directly to judge whether the utterances are indistinguishable.

In the fifties a general acceptance of new ends and new means of understanding language and computers was abroad. Machines that could converse, preferably verbally, were mooted and the impending achievement of such practically useful and theoretically revealing procedures as machine translation was not, initially, much queried. Linguists, the guardians of the then current wisdom on language, were not wildly enthusiastic about machine translation, but their intuitive scepticism was not going to overthrow the enthusiasm for technological developments to which millions of dollars had already been committed. The logical and incisive criticisms of machine translation by Bar-Hillel (cf. Bar-Hillel, 1964) had more effect.

Caution and even disillusion now replace the euphoria which permeated much of the earlier writings on computers and language. Many of the results raised problems now at the centre of discussion. Current work when it does relate to themes now largely abandoned is mainly a clear reaction to them. For example, the computer model of syntax perception described by Thorne (1968) seems partly to originate from a refusal to employ certain techniques practical in machine translation (cf. Rhodes, 1959). These techniques struck Thorne (1964) as irrelevant to the 'organizing power capable of producing that kind of data' which has traditionally concerned linguists. In a wider way Chomsky's work also carries an assertion of the need to use new means to achieve different ends; as his work is influential in attempts to program computers to converse in natural language some of its important features will be sketched.

In a 1956 contribution Chomsky discussed finite state or regular grammars. These abstraction involve defined states that can be traversed in accordance with the structure of the grammar. They are presented as maps like the one shown in Figure 7.1.

Stringing together any sequence of words found on following the arrows in a map like that shown in Figure 7.1, gives a sentence violating no rules of the grammar. Our example employing English words will produce such sentences as:

The aged horse drank from the lake.
The little laughing man slowly slowly swam.

Chomsky has stressed that for a linguist any complete account of a language must be capable of generating, in the sense exemplified above, all, and only, the sentences of the language. Given that goal, regular grammars show promise as they can generate some sentences of English. The 1956 contribution of Chomsky ended that promise; it includes a proof that certain grammatical sentences are logically beyond the generative capacity of any regular grammar.

Pursuing other kinds of grammar Chomsky (e.g. 1957, 1963) considered phrase structure grammars. These do not produce sentences in a left to right pass as regular grammars do. They are, as their name suggests, structural, and larger units contain or dominate smaller ones. These two verbs correspond to two conventions for illustrating phrase structures: bracketing and tree diagrams. The two conventions are, however, formally exactly equivalent, compare examples (*a*) and (*b*) in Figure 7.2.

Given what are called lexical rules, like those below, a number of distinct and grammatical sentences with a common structure can be derived from a phrase structure.

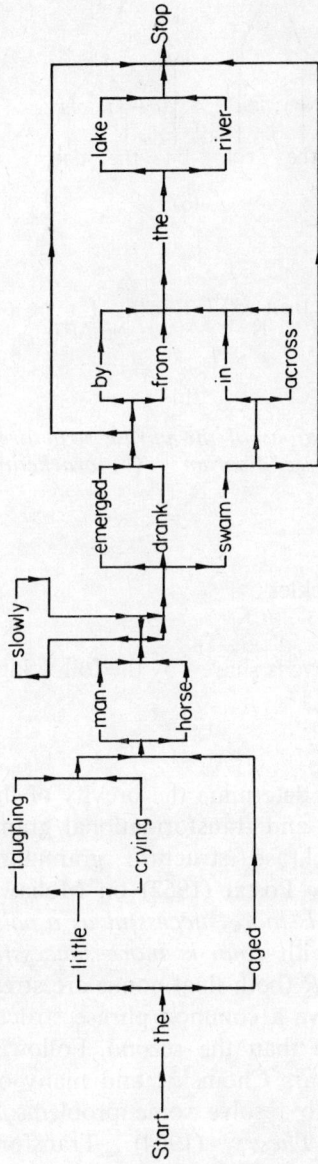

Figure 7.1—An example of a regular grammar

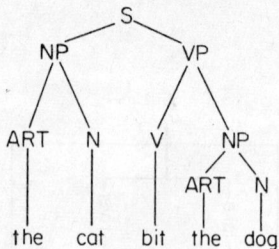

(a)

(b)

Figure 7.2—Two presentations of the phrase structure of a simple sentence.
(a) tree diagram   (b) bracketing

Lexical rules:
  N → cat, dog, baby
  V → bit, sees, likes, tickles
  Art → the, a

The structure shown above is shared by the following sentences:

The dog sees the cat.
A baby bit a dog.

Considerations of space determine the brevity of this account as well as the accounts of regular and transformational grammars. In arriving at the conclusion that phrase structure grammars were inadequate, Chomsky cited work by Postal (1962) on Mohawk and the oddity of such sentences as *John is more successful as a painter than Bill is as a PAINTER* compared with *John is more successful as a painter than John is as a SCULPTOR* (both final nouns are stressed). The point here is that the sentences have a common phrase structure but the first is a less acceptable sentence than the second. Following his discussion of phrase structure grammars Chomsky, and many others, look to transformational grammars to resolve some problems he raised in *Current Issues in Linguistic Theory* (1964). Transformational grammars acknowledge relations between the structural descriptions of phrase structure grammars. A simple illustration is the singular transformation of permutation shown below in Figure 7.3.

```
           S                                    S
         /   \                              /   |   \
       VP      NP                          V    NP    Particle
      /  \     / \                         |   /  \      |
     V  Particle Possess N              take Possess N   off
     |    |      |    |                       |    |
   take  off   your clothes               your clothes
```

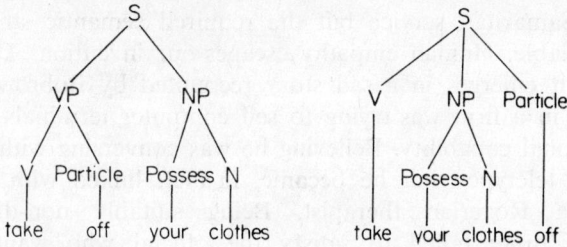

Figure 7.3—*A simple transformation of permutation*

The above review of developments in Chomsky-type theoretical linguistics is certainly not irrelevant to the psychology of language; it offers a description of what people are able to do when they acquire a language. Chomsky considers that his later formulations (e.g. 1965, 1968) put forward a general, if incomplete, theory of language, and this for him means a theory including even what an infant does in acquiring its native tongue. This brief summary leaves unmentioned Chomsky's developing views on the role of transformations in changing, or not changing, meaning, and his arguments for innate and uniquely human structures which process linguistic data in certain wide but still constrained ways. To follow the argument further the reader should consult Chomsky (1965, 1968).

A theory of language can be central to the efforts of a computer programmer when it is sufficiently formalized. As Clowes, Langridge and Zatorski (1970) note, several workers have used Chomskian formalisms in developing a natural language conversation facility between a computer and a person. Other contributions to theoretical linguistics have been similarly used. Chomsky's work is cited here because, besides laying a psychological claim, it looms large in the overlap of theoretical linguistics and computer programs for natural language conversations.

There have been natural language conversation programs for about a decade. In that time their capabilities have been considerably developed. Sometimes their limitations have had a uniformity and recently these weaknesses have become more obviously semantic than syntactic, for while useful formalizations of grammatical structures are available those for referential structures are less advanced. To illustrate this trend four representative programs will be described. Notice that all four programs *answer* questions, but only one (STUDENT) *asks* questions of its human partner. STUDENT's queries are aimed at solving the problem originally posed, rather than at broaching a fresh topic. The grammatical devices in these programs might help in developing, say, an

automated Samaritan service but the required semantic structures are
not yet available. Human empathy escapes our invention. The force of
this comment emerges in a sad story recounted by Bobrow (1970). A
high official in a firm was trying to sell computer terminals which had
a conversational capability. Believing he was conversing with one of his
staff on the teletypewriter he became, in fact, linked with a program
simulating a Rogerian therapist. Being suitably non-directive its
conversation quite failed to satisfy the official who wanted explicit
information quickly: the clash of style was, we are told, decidedly
provoking. Obviously such a clash could sometimes have unhappy consequences. Of course, not all human conversations are necessarily, or only,
communicative and this draws attention to the present severe limitations
in conversations between machines and people which will certainly
continue until we improve understanding of what Bobrow (1964) called
the 'semantic base' of a topic of utterance. (For an account of the
Rogerian therapy program see Weizenbaum, 1966 and pp. 226–7.)

A program called BASEBALL and written by Green, Wolf, Carol
Chomsky and Laughery (1961) was one of the first to answer questions.
It replied to queries phrased in simple English and concerning games
played during a season of American League baseball. Such enquiries as
'How many games did the Red Sox win in June?' were answered. Its
sentence structure analysis was not powerful and unlike our own pro-
ceeded from final to first word (it was based on some work by Harris,
1960). Among its limitations BASEBALL suffered from: an inability to
deal with logical connectives or implicit relations in questions, and
answers that were rarely in grammatical English. It could accommodate
some passive constructions and would be fairly easily open to some
improvements.

Lindsay (1963) wrote another early question answering program with
the acronym SAD SAM. This accepted statements about named
individuals and their relatives and answered questions on kinship. The
questions asked were fairly circumscribed and the limitation of vocabulary to Basic English, which extends to some 1,700 words, was practical.
The input sentences could be compound ones and even if their grammar was dubious a decision on their structure was always reached. The
parsing of the structural analyses ran from first to last item and so was
less clearly contrary to human processing; it was based on Chomsky's
early work.

STUDENT, a program written by Bobrow (1964), solved story
algebra problems, that is algebra problems presented in prose.
STUDENT even solved problems on ages; people often baulk at the
sentences in age problems like 'Mary is twice as old as Ann was when

Mary was as old as Ann is now. If Mary is 24 years old, how old is Ann?' A special set of substitutions are used by STUDENT for the terms characteristic of age problems, for example 'as old as'. Another set of substitutions is used with all problems. The basic method is to render questions into one of seven formats, for example, 'How many £ does £ have?' where £ stands for any string of letters. This rendering into a standard form involves first mandatory substitutions, and then optional ones might be tried if no standard format has been reached. To enable more questions to be reduced to a standard format STUDENT includes a table of equivalent forms which is called REMEMBER. From REMEMBER, STUDENT can, for instance, discover that distance equals speed multiplied by time. The algebraic equations derived from the standard format sentences are solved using several recursive routines whose detailed nature is unimportant here. One point, however, is worth comment. The routines were generally successful but certain problems, even though mathematically similar to solvable ones, are beyond them. This restriction parallels limitations in human processing that sometimes arise when making one sort of substitution and not another: formal integration in calculus provides examples. STUDENT would, if unable to proceed, ask for more information, sometimes requesting the answer! This occurred when the equations derived from the sentences were non-linear or not reducible to an equation linear in the required unknown. STUDENT did avoid giving incorrect answers; instead it printed out an assessment of the inadequacy in the given information. Obviously conversation with STUDENT is more flexible than with the two programs mentioned earlier. Its limitations again include a restricted universe of discourse and some grammatical difficulties; thus a sentence with a coordinate phrase would be taken as structurally similar to one formed from simple sentences. However, *He is tall, and young, too* and *He is tall and she is young* are clearly not structurally equivalent but differ in their numbers of subjects.

Our fourth example is the (1967) Woods program which answers questions about air-line routes and time-tables. The program shares some noticeable improvements with STUDENT and has new features too. It is unusual in having no published acronym or name and remarkable for a parsing system giving a deep structure. (Briefly and after Chomsky (1965), deep structure is about the meaning of a sentence, and surface structure is about its utterance.) The Woods program has transformational components; one use for these is to store new information so that subsequent questions can differ in only one way from the stored forms. The example below differs in exact form from the program but illustrates the principle.

(a)   The plane going to Tokyo leaves at 2030.
(b)   The plane leaving at 2030 goes to Tokyo.
(c)   The plane leaving at 2030 goes where?
Storing input (a) in form (b) aids answering query (c).

The sentences (a) and (b) are transformationally related.

The four question-and-answer programs had small areas for enquiry and often capitalized on an accompanying restriction of style: there are few deeply self-embedded sentences in the story algebra problems that Bobrow used. Thorne and his co-workers, and Bratley, Dewar, and Whitfield, have produced programs on one aspect of linguistic communication, but have generally avoided limitations of topic. Given text input relying on the English alphabet their programs process even nonsense poetry, as long as it might be said to have an English language flavour, like the poems of Edward Lear. Thorne is a linguist who stresses the linguistic intuitions of a fluent speaker. He is wary of what he takes to be more algorithmically statable than humanly apt and is prepared to seek seriously for a wide account of language. In his papers Thorne has suggested that accounts which can lead to computer-human conversation but are unable to throw light on human language mechanisms, by for example, illuminating the deficits of the aphasias, are only a limited success. The perception of syntax is the problem Thorne and his colleagues have attacked in several computer programs. They aim to achieve automated syntax perception in a way that will elucidate human language abilities.

There are now two pre-conditions marking the Edinburgh syntax perception programs (Thorne, Dewar, Whitfield and Bratley, 1966; Bratley, Dewar and Thorne, 1967; and Thorne, 1968). One pre-condition is that sentence analysis runs from first to final item in a single pass. The other is that program dictionaries are small. These dictionaries principally list closed class items such as articles, prepositions, conjunctions, and pronouns, which cannot be as readily or briefly extended as open class items such as adverbs, nouns and adjectives. The remaining entries are anomalous open class items: for example most words used in English and ending -ous are adjectives but, as Bratley remarked, the word caribous is a plural noun.

These two pre-conditions reflect everyday observations of our experience of understanding sentences. The 'first-to-final-item-single-pass-analysis' accords with our comprehending a spoken sentence as we hear it, even though we may retain options on its final meaning. To wait until the end of hearing an utterance before starting to understand it, is not how comprehension generally occurs—and just as well, for many utterances are not wholly grammatical. Note how the concurrence of our analyses can avoid the need for re-analysis to uncover ambiguity; all the acceptable versions should be available as the single pass ends. These points are crucial and were basic to the Edinburgh programs. As research on ambiguity continues however, their generality becomes suspect Garrett (in Flores d' Arcais and Levelt, 1970) gives one useful review of studies of ambiguity.

The aptness of the second pre-condition, of a small dictionary, was indicated in the mention of nonsense poetry. Including in this dictionary such bounded morphemes as -ly, -s, and -ful permits the analysis of linguistic inventions exemplied in a sentence such as:

The vags quootly kasling the wobs were gogthful.

It seems likely that *quootly* would be widely judged to be an adverb because it ends -*ly* and precedes a word ending -*ing*; the articles are plausibly positioned for *quootly* to be an adverb with *kasling* an infinitive. Note that to achieve some certainty in such categorizations may need more than one cue: several words ending -*ly* are not always adverbs—for example, *burly, slovenly, friendly* and *early*. Openness to other information is a strength of 'first-to-final-item-single-pass-analysis' that retains possible structures until they are inconsistent with current input.

The heart of the program analysis is the continuing development of structures. There are three possibilities: to start a new structure, to continue an existing one and to end an inconsistent one. Thorne illustrated the analysis with numerous examples of which this is one: *The boy smokes.* The dictionary lists *The* as the definite article and the role of articles in noun phrases is coded in the program. A terminal -*s* is listed as a noun and a verb inflexion; *boy* can be an adjective, as in *the boy hero.* If *boy* were an adjective here the string of words could not be a sentence: by modifying *smokes boy* would show it to be a noun and a sentence must have a verb. As no other word in the string is a verb *boy* must be the subject of the intransitive verb *smokes,* this completing the analysis of the sentence given. This illustration indicates how the analysis proceeds. Recent programs are sufficiently thorough to give deep as well as surface structure. With surface structure alone, Bratley had found over sixty parsings of one sentence, a quantity uncharacteristic of human syntax perception. These outpourings could be pruned on a second pass. Unfortunately, the analyses ordinarily seen as correct were then often lost—along with improbable unwanted oddities. The print-out of the deep structure includes the inversion of elements in the surface structure for some sentence types (for example, questions) and the indication of elements deleted from surface structure. The analysis output for one sentence is shown below with its original abbreviations expanded:

Sentence	Playing cards intrigues me.	
Analysis	Level 1	Sentence is a statement
of	Level 2	Subject (qualified by a gerund); Active verb: *intrigues;* Object: *me*
Sentence		
	Level 3	Subject (deleted in surface structure); Active verb: *playing.* Head of noun phrase: *cards*

Such deep structure analyses are obtained by specifying transformations in the program, but these and other features of the syntax perception program will be omitted here.

Computers in on-line experiments on the psychology of language

Important distinctions must be made in the various uses of computers in those studies of language which interest psychologists; calculation differs from conversation which again differs from automated syntax perception. On-line experiments can bring together some distinguishable aspects of language use under experimental control. Recent discussions have clearly doubted the adequacy of always subsuming first and later language acquisition under one paradigm (cf. Lenneberg, 1964; and more briefly Lyons, 1970, p. 111). Practical problems, such as access to infants, as well as technical difficulties in building equipment for use with toddlers at play, make first language acquisition peculiarly suited to investigations more observational than experimental. As on-line studies of acquisition are characteristically restricted to the laboratory, their findings cannot be expected to hold always. Their strength seems greater, however, for work on second language acquisition: consider, for example, an experiment by Torrey (1969) who taught adults three Russian constructions by explicit instruction in the relevant grammar and, to a significantly better extent, by having them rehearse a number of grammatically correct sentences that exemplified the constructions. Two limitations of her experimental situation may be amenable to computer assistance. One is the size of the vocabulary used; Russian is a natural language, and its vocabulary accordingly extends to more than the 66 words Torrey used; similarly its sentences, unlike hers, are usually more than four words long. The second point is that the rules her subjects satisfied, concern 'form-class sequences' (for example, with few exceptions adjectives precede nouns in English: *the red windmill;* in French they normally follow them: *le moulin rouge*). As Torrey clearly noted (see especially her 1966 publication) there are other kinds of grammatical rule. For an apt example consider the writer's elder son's remark: **A girl called Avril's dog in my class joined the police.* This utterance is clearly, even disturbingly, ill-formed. It is ungrammatical because the inflexion on Avril is overworked (cf. *A girl called Avril's in my class; Avril's dog joined the police*). Correction depends on separating the inflected uses and re-ordering the results.

To realize a wide selection of rules needs more than a tiny sample of the vocabulary of a language. The syntax perception program, discussed above, had a closed class dictionary running into 1,000 items and many were involved in grammatical structure. Richer facilities, like those that Thorne *et al.* have already developed, can be imported into laboratory studies of second language acquisition. Such importation looks promising because experiments become more comparable to everyday second language acquisition by initially monolingual speakers in a community predominantly using that second language. Admittedly, spoken and orthographic forms of language differ, but the order of acquisition of rules would, for example, be far more open to scrutiny than in non-computer extensions of work like Torrey's. Wright and Kahneman (1971) have remarked 'it may be time that some of us who are interested in the psychology of language shifted the focus of our research from examining what people *can* do, in the extremity of a laboratory environment, to discovering what people *do* do, unselfconsciously, when processing language.' Making laboratory environments less simple in their linguistic possibilities may help achieve that shift. As observational studies of first language acquisition suggest there will be other ways, too, that will not need computer facilities.

The experiments in the interesting 'Project Grammarama' directed by Miller (1967), and 'Jabberish', invented by Green (1973) may seem incompatible with the advice of Wright and Kahneman. These on-line studies are just intermediate, in their linguistic complexity, between classical laboratory simplicity and language in everyday use; this is so even if the subject's situation, that is, facing a teletypewriter, has a complexity of its own. The further enrichment of on-line studies in the psychology of language will be considered after sketching the studies by Miller and by Green.

A description of the situation and task Miller devised appears in Chapter 4. To recapitulate: subjects produced letter sequences on an on-line teletypewriter which were to meet rules specified in the computer program and of which subjects were unaware. Knowledge of results was given after each sequence. When the subject instructed it, the computer ran a short test assessing how accurately subjects recognized the correctness, or incorrectness of computer generated sequences. Ninety-eight subjects attempted to generate sequences conforming to the rules characterizing the presented sequences. The results showed that over half these subjects opted to take the test at a time when they could not pass it; there was good evidence that this premature choice was not motivated by boredom or inability. In a variation of this task by Norman (cited by Miller, 1967) one important distinction was that strings had referents. The strings had to be of letters only. The referential aspect of Norman's language was the relation between sequences of letters that subjects produced and the subsequent actions of their teletype-writers. Norman arranged that grammatical sequences of letters and runs of several such sequences caused the computer to print 'hash' marks ($\neq$) and move the teletypewriter head through spaces; un-grammatical sequences simply returned it to the left margin after printing WRONG. The number of spaces and hash marks depended on the grammatical sequences subjects entered. Thus subjects could use the language to produce patterns; the language was of small complexity and its vocabulary was impoverished but it provided a means of constructing sequences distinct from itself but dependent upon it. Norman had 24 subjects and none took the test before they could pass it. Even if one does not agree that learning a language is the same as learning the rules of the language (cf. Wright and Kahneman, 1971; Herriot, 1970, p. 58; and most of all Esper, 1968) it still seems that subjects in the with-referents experiment were better at knowing when they knew the structure of the language, or even that they knew rules equivalent to those that Norman had asked them to exemplify.

Green wrote a program to present sentences in 'Jabberish'. This is a nonsense language he invented. Its grammar is a subset of the rules of grammar of English; its lexicon is of nonsense words easily pronounced by native English speakers. Some of Green's subjects acquired Jabberish using only an interactive on-line teletypewriter. These subjects thus came to express unknowable nonsense grammatically: they knew not what they meant when they uttered Jabberish; their utterances did however conform to rules even if lacking referents. Others of Green's subjects saw simple diagrams displayed on an oscilloscope output; grammatically correct sentences in Jabberish were given, accurately describing the diagrams. This addition to the interactive facility had no significant effect on acquiring Jabberish.

The contradictory results of these two experiments are perhaps not as surprising as they initially appear. Obviously there were differences between the two experiments, which are unmentioned in our summaries and one outstanding difference lies in their semantic aspects. Norman's subjects manipulated part of their world; Green's only received descriptions of part of theirs. Directly to enter a hash mark on the teletypewriter in Norman's study was ungrammatical as hash marks are not letters, which the input has to be. In consequence, hash marks caused the return of the teletypewriter head to its left margin. Simply to describe a diagram using English in Green's study affected nothing and was without consequence. Thus Norman's subjects had to master the grammar of his language if they were to make patterns but Green's could know nothing of Jabberish and yet have a description of a diagram. Only experiment will show how apt is this distinction between action and reception in elucidating the different roles of semantics in acquiring languages even as impoverished and artificial as these. It is the present writer's suspicion that such experiments would be about a characteristic attribute of the use of natural languages: changing our environment.

Language experiments employing computers and including subjects have been few. In what directions do such experiments promise most? Linguistics is studied both analytically and generatively. Analytic linguistics asks what makes up an utterance. Generative linguistics attempts to specify how to make grammatical utterances. In its development, psychology has predominantly been formulated in the traditions of analysis; its experiments characteristically consider the effects of the separable aspects of a situation in determining the behaviour of subjects. Studies asking how to select one behaviour rather than some other are not so much the experimentalists' stock-in-trade. Specify a behaviour and the psychology of learning may be relevant in producing it; ask what behaviour is adaptive in a situation and there is no comparable specialization to consult. The distinction between analytic and generative linguistics is one of several made by linguists when describing different approaches within their study and, though important, it is not paramount among their distinctions. However the psychology of language is likely to benefit much from borrowing the analytic/generative distinction when devising on-line experiments.

Given rules, computers can generate examples of the rules and generative linguistics holds that we do the same in talking. Computers can also, of course, rapidly process large numbers of symbols. This latter facility is frequently used by psychologists obtaining very fine grain analyses of simple responses, for example obtaining one thousand readings of the position of a joystick moved from left to right; it is also used for more simple analyses of many simple responses, for example one thousand key-pressings in a choice reaction task. Language with its continuity, structure, semantics, and ambiguity is far from simple. This is one reason why subjects in psycholinguistic experiments are usually asked to respond simply to precisely specified material, for example by rating on a seven point scale the relatedness of words in a sentence (cf. Levelt, 1969). When experimenters ask subjects to generate language such as sentences the measure taken is likely to be response latency, while the sentences uttered will closely resemble those presented (cf. Miller and McKean, 1964). There is no doubt that with such studies we have gained enormously: analysis continues to be potent. It may apply in language experiments less circumscribed, and more generative even, than those in which it has been so successful. Here computers promise to be crucial.

There are two bases for this hope: first, the impressive success of observational studies of first language acquisition (cf. Huxley, 1970; Brown, 1964; McNeil, 1966 and others); second, an acknowledgement of the scope and variety of language, a point made when discussing the work of Torrey (1969) but also relevant here.

Sociolinguists provide an illustration of this variety that may be especially suited for the psychologist's appreciation. Tanner (1967) noted that Javanese speakers who are young, adult, friends, faithful Moslems, comparably educated and of like age, use Low Javanese in a conversation; High Javanese is used by speakers who are married, of different sex, and different class. None of the nine attributes are mutually exclusive even if some are not very likely to occur together. For example, different class and comparable education are unusual. When speakers with attributes calling for both Low Javanese and High Javanese converse, they resolve the conflict by using Indonesian. Now the social attributes of pairs of speakers is manipulable and so open to experiment: it happens that fieldwork will often permit assembling results that effectively constitute 'an experiment by nature' or by social history. Such an 'experiment' will reduce experimenter effects if the sociolinguist is skilled and thus rather than manipulate conditions he may select examples from them.

For the psycholinguist the cognitive context of a speaker is manipulable. We can, for example, enquire how language differs when all of a speaker's utterances are met by queries rather than by acceptance, and indeed can vary the proportions of these two kinds of replies. The sad tale of the American salesman of conversational terminals (p. 196) showed that computers can adopt a particular conversational style. The cognitive task of a speaker can, of course, be varied without using a computer, e.g. Goldman Eisler (1960) asked her subjects to describe cartoon drawings and also to summarize the points of their humour. However, manipulating particular attributes of such cognitive tasks according to clearly formulated rules is work more suited to a computer program than to an experimenter's best efforts: programs are less labile. The task of editing prose writings also illustrates the practical usefulness of computers for examining a skill little studied by psychologists and having a generative aspect. This task, unlike those normally involving speech, need not suffer from the recurrent computer constraint resulting from an on-line teletypewriter input being used to link the subject with a machine: many authors normally type their drafts. The problem in studying editing is not lack of edited drafts; it is that their perusal would reveal relatively little of the changes occurring in arriving at a final version. Erasures, insertions and crossings out obscure their own identity, sequence and content. Observing somebody editing would often fail when the editor was delayed by the recording of details that might need enquiry and which, if postponed until after editing was complete, might be forgotten. Such interruptions for enquiry, however, would probably detract from the editing, which is the object of study. Given an oscilloscope display under keyboard control these intrinsic difficulties disappear: computer memory can record the sequence and identity of a subject's revisions and without at all impeding his natural pace and scope if he usually types his drafts. That this scenario is not an impractical situation for empirical study, can be appreciated on learning that the author Len Deighton already uses computer facilities in writing his books.

The study of the psychology of language has had too many simplistic contributions. It has not been much advanced, moreover, by some linguists whose justified wonder at its mysteries has seemed all too likely to be perpetual. Hopeful looking approaches are developing however, some of which we have described. Other areas of research unmentioned include speech perception studies relying on speech synthesis or synchronization, and computer monitoring of the electromyographic aspects of speech production (cf. Fromkin and Ladefoged, 1966). Whatever the limitations of early work, it should be clear from what has been cited here that more aspects of languge are emerging to claim our attention than emerged before computers. There are also already more concepts within which to unify data. Similar changes might well have come about without computers but often computers have been important in making recent advances. It seems certain that at least a few computer studies of psycholinguistic interest will, in the next decade or two, avoid the obscurity of safe triviality and chart a broader path of progress.

Further Reading

Kaneff, S. (Ed.) (1970) *Picture Language Machines,* Academic Press, New
    York. Report of a symposium with interesting but sometimes abstruse
    papers.
Lyons, J. (1968) *Introduction to Theoretical Linguistics,* Cambridge
    University Press. A lucid book that goes a long way to recognizing
    continuing difficulties. A 'good buy.'
Lyons, J. (Ed.) (1970) *New Horizons in Linguistics*, Penguin, London. An
    anthology of wide scope and varying penetration but one sensible place
    to start to find out more about linguistics.
Winograd, T. (1972) *Understanding Natural Language*, Edinburgh University
    Press, Edinburgh; *or Cognitive Psychology*, **1**, 1, 1972. Not perfect, but
    probably the best computer conversations yet are reported in this book.

Chapter 8

The Computer in Comparative Psychology

Stuart J. Dimond

Introduction

Within the last two decades computers have had an increasing influence upon the study of animal behaviour. Not only have the techniques resulted in a considerable facilitation of existing types of investigation but they have also extended investigations into fields of research in ways which may not have been possible before.

Computer control of experiments

Automated experiments

The origin of the application of computer methods lies in experiments which have been automated in other ways. These have largely been operant experiments employing automatic feeding or reinforcement schedules which the animal implements by the depression of a lever.

Emitted behaviour in these experiments is brought under control by reinforcement. The experimenter initially reinforces some patterns of behaviour but not others. Reinforcement may take the form of food, water or other types of reward. Thus a pigeon may be placed in a special box of restricted area (Skinner box); each time it moves towards a key in this box it is provided with food. Once it has learned to peck the key it is a simple matter to use the key as a switch to trigger electrical systems. The number of pecks made at the key can be registered using the key to activate a pen recorder. The key can also be used to operate the food magazine.

It may be that a complex relationship between key pecking and the operation of the food magazine is essential for the purposes of an experiment. For example, the pigeon receives food after every five pecks or the pigeon receives food at random, in which case a direct link between the key and food magazine is no longer sufficient and a more advanced link becomes necessary. The Skinner box therefore usually has an accompanying electronic switch system controlling these contingencies of reinforcement.

A system for presenting stimuli to the pigeon is also required and if the arrangement of these stimuli is contingent upon the presence of reward, this demands a system of complex electronic control. The pigeon's behaviour is automatically registered, recorded and analysed, and the subsequent events of the environment, e.g. the presence of food or patterns of stimulation, are programmed to be dependent on the animal's response.

In order to carry out simple operant conditioning experiments a minimum of basic equipment is necessary. Environmental chambers should be durable and soundproof. These are often enclosed in special cubicles which can, when longer-term experiments are undertaken, provide a sustaining living environment for the animal. They are temperature-controlled and air-conditioned. The test chamber contains a grill floor which can be employed to give shock, and the lever and the food or the water magazine are placed on one wall. The experiment is controlled mechanically by automatic systems linked to the test chamber. The essential elements for this are a power supply and a pulse former which is a means for converting a variable signal into a pulse of constant length. For example, this would count lever presses by the animal of different lengths of time as single lever depressions. The pulse when formed is then used to activate the rest of the equipment. Lever presses are recorded cumulatively, each pulse putting a mark on the recorder which moves in a step-wise fashion.

Next we come to the central concern which is the apparatus which ensures that the experiment is carried out automatically. We consider the means by which it is programmed and also the way in which the consequences of signalling and reward are made dependent on behaviour. This is achieved by the use of logic systems, which present stimuli in a particular pattern, at specified intervals and to a predetermined plan, as well as programming reinforcements at fixed, variable or contingent intervals.

The use of logic systems for experimental control

During recent years the technology of automatic control has changed considerably. Many of the processes were at first carried out by electro-mechanical relays (Thompson, 1964; Farmer and Schoenfeld, 1964). Apparatus was constructed in units which could be interlinked with one another to provide the necessary functions. This equipment in fact works well and where available can be usefully employed. It uses combinations of components of a number of different kinds. One such component is a stepper which allows control to pass from point to point along a bank of terminals and each terminal may be connected to a particular piece of equipment (e.g. a stimulus lamp or food magazine). Other components are counting relays (relays which fire after a certain number of impulses), pulse formers (defined above), recycling timers (devices to return the series of operations back to the beginning). The next step was to provide for control by the use of electronic modules which effect basic logic operations. These take the form of AND gates, OR gates, flip-flops or bistable states and so on.

The next advance still maintained the modular approach, but with the advent of solid-state electronics not only did the modules become smaller but they achieved a compactness and comprehensiveness which made them suitable for a wider range of applications. Instead of each individual operation being carried out by individual modules, they were now combined *within* modules. This kind of combination can be described as macro-logic. A single module can contain functions such as predetermining counting, buffer storage (storage whilst other operations are in progress), delay timing, etc. The use of solid state digital elements (modules) has been described by Herrick and Denelsbeck (1963) and by Weiner (1963). Even a complete program for standard reinforcement schedules can be built into a single module which is used as the controller.

Computer uses

Controlling solid state modules might be thought to be all that could be desired by the experimenter. However, there is still the problem of data analysis which is a different one from that of experimental control. There is also the problem of the laborious modification of existing equipment when the investigator advances to fresh areas of study. The use of the integrated module, whilst representing a high level of sophistication, does have the disadvantage that it lacks flexibility. Here the computer comes into its own. It was at the point where the need for complex control became apparent, and where at the same time flexibility was an advantage, that computer techniques seemed to provide the greatest spur to further development.

A general purpose computer has the advantages of high information rates and precise timing, simultaneous data analysis, large storage capacity for programs and data as well as flexibility in use. Experimental control can be established by the use of a general purpose computer on-line (i.e. directly connected to the experimental subjects as the data source), and in real-time (i.e the natural time scale of the experiment is matched by the machine).

The interface

The interface relates environmental modifications to computer control. It is the region through which the links are made between the animal and the computer. It is the channel through which the computer gathers information about the animal and dispatches signals to it. The problem of providing an information display in animal work is not as great as that of obtaining information from the animal and rendering it in an appropriate form for computer analysis. In this respect the value of operant studies lies in the fact that the lever press provides a convenient means of translating the animal's actions into a readily encoded signal. Small computers have many uses in this context. The LINC is an example of a small computer specifically designed for on-line use and suited to this kind of data (Clark and Molnar, 1965). The successor to the LINC is the PDP-12. This machine incorporates the interfacing facilities of a LINC with the arithmetic ones of a PDP-8. In doing this, two processors are available and time-sharing possibilities are multiplied.

Laboratories may possess their own computer but where this is impracticable a link can be established between central computer facilities and more remote experimental stations. Uber and Weiss (1966), for example, describe one means of coding information in frequency modulated tones to be transmitted by cable and decoded at the other end. Although input/output rates tend to be slow this need be no great handicap in operant experiments.

It is commonly a problem for the human observer in recording the recurrence of specifically defined behaviour patterns in ethological studies to register and code these whilst at the same time carrying out the necessary observation. Tobach et al. (1962) suggest one way in which this difficulty may be overcome. They employed a keyboard using each key to represent a behavioural item. The keyboard was coupled to a Laupheimer converter which linked the keyboard to a standard tape punch to produce a paper-tape usable in the IBM 1620 computer.

Control systems

The central processor usually consists of a general purpose computer with unit time and random number generators. This unit is linked to magnetic tape readers and recorders providing storage and memory facilities. The input/output functions may be implemented by teletypewriter, high-speed paper tape readers, tape punches or other equipment.

If individual experiments have to run at a low information rate much computer time will be wasted. It is possible to control several experimental stations simultaneously by switching rapidly back and forth between them. As examples of the types of system which might be employed we cite those used by Ellen and Wilson (1964), Barry *et al.* (1966), and Sutherland *et al.* (1969).

Ellen and Wilson (1964) applied digital logic techniques to the recording of events taking place within simultaneously operating chambers. Responses, reinforcements and time data for each chamber were recorded and problems were encountered in registering this amount of data on a limited number of input channels. The solution was to record the responses from each chamber on to paper tape directly, whereas reinforcement signals and time data from each chamber were applied for memory storage to flip-flop elements capable of assuming one of two states at any given time. The outputs from these flip-flops were scanned at every 1/5 second. If a signal was present a coincidence gate was enabled (AND gate) and the signal was passed into an encoding network. It was encoded into its binary equivalent by passing through a system of coincidence gates and finally put on to tape. In other words, some of the information from the chambers—information concerning reinforcements and time data—is translated into a more compact form. The logic system which does this provides capacity which is not on the tape. This shows that a logic system can be used to overcome the problem of dealing with large amounts of data over limited channels.

Barry *et al.* (1966) also used a system in which they were faced with the same kind of problem. They tested rats on a Sidman avoidance schedule which required separate avoidance and escape responses. Depression of an escape lever turned off shock. Presses on the separate avoidance lever postponed the onset of the next shock by 20 seconds if the shock was currently off. Twenty-four different event codes were necessary in an eight-chamber test situation. In this case the codes for the 24 events as well as 40 time intervals were recorded in binary form. By use of coding systems, not only was control established over a number of separate stations, but economy of computer time was also effected.

The advantages of equipment capable of running experiments on many animals at the same time has been pointed out by Sutherland *et al.* (1969). They describe a system for running up to 20 animals at a time on-line, controlled by an Elliott 4130 computer. The interface between the computer and the animals consists of a peripheral animal controller to which each test chamber is linked. Each test chamber receives 12 output lines from the computer through the controller and returns four input lines back to the computer. Sampling of the state of the inputs is carried out by the computer once every 16 milliseconds on receipt of an interrupt from a real-time clock to the central processor. Storage of incoming data takes place and outputs to the experiment are made. When the necessary actions have been taken the central processor is freed to continue running background programmes for the remainder of the 16-millisecond interval. Data output can occur on paper tape, on a visual display or through the teletypewriter. Experimental control programs are written in the Elliott assembly language. Francis and Sutherland (1969) have reported on a higher level control language which has been described in Chapter 3.

It is possible to fabricate schedules of reinforcement using computers, which are impossible to program by conventional methods, and thus observe aspects of the finer structure of behaviour. One example quoted by Weiss and Laties (1965) is that of the problem of differentially reinforcing low variability in response rate, or in other words reinforcing for stable rates of response. They describe a computer-generated schedule which controls variability directly and they demonstrate how a detailed analysis of the data reveals multiple effects. Both the programming and the analysis were performed by a small high-speed LINC computer. They used an autoregressive reinforcement schedule, a stochastic schedule which takes its name from a time series in which successive observations depend on a function of the previous term or terms, plus a random additive error. It reinforces low variability by promoting consistency in the intervals between responses. The closer the similarity of inter-response times the greater the probability of reinforcement. The organism's own behaviour then becomes the basis of the response-reinforcement correlation.

To determine whether the conditions for reinforcement are met, the program first computes the quotient of the two successive interresponse times, always placing the larger value in the numerator. The quotient corresponds to a number equivalent to a certain *p-value* in a table stored in the computer memory. A random number is then generated and compared with the table entry. If the table entry is greater, reinforcement is programmed. The behaviour of monkeys reinforced with a fruit drink came under the control of the schedule in a short time, the monkeys rapidly reducing the variability between their interresponse times.

In a further experiment Weiss *et al.* (1966) also describe in detail computer applications to behaviour when the animals were required to respond to short intervals for certain periods and long intervals for other periods. The effects appeared as a tendency to drift up and down in long wavelength periods around the minimum interval required for reinforcement. The three monkeys were interfaced to a LINC computer through their levers. The levers were connected to the external sense lines of the LINC through Schmitt triggers and flip-flops. The LINC programmed the schedule and recorded all interresponse times to the nearest 40 millisecond. Reinforcement occurred each time a response terminated an interresponse interval of 20 seconds or more.

We have quoted a few examples of the use of on-line methods in behavioural studies. The control of such experiments is achieved by the use either of general purpose equipment or by small special purpose computers. The advantages of enhanced flexibility, experimental control and economy of time have already been stressed.

Computer modelling of behaviour systems

In this section we are concerned with the capacity of the computer to model functions of significance to a theoretical understanding of behaviour. It is possible to construct analogs of brain processes, including physiological functions, perceiving, learning, remembering, etc., and also evolutionary systems, ecological networks, genetic processes, and the systems concerned with the regulation of animal numbers.

Physical limitations

The physical constraints on behaviour may be structural (Oxnard, 1969; Ede and Law, 1969), or act through functional means to limit expression. There is little doubt, for example, that the range of behaviour is restricted by ballistic properties of the limbs, skeletal arrangements and neuromuscular effectiveness as well as by the mechanisms for nervous control. Certain patterns are beyond the scope of the organisms because of these limitations. Computer simulation can reveal those types of behaviour available to an organism and those which are not, in the light of these physical restraints. An example can be quoted from the study of vocal activity in the chimpanzee (*Leiberman et al.*, 1969).

This problem concerns the capacity of non-human primates to talk. Whilst there is evidence of linguistic capacity in chimpanzees there is little evidence for any direct capacity to speak. If the vocal tract is examined it may be determined whether the limitation is one which operates at this point or whether this limitation must be traced to an incapacity of the brain itself.

Lieberman *et al*. (1969) used a computer program that calculated pattern frequencies to simulate such frequencies from the area function of the animal's supralaryngeal vocal tract. This simulation was systematically varied within the limits imposed by anatomical constraints. The resulting levels were compared with those of humans and with recorded vocalizations of non-human primates. The computer model indicated that the acoustic vowel space of a rhesus monkey is quite restricted compared to that of the human. This limitation results from the lack of a pharyngeal region that can change its cross-sectional area. Primates can thus be shown to lack the complex output mechanisms necessary for the production of human speech. In the use of a computer-implemented model of the supralaryngeal vocal tract it was possible to determine that there are physical limitations which would prevent the production of speech in these animals.

Population studies

Computer assistance is also of very great value in the study of factors regulating animal numbers. Pennycuick (1969) describes the use of a computer model in the study of population fluctations in a great tit population. Fecundity and mortality in these animals were related to a variety of factors extracted from population data. The program calculates the number of birds in the population over any number of years; it enables the factors affecting fecundity and survival to be tested alone and in various combinations for their effects on the population. It was argued on the basis of this model that density independent factors would not control the population for any length of time. The effect of the calculated fecundity functions on the number of tits was shown to be small compared with the effect of the functions relating to juvenile survival.

The problems of ecology are particularly complex and it is in areas such as these that it is important to resort to aids from computer systems (Conrad and Pattee, 1970; Watt, 1964).

Innate behaviour

Computer analogies can represent the ideas of complex chains of preset patterns of behaviour as described by Tinbergen (1951). The sequence envisaged by the early ethologists was triggered by various types of environmental stimuli. The organism could appear as being programmed in certain ways and internal states or appropriate environmental stimuli each could have access to the register of tapes, selecting some but not others to be put into operation (Dimond, 1970 a and b). The relationships of instinctive patterns to computer technology have been stressed by Friedman (1967). Evidence that sequences of actions last longer than the duration of the stimulus itself is to be obtained from the studies of electrical stimulation of the brain (van Holst and van St. Paul, 1963). This suggests that because of the neural arrangements the organism follows a program through to its conclusion. It has to be remembered however that this is still an argument by analogy. Perhaps the principal value of the computer analogy lies not in that it teaches us new facts but that it provides a framework and a terminology within which to discuss the problems of control. It may not help to know that it is possible to construct an analog of Tinbergen's model but the process of constructing a model can provide for refinement of the original concept.

Some of the most important attempts to construct a grammar for use in the explanation of behaviour has taken place in the use of logical nets. The modelling process is represented by the assembly of logic elements performing different functions. Just as it is possible to assemble a series of logic elements to exert control over automatic experiments, so the possibility exists of assembling logic elements to form an analog of behavioural systems. Thus the stages in Tinbergen's hierarchical model could be seen as a series of OR gates. It is possible to model many different behavioural functions using logic elements and the principal value lies in the development of parallel systems to living organisms— artificial automatons and intelligences. Horridge (1968) has argued that it may not be possible to predict on the basis of input/output data the nature of the complex logical arrangements of a system if that system consists of something more than a single channel. Any given computer model even if it works in the way required is still only one of many possible approaches to the system and it may not be the correct one, but there is a value in simulation: it forces the investigator to think not only in detail but also in logic about the system itself.

One of the most appropriate models for ethological theory is the McCulloch and Pitts (1943) stimulus-response system described as the nerve net. This is a finite number of neurones in which the axon of one cell leads to the cell body of another.

Neural nets were envisaged originally as a series of elements having finite states producing specifiable output on the basis of input data. They form a class of automata. At a lower phyletic level we may expect the analogy with innate patterns of behaviour to hold most strongly. Logical nets represent regular events and can be defined by a set of matrices. Kleene (1951) points out that they are both logical and realizable. They can be regarded as pre-wiring, i.e. as the fixed con- nexions of the nervous system.

One feature which we might describe as economic is that the model should respond in a direct way to specific signals. Such a system may well show behavioural mistakes if response is triggered in an automatic fashion or if it is unable to avoid responding when other features are present in addition to the original signal. This suggests a parallel to the stimulus releaser and super-normal releasing stimulus. The response to primitive stimulus features is evoked irrespective of the other features in the environment. The mechanisms of these systems is coarse grained and relatively fixed. It has the appearance of being governed by pre-wired logical nets. Svoboda (1960) and Pelikan (1964) describe devices which behave in a stereotyped predetermined fashion and which to some extent simulate the instinctive behaviour of lower organisms. Raichl (1966) also describes properties of a similar organism simulated by computer. Whilst showing a limited range of behaviour in its original state, it learns little because the signals which disturb its function have a random character. Learning capacity can be increased however by reducing the random effect of signals and by enhancing the control which the organism can exercise in relation to the environment. Friedman (1967) also describes the computer simulation of the behaviour of an organism designed to approach a target. He points out that this system, because of its construction, can persist in committing the same error despite repeated corrections and thus resembles an organism with an innate releasing mechanism in perceptual organization.

Learning

The nerve net stimulus-response system of McCulloch and Pitts (1943) was the forerunner of a number of adaptive systems which reflected a capacity to learn. This is highlighted in the study of finite automata and the more recent movement to the study of artificial intelligence (Swigert, 1967; Kilmer *et al.*, 1969).

Theories of learning have been subject to critical analyses by the use of computer simulations. Perhaps the most elaborate and systematic theory of learning to be formulated from studies of maze learning was that of Hull (1943). It was immediately appreciated by Hull's critics that this extensive theory was inadequate as an explanation of learning, even in rats in simple maze-running situations. This view was reinforced by Dunham (1957) who carried out a computer simulation of the theory which revealed not only the difficulties of formalization but also the inadequacies of that theory as it stood. Rochester *et al.* (1956), in a paper which has already been mentioned in Chapter 5, also simulated neurone nets on an IBM Electronic calculator to resemble the cell assembly of Hebb (1949). During any given run the neurones were connected in a particular net. Each neurone stimulated 10 other neurones. Diffuse reverberation was a feature of networks of this kind. An artificial change in the refractory state of one neurone produced profound changes in subsequent network reverberation—a situation which miti-gated against the formation of cell assemblies. It was appreciated that both inhibitory and excitatory synapses were essential to network stability and this led Milner (1957) to prepare the revised model of cell-assembly Mark II which unlike the earlier model included inhibitory synapses to stop total reverberation throughout the system. Since that time Rosenblatt (1964) has examined closed-loop cross-coupled systems in which all the association units are interconnected. Simulation of system dynamics in this context is an important aid to thought about the nature of the learning process itself.

Computer simulation can indicate the unsatisfactory nature of formerly respectable learning theories and the simulator may become involved not only in the construction of the program but in the revision of the theory itself.

Stimulus response theory in the study of animal learning has received many criticisms. Not least of these was that of Miller *et al.* (1960) who objected to this approach on the ground that it could not account for intentions or the capacity to plan for the future. They formulated the TOTE model (test-operate-test-exit). Chomsky (1963) has shown that the TOTE hierarchy itself may be viewed as a finite automaton and Suppes (1969) has argued that automata theory may also be deduced from stimulus-response theory and goes on to claim that it may be that the differences between these classes of models are not as pronounced as was first believed. In relation to this, Holder and King (1970) were able to construct a computer program which was effective as a model of classical and instrumental conditioning procedures. Not only did it summarize large amounts of data but it also generated anticipatory response sequences, though admittedly of a simple type.

There is a sense also in which simulation can be used as a tool in the evolution of a theoretical viewpoint. Successive approximations can result in the production of a model which may fit the facts better than most. Ledley (1965) describes the Monte Carlo simulation. The learning process is studied by successive approximations. The model is adjusted until it agrees with the laboratory results and the data can be compared. After an accurate model has been obtained the effects of different parameter changes may be studied by varying these on the computer. Walker (1967) also points out the virtues of this type of simulation. Without simulation it is often difficult or impossible to anticipate whether the set of principles selected for the program will actually fit the results. The program may need to be refined from the original, and ingenuity may be required to find what part of the program is unnecessary and what factor is adding the extra complication. Walker (1967) describes a simple computer model of learning programs and run on a large computer by S. H. Robinowitz. The program simulated the rat's capacity to learn to go to one side of a simple T-maze for food. The initial tendency to go to each side was assumed to be equal. It was necessary to build variability into the probabilities of going to either side. One side was chosen to be rewarded. Superimposed over the existing variability the computer was instructed to reward the hypothetical rat whenever it chose side one, but adding to the probability a certain calculated amount. Each time the computer chose side one the tendency to go to that side was again increased. Using simulated animals, it was possible to plot learning curves indistinguishable from results obtained in experiments involving real rats. These examples illustrate both the strengths and weaknesses of simulation methods. They show that a model does not always provide fresh facts about the behaviour studies, but on the other hand the process of simulation can clarify difficult and otherwise intractable problems and having once attained a simulation it is then possible to work with this to explore the parameters. 'The computer with its potentiality for simulation is neither a substitute for thinking nor a replacement for experimentation but an important aid in improving both processes'. (Walker, 1967)

There are of course many further developments of these ideas particularly in relation to problem-solving and advanced forms of human learning. However, these lie outside the scope of this chapter.

Conclusions

The fact that computer studies have a relevance to the study of animal behaviour is beyond doubt. It is possible to feel a qualified optimism about the use of these techniques and a hope that our knowledge of comparative psychology will be extended by their use. The main advantages lie in the potential for the automatic control of experiments and the capacity for modelling of behaviour as well as the more customary use for data analysis. Perhaps the greatest significance lies in the possibility of investigating complex problems which have so far proved to be intractable. Principal on the list are those of brain organization, perception, learning and remembering, but there are also the problems of autonomic function and physiological regulation of behaviour as well as the problems of the integration of muscle synergies. High on the list at the group level are the problems of population dynamics, regulation of animal numbers as well as the problems of interaction between one animal and another—communication and signalling systems, and the mechanisms which develop to make human group living possible.

Further Reading

Arbib, M. A., (1965) *Brains, Machines and Mathematics.* McGraw-Hill
    Paperbacks, New York. A description of cybernetic approaches to the
    study of brain functions.
Dimond, S. J., (1970) *The Social Behaviour of Animals.* B. T. Batsford,
    London. This book describes the use of experimental methods in the
    study of animal behaviour.
Ledley, R. S., (1965) *Use of Computers in Biology and Medicine.* McGraw-
    Hill, New York. A general account of computer applications in biology
    and medicine, including the use of Monte Carlo methods.
Stacy, R. W. and B. D. Waxman (1965) *Computers in Biomedical Research.*
    Academic Press, New York. An introduction to computer applications,
    especially in the area of physiology.
Walker, E. L. (1967) *Conditioning and Instrumental Learning.* Brooks/Cole
    Belmont, California. Looks at the processes of learning and describes a
    computer application.

CHAPTER 9

The Computer in Clinical Psychology

James O. Robinson

This chapter reviews some of the ways in which computers have been used in clinical work. It does not pretend to be exhaustive but the examples chosen are some of the better known applications and an attempt has been made to give a clear and fairly detailed description of the logical principles involved in these applications. Thus, whilst it is more than a brief review, it concerns itself with these logical principles rather than details of programming beyond the flow-chart stage.

Computers and the storage of clinical information

The storage of clinical data in the form of case notes, the format of which may not even be standardized within an institution, may suffice for the treatment of a particular patient during one episode of illness, but it is usually inadequate when several spells of illness or several institutions are involved. Records are lost, are not sent from one institution to another, or are so different in form that comparisons are difficult. In addition clinical information used for research purposes almost always needs to be collected in known and standard ways. The use of computers for data storage means that case records are easy to find and reproduce. Such storage entails the use of standard format and thus the needs of comparison and research generally are incidentally met.

The example of such a system which will be described here, devised by Eiduson, Brooks and Motto (1966), requires surprisingly little formalization of information. Information is retrieved from the system by asking questions which are answered in an extremely flexible way. The system takes as its basis 'events' in the lives of patients or people related to them. An 'event' can be practically anything that happens to a patient or his immediate environment, from the birth of a sibling to events in the contents of his thoughts. Clearly, events must be considered relevant by the clinician before they are entered on the patient's record. To each event a statement is attached giving information qualifying it, for example the time and place of its occurrence, who reported it, the

221

patient's reaction to it, the reaction of other key individuals to it, and so on. The computer can be interrogated about particular sorts of events, for example all events involving the patient's mother or all events in their time sequence. Not only can events within a patient's record be picked out but also similar sorts of events can be selected from many records. Thus patients with certain common characteristics can be identified. The potential of this feature for research is clear.

Computers and the collection of clinical data

Introduction

The collection of clinical data, particularly that done by means of psychological tests, was probably the first part of the diagnostic process to be made automatic. Subjects gave their responses to the test by punching a hole in an appropriate place on a card or by making a mark with a special pencil which was 'visible' to an automatic scoring device Such a device, a fairly simple counting machine, could produce total scores or various sets of sub-totals or even results processed in a simple way, averages for example. The computational part of such a process was very elementary but considerable labour and error was avoided when such counting of responses was made automatic. It is a short additional step to have the subject interact directly with the computer, reading the questions from the computer display (for example, a tele-typewriter) and typing in his responses. This avoids even the handling of response cards.

However, the real power of a computer in this sphere becomes apparent when the computer makes decisions and is not merely used as a calculator. Subsequent questions put to the subject can be made conditional on his replies to earlier questions. Thus the computer can automatically carry out a test procedure which involves 'focusing down', that is, introducing a more detailed test of a particular area only when the seeking of such further detail is appropriate. The complexity of chains of such decisions can be very great and the greater it is the more closely such automated testing approximates to interviewing.

The automation of psychological testing

The automation of group paper and pencil tests is a fairly simple process. It probably saves the time of the administrator but may also tie up for that time a lot of expensive machinery. A greater challenge is the automation of a test which usually has to be administered indi-vidually, such as the Wechsler Adult Intelligence Scale (WAIS). The saving of time is much greater for such a test and automation has the added advantage of presenting the test in a standard form; there are no complications stemming from the tester's part in the person-to-person interaction which takes place in the usual test procedure. However, there is still the machine-to-person interaction and this may introduce variance into the test results, but at least the machine will not vary in its presentation of the test to different subjects. The human tester almost certainly does. Most testers would defend such variability as the wholly desirable process of establishing *rapport* and the question of *rapport* still cannot be neglected in the use of automated techniques.

A project to automate the WAIS is reported by Elwood (1969). This test involves much more than the simple marking of responses on an answer sheet and so is a good example of more sophisticated automatic testing. At the time Elwood's paper was written, the project was not complete but scores for the Block Design, Picture Arrangement and Object Assembly sub-tests could be produced automatically. However, no computer was used, only a timer activated by the solenoid latches on the various drawers containing the sub-tests. The subject pressed a button to start and the latch of the first of a panel of drawers was released. He then did the sub-test within the drawer; for example, he rearranged the Picture Arrangement items which rested in $\frac{1}{4}$-inch deep cut-out areas in the floor of the drawer, and then closed the drawer. The time for which the drawer was open was recorded.

At the end of the test an assistant looked in all the drawers and scored the results. It would be a relatively simple matter with the aid of a little electronic logic to make the scoring automatic too, but a computer is not necessary. The sort of technique just described might be carried out by a computer as part of a larger scheme in which it would be responsible for the decision as to which test to use and would select the WAIS from a number of possible tests. Such an immense system, with a repertoire of tests, has not yet been evolved but very flexible systems of medical and psychiatric interrogation certainly have.

The automation of interviews

These are basically inventories containing a large number of fairly general questions. A positive reply to one of these questions elicits from the computer sub-sets of relevant questions which enlarge on the positive reply.

Such a system on-line to an IBM 360/50 computer and given the name Computer Assisted Special Enquirer (CASE) is described by Stillman *et al.* (1969). It is used, according to the authors, for eliciting mental status, psychometric and personal history information without

the aid of an interviewer. The patient sits before a teletypewriter on
which he responds. The questions are printed out by the teletypewriter
or else appear on a video screen in front of the patient.

An example of a flow-chart of branching questions is shown in Figure
9.1. The authors state that the design of such a chart of questions can

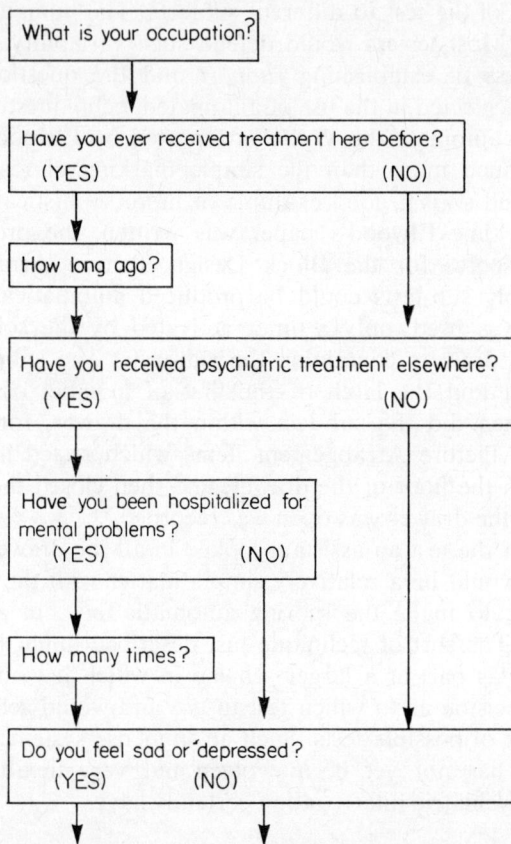

Figure 9.1—*Sample flow-chart for questions and branching (from Stillman*
et al., *1969)*

be a lengthy and complex task. It is indeed the whole difficulty of such
a system. The computer can ask the questions automatically but it
cannot yet make up its own questions and the chief problem in psychological or psychiatric interviewing is to decide what questions ought to
be asked. This point will be taken up later with reference to diagnosis.
Clearly the design of such a system for collecting demographic informa-

tion, facts about life history and the broad outline of the sort of difficulty that has prompted the patient to seek help is fairly straightforward. The information could be used to call in various sorts of automated test procedures but although the authors indicated this possibility they did not report its having been done. The system's chief advantage appears to have been the saving of interviewing time. The psychiatrist had to retrieve the results of the interview and read them before he could make a diagnosis. Clearly the time spent in reading the computer output must be set against the time saved on the interview. The method has the advantage that the interview is standardized and so increases comparability between interviews. The authors claim that much of the variance in psychiatric diagnosis is due to variations in interview technique.

In such an automated interview information can be obtained about the patient from relatives or from hospital staff and all the information can be gathered together on the patient's computer-stored file. Nor is the interview restricted to verbal data. There is no reason in principle why measures such as the E.E.G. should not be included, or indeed any of a large range of physiological variables. Slack (1971) has included a measure of heart rate in such an interview scheme and made some branching of the program contingent on it. Thus, when the heart rate shows a marked rise the patient is given reassurance and told to relax.

Another advantage of automation is that several interviews with the patient can be carried out during his course of treatment and so an estimate can be made of his progress. It would be possible to design such a system of multiple interviews so that it could warn staff of impending crises or would provide day-to-day information by which, for example, drug dosages could be adjusted.

Systems of this kind could carry out any of a large range of data-gathering procedures and, apart from savings of time, their effectiveness would depend on the data sought. A psychiatrist or psychologist who is successful in old-fashioned interviewing could reasonably hope to use the same questions for both the two kinds of interviews and that their interpretation would be similar.

Slack and von Cura (1968) report that computer-based interviewing is well accepted by patients. They allowed patients to answer 'yes', 'no', 'don't know', or 'don't understand' to questions about the interview. Patients' responses indicated that they did not find it difficult, did not dislike it, found it interesting and not boring, and did not find it tiring. Responses to questions about preference for automated interviews and about the thoroughness of the interviewer and the machine were not markedly in favour of either. It is worth adding too that Coombs,

Murray and Krahn (1970) found that difficulties in coping with computer-based interviews were related to age and education. Young people and well educated people coped best.

The example of automated interview given by Stillman *et al.* provides for branching in the sense that the response 'yes' to a particular question will switch the computer into one set of subsequent questions and the response 'no' will switch it into another. The two streams of questions may come together again into one stream by means of subsequent branching, but this does not exhaust the subtlety of this sort of program. In live interviews it is not necessarily a 'yes' or 'no' that elicits a particular question from the interviewer. It is something in the content of a more complex answer. Kleinmuntz (1969) quotes part of an interview conducted by ELIZA, a computer program devised by Weizenbaum (1966) to carry on a conversation with a human subject. This program was not designed to conduct psychiatric interviews but to make responses to human verbal statements which were linked to those statements in the sorts of ways human response would be linked. The result is the following kind of conversation.

Patient (Pt): Men are all alike.
Therapist (Th): In what way?
Pt: They're always bugging us about something or other.
Th: Can you think of a specific example?
Pt: Well my boyfriend made me come here.
Th: Your boyfriend made you come here?
Pt: He says I'm depressed much of the time.
Th: I am sorry to hear you are depressed.
Pt: It's true. I am unhappy.
Th: Do you think coming here will help you not to be unhappy?
Pt: I need some help, that much seems certain.
Th: What would it mean to you if you got some help?
Pt: Perhaps I could learn to get along with my mother.
Th: Tell me more about your family.
Pt: My mother takes care of me.
Th: Who else in your family takes care of you?
Pt: My father.
Th: Your father?
Pt: You are like my father in some ways.
Th: What resemblance do you see?
Pt: You are not very aggressive but I think you don't want me to notice that.

Th: What makes you think I am not very aggressive?
Pt: You don't argue with me.
Th: Why do you think I don't argue with you?
Pt: You are afraid of me.
Th: Does it please you to believe I am afraid of you?
Pt: My father is afraid of everybody.
Th: What else comes to mind when you think of your father?
Pt: Bullies.
Th: Does that have anything to do with the fact that your boyfriend made you come here?

Kleinmuntz points out that this program demonstrates the ability to interpret replies made in natural language and to generate responses in a very flexible way. It identifies key words in the input material and responds to them according to relatively few rules which are based on common modes of response to such words in certain contexts. Thus the word 'everybody', a general term, elicits a question asking for detail; mention of the respondent's mother elicits questions about her family.

The capacity to generate entirely new statements according to certain rules is an exciting feature of this system because it is likely to produce chains of verbal exchange which have not been foreseen by its creator. Where questions are all completely specified, as in the system of Stillman and others, all possible outcomes are fairly easily specified. A system which generates its own questions, even if the rules by which it does this are fairly simple, has so many possible outcomes that it would probably not be possible to specify them, especially as one cannot predict all possible input statements that a patient is likely to give.

Such a system has not yet been established for psychological interviewing and the main difficulty of doing so would be deciding on the rules. Most experienced interviewers in this field would have difficulty in specifying how one question leads to another in an interview. However, it is probably not profitable to worry about having the rules conform to a particular interviewer's procedure. With a system of this sort of complexity it would probably be better to build in a likely looking set of rules and then see how the machine performed in some particular role. If the role were that of the initial psychodiagnostic interview, then the system's adequacy could be judged by comparison with live interviewers in the ease with which diagnosis could be made from a transcript of the interview. Its shortcomings could be assessed and the rules for generating the computer output to the patient could be modified.

Computers and the interpretation of clinical data

Introduction

If a set of rules can be specified for the interpretation of any mass of data then the computer can in principle be made to interpret the data as well as the rules themselves will allow. Thus the computer interpretation of the results of objective tests is relatively easy. A distinction can be made between interpretation according to a specified set of rules on the one hand and diagnosis on the other. In diagnosis it is not at all clear by what rules most decisions are made. The clinician may be able to describe broad general strategies which he adopts in seeking information and approximately what weight he gives to different sorts of information, but the exact details of how he arrives at a diagnosis may be something of a mystery even to him. There is little doubt that the human brain can usefully process and give appropriate weight to information without the processes ever coming into consciousness, so that a clinician can arrive at a diagnosis feeling that some guesswork has gone into his decision and yet over time his diagnoses can fulfil successfully whatever need they serve. This is one of the biggest problems of computer diagnosis.

The approach usually followed is to make some model of how diagnosis *might* be made, perhaps a model based on the use of past observed frequencies of symptoms and the diagnoses that have resulted. The model is then tested by calculation of the extent to which it agrees with clinicians over a large number of diagnoses. Such a method assumes that the diagnoses of clinicians are the best standard against which to test a computer program. But a computer program could be better than a clinician in two ways; it could diagnose more effectively using the same rules and the same diagnostic categories; or it could lead to the establishment of new rules or even new diagnostic categories.

The interpretation of psychological tests

When computers were first used to perform factor analyses this use could legitimately be seen as that of interpreting psychological tests, but the actual interpretation in that case was made by a human being after the output from the computer had been studied. More recently the computer has itself been the decision-maker. Most work has been done using the Minnesota Multiphasic Personality Inventory (MMPI), a widely used test which also has the advantage of having generated a large mass of research literature from which can be gleaned all sorts of material useful in forming a set of rules by which interpretation can be made. Two programs will be described.

The first of these, devised at the Mayo clinic and described by Rome *et al.* (1962), scans an answer sheet which is specially prepared for use with the program. It scores the inventory according to the usual rules and derives the usual clinical scales. The scores on these scales are then scanned and statements describing the patient's position on the scales are printed out. Thus, for example, for a person scoring between 11 and 14 on the *Pa* (paranoid) scale, the computer prints out, 'sensitive, alive to the opinions of others'. For a score of 15 to 19 it prints out, 'touchy, overly responsive to the opinions of others. Inclined to blame others for own difficulties'. For a score of more than 20 it prints out, 'resentful and suspicious of others, perhaps to the point of fixed false beliefs'. Thus the program chiefly performs the task of reading the score on a particular scale and printing out a predetermined statement elicited by that score. As well as assessing individual scores the program also makes certain standard evaluations of score patterns. For example, if four or more scale scores exceed 70 it recommends psychiatric consultation, if the *Ma* (hypomania) scale is less than 15 in an old patient it discounts such low motivation as typical of a patient of that age. It also operates the validating scales, for example by indicating that the scale is invalid if the F (validity) score is less than 22.

Administratively a much more ambitious scheme, though in other ways broadly similar, has been established by the Roche Psychiatric Service Institute in Alabama. It is described by Fowler (1969). The scheme provides clinicians with a kit of MMPI test material complete with instructions. The test is presented to the patient and the results sent by mail to the Roche Institute. The computer carries out an analysis of the test results and provides a report made up of statements output in response to various score patterns. The striking feature of this report is that it appears in normal language with variously formed sentences suitably composed into paragraphs. To the reader it might be a report written by a human interpreter.

Another program designed to interpret the MMPI was devised at the Carnegie-Mellon University and is briefly described by Kleinmuntz (1969). Its main immediate purpose was to screen college students for likelihood of emotional difficulties and the rules used in the program were a good deal more complex than those of the Mayo Clinic program.

A number of experienced interpreters of the MMPI were asked to sort 126 MMPI profiles into a number of categories by making a general judgement of the profile. The categories ran from highly adjusted to poorly adjusted and the actual condition of the individuals from which the profiles came was known in terms of whether they were well or ill. If they were ill then a full diagnosis, based on a full psychiatric interrogation, was available.

The interpreter who did best in correctly identifying the profiles of ill and well individuals was asked to carry out the sorting procedure again, thinking aloud throughout. He did this, and from the tape recording of what he said it was found possible to generate a large set of rules which could be built up into a program. For example, one statement ran 'here's a paranoid character . . . I wish his K score were not quite so high . . . and he could use more Mt. . . . When that Mt score is less than 10, I figure something must be stabilizing him. . . . I like an inverted 'V' with F high on the validity scales.' From this statement was generated the rule 'Call maladjusted if $Pa > 70$ unless $Mt \leqslant 6$ (raw score) and $K \geqslant 65$.

Up to this point the programmers had created an automated version of the interpretation scheme of their selected expert. It worked nearly as well as he did. With the 126 profiles it achieved 63 per cent correct identification of maladjustment and 88 per cent correct declarations of absence of maladjustment. The figures for the expert were 80 per cent and 67 per cent respectively. Next, the program was modified by the introduction of various sets of new tentative rules and its performance, in terms of identification of maladjustment in the same set of existing profiles, was tested. This process is described below. The result was a considerable increase in complexity of the program and also an increase of the two criterion figures to 90 per cent and 84 per cent respectively. Thus the program was now doing better than the expert in the rather limited sense of allocating more correctly diagnoses based on this set of profiles. In view of this, it is worth looking at the detail of this second stage of its design.

One technique used was to instruct the computer to withhold a maladjusted/adjusted decision after all the existing rules had been applied whilst it calculated the number of rules which had worked in favour of the two possible decisions. This total was then made to contribute to the final decision. Another technique was to find rules that were relatively strong or weak in their contribution to decisions. Thus a strong rule would be found to be practically always associated with one final decision whereas a weak rule would sometimes be associated with one decision and sometimes with the other. The situation finally created was one in which the computer not only applied the rules but also allowed its final decision to be influenced by the *pattern* of the decisions stemming from the application of the rules. This made use of the enormous storage capacity of the computer in which items are quickly and certainly available. Human storage capacity is probably greater but is less certainly available, so that even though an expert might have some inkling of the relative potency of the various rules he applies he cannot use his knowledge in a very sophisticated way. The computer on the other hand can retain and use profiles of this type which amount to a kind of 'super-experience' which the human expert probably could not acquire.

It is interesting and important that the success rate achieved by this program for subsequent new samples of profiles, even samples taken from the same (student) population, were much lower. I believe that this is an instance of the same problem which occurs in attempts to use discriminant functions derived from data obtained from groups of individuals to classify new individuals. This problem will be raised again later. It is enough to say here that provided the patterns of scores for the members of a sample are large enough and all different then it is logically possible to derive a set of rules which will not only correctly classify them into sub-groups but will even identify individuals. But such a set of rules would be unique for that sample and could not be expected to work for any other sample. So, while the computer achieved super-human results in this restricted situation, when presented with problems as new as the problems usually dealt with by a skilled interpreter, it did not do noticeably better than the man.

Although the MMPI has been favoured, attempts have been made at automatic interpretation of other tests. The Rorschach Test could be seen as a particularly difficult test to automate, yet Piotrowski (1964) has published an account of a program for its interpretation once the scoring has been done. The test is scored and the profiles presented to the computer. It carries out the interpretation by the operation of a large number of rules and prints out interpretative statements. Such a program is something like the MMPI interpretative system developed at the Mayo Clinic and described above. If the rules for interpretation are explicit then the design of a program to operate them is not difficult.

Diagnosis by computer

In diagnosis, where there are no explicit rules for the interpretation of information, problems are more difficult. Computer programs designed to make diagnostic decisions rest chiefly on two sorts of principle: some are based on the human clinical decision processes and some have an actuarial basis, that is they try to specify the prior probability of a particular diagnosis. Clearly, human clinical decisions are partly actuarial in that some estimate of the prior probability of a diagnosis is bound to enter into the decision. Thus a clinician faced with symptoms of upper respiratory discomfort will begin with a different set of hypotheses in the summer-time from the ones he begins with in the winter. The reason for this is that colds are much more prevalent in the winter and hay fever is more prevalent in the summer.

However, such actuarial characteristics of human decision-making are informal and limited. Computer programs with an actuarial basis use prior probabilities much more exactly and explicitly. Such probabilities are usually generated from a large group of patients whose symptoms are known and for whom diagnoses have been arrived at in traditional ways. Methods are then found of predicting from a given pattern of symptoms what the most likely diagnosis would be in the group from which the probabilities were calculated. Let us examine in detail first a program based on a decision tree, and then two actuarially based programs.

A scheme devised by Spitzer and Endicott (1968, 1969) and known as DIAGNO is based on a logical decision tree. This is to say that it proceeds through a large number of decisions which branch out in a tree-like way from an initial decision. The flow-chart for DIAGNO II is shown in Figure 9.2.

The basic information for this program comes from the Current and Past Psychopathology Scales (CAPPS) which is a combination of the Psychiatric Evaluation Form (Diagnostic Version) and the Psychiatric History Schedule, both of which were designed by Spitzer, Endicott and their collaborators. The former contains 41 scales by which are recorded judgements of the patient's psychopathology over the past month and the latter contains 130 scales and other items by which are recorded judgements of psychopathology, personality and adjustment in various contexts from the age of twelve up to the past month, with some scales referring to specific periods within that range. The scales are seven-point rating scales and the rating is done by the interviewer. The completion of most of the scales would require psychological or psychiatric training and so the data used by this program is by no means raw data. Some examples of the scales are shown in Table 9.1.

The first question the program asks of the CAPPS data is whether or not there is evidence of organic brain disorder. The answer is obtained by scanning relevant scales (the relevant scales were predetermined by the programmer on the basis of clinical experience). The question takes the form of cut-off levels on scales coupled with logical operators NOT, AND and OR. A question could be put into words thus: 'Is scale $X > 5$ and scale $Y > 4$ or scale $Z < 3$? If so go to question C, otherwise go to question F'. Most actual questions were much more complex than this hypothetical example.

The program can make any of 46 diagnoses of which 44 are diagnoses set out in the standard nomenclature of the American Psychiatric

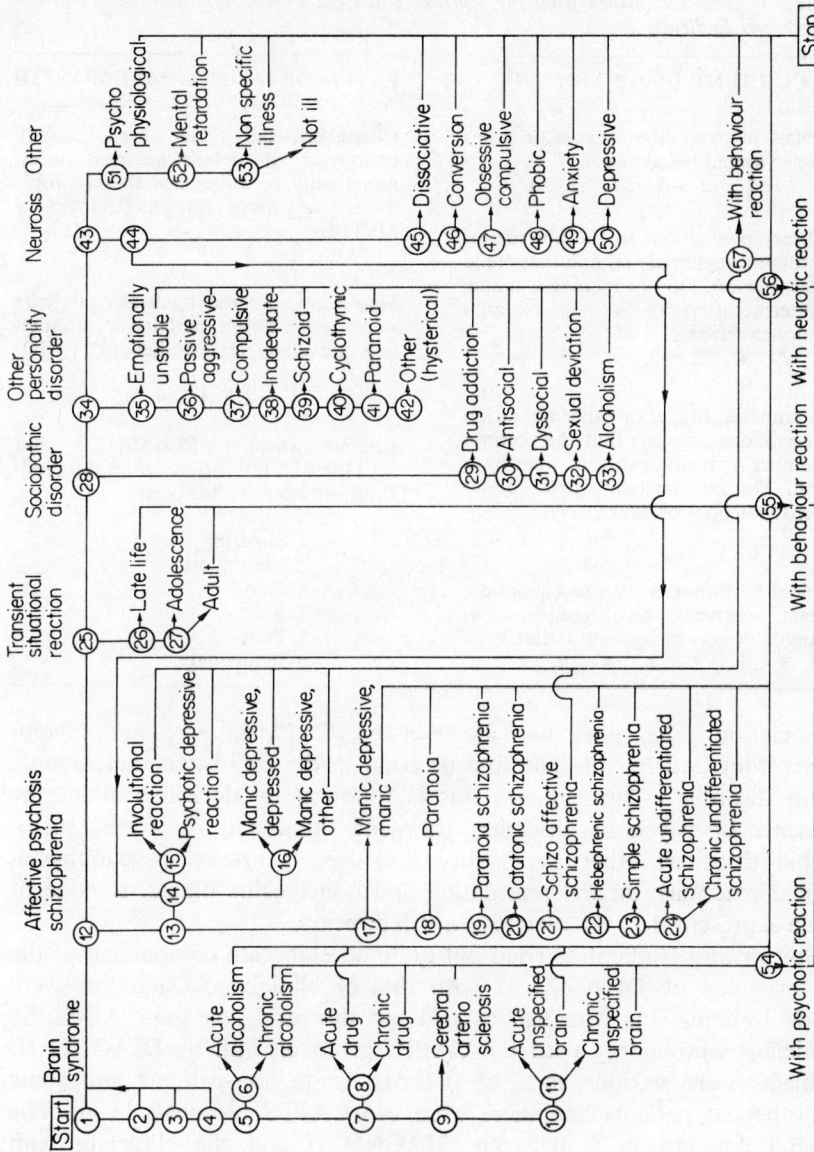

Figure 9.2—Schematic flow-chart for DIAGNO II computer program (from Spitzer and Endicott, 1969)

Table 9.1—*Selected Scales from the Current and Past Psychopathology Scales (from Spitzer and Endicott, 1969)*

CURRENT (PAST MONTH)	PAST (AGE 12 UP TO PAST MONTH)

Engages in overt homosexual or other perverse sexual behaviour.
   ?   1   2   3   4   5   6
	Characteristically has been unduly concerned with details, neatness, order, punctuality or adherence to set procedures for doing things. (COMPULSIVITY)
	   ? 1 2 3 4 5 6

Auditory perceptions in the absence of identifiable external stimulation (e.g. voices, noises). Do not include a simple misinterpretation of a real external sensory experience.
   ?   1   2   3   4   5   6
	Has been bothered by irrational fears of a specific object, activity or situation (e.g., travelling, crowds, heights). (PHOBIA).
	   ? 1 2 3 4 5 6

Has amnesia, fugue, or other alteration in consciousness so that he cannot remember or is not aware of what he is doing. Do not include when due to epilepsy, alcohol or drugs.
   ?   1   2   3   4   5   6
	Characteristically, PLEASURE and SATISFACTION in activities, relationships, or interests has been:
	   ?
	   1 Superior
	   2 Very good
	   3 Good

Suicidal thoughts, preoccupation, threats, gestures or attempts, and thoughts or acts of self-mutilation.
   ?   1   2   3   4   5   6
	4 Fair
	   5 Poor
	   6 Inadequate

Association. The other two are *non-specific illness with mild symptomatology* and *not ill*. The first decision in the tree is whether organic brain disorder is present and this is followed by decisions about the presence of psychotic disorder, transient situational disorders, sociopathic disorder, other personality disorders, neuroses, psychophysiological reactions, mental retardation and non-specific illness. If none of these is present then the diagnosis *not ill* appears.

Spitzer and Endicott carried out quite an elaborate comparison of the performance of DIAGNO II with that of clinicians. Diagnoses were made by clinicians who had carried out the rating on the CAPPS, by clinicians who simply used the CAPPS protocols and by DIAGNO II. Subjects were various sorts of patients, some non-patients and some hypothetical patients and there were 146 CAPPS protocols in all. The crucial comparison is between DIAGNO II and the clinicians who simply used the CAPPS protocols, since exactly the same information was available to each, whereas the raters had seen the patients themselves (with the exception of the hypothetical patients, who were not interviewed!). The level of agreement between clinicians and DIAGNO II was very close to the level of agreement between clinicians. The latter was low enough to make a prospective patient feel a little insecure, but it was clear that using current psychiatric methods and current psychiatric categories DIAGNO II agreed well with psychiatrists in diagnosis. The greatest disagreement between the two was in the category 'not ill': DIAGNO II put 18 patients into this category against the clinicians' 8. Presumably the clinicians formed their judgements on scale scores below the cut-off levels used by DIAGNO II.

Discriminant analysis is an example of a technique with an actuarial basis. It is a process in which the best possible discrimination is obtained between two or more groups. If there are several measures for each member of several groups, then a discriminant function can be calculated which maximizes the ratio of the variance between groups to the

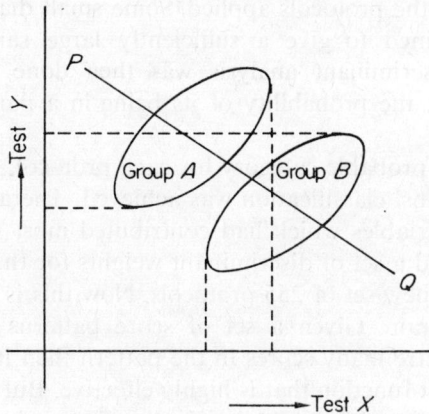

Figure 9.3—*Discriminant analysis*

variance within groups. In practice a set of weights is obtained, one for each measure, and measures are multiplied by weights and summed. Cut-off points can be determined for the resulting totals which will give minimal misclassification. Such cut-off points constitute simple rules of classification so that, for example, individuals with a discriminant function score of greater than x and smaller than y are allocated to category b. A simple and idealized example, using only two tests and two groups, is shown in Figure 9.3. There is considerable overlap between the groups on both dimension X and dimension Y. What discriminant analysis does is to transpose the data on to another dimension on which the groups are better separated, such as the dimension PQ in Figure 9.3. It can do this with many dimensions and several groups. Discriminant analysis is the method used by Melrose, Stroebel and Glueck (1970).

In writing about this model earlier (Glueck and Stroebel, 1969), two of these authors ask an important question about how clinicians make diagnoses. Do they follow through a logical decision tree or do they have a sort of 'template' of a disorder which is composed of various intensities of various symptoms, with which they compare the particular pattern of the patient? This question embodies two models of the diagnostic process: the latter is the discriminant model and the former is the logical decision tree model just described.

Melrose, Stroebel and Glueck described a type of discriminant analysis which they compared with DIAGNO II. To make a good comparison possible they used 413 CAPPS protocols supplied by Spitzer and derived from psychiatric patients. These were grouped according to diagnoses which had already been made by the clinicians attending the patients to whom the protocols applied. Some small diagnostic categories had to be combined to give a sufficiently large sample in any one category. The discriminant analysis was then done and it provided, for each protocol, the probability of its being in a particular diagnostic group.

Using the most probable category for each protocol, 75 per cent agreement with clinicians' classification was achieved. The authors then chose the 70 CAPPS variables which had contributed most to the discrimination and calculated a set of discriminant weights for them. These weights they applied to a new set of 255 protocols. Now this is the crucial test of this sort of program. Given a set of score patterns all of which are different, if there are many scores in the pattern then it is not difficult to find a discriminant function that is highly effective. But the chief question is whether such a function has generality or whether it can only correctly classify the patterns from which it was calculated. For the new protocols there was overall agreement between the discriminant program and the clinicians, of only 29·7 per cent. DIAGNO II, with the same protocols, achieved 40·1 per cent agreement with the clinicians. The agreement was improved to 43·8 per cent between the discriminant analysis and clinicians if a classification by the latter was taken as an agreement if it corresponded to any of the three most probable categories proposed by the former.

The agreement for most probable categories will seem to the reader to be small. It is worth indicating that agreement varies very much from category to category. For example, the discriminant program did much better with obsessive-compulsive disorders, neurotic depression and some varieties of schizophrenia than with the rest.

An advantage of this sort of classification procedure over a decision tree procedure is that it provides probabilities of membership of other categories besides the most probable. It thus leaves room for skilled judgement at the end of the process and guides the clinician towards likely alternatives. On the other hand it is not yet of great practical use because even the three most probable categories do not contain diagnoses in very close agreement with clinicians. However, the authors claim that this is a good beginning, and such a claim is probably valid. If the range of information originally processed is increased and that found to be most predictive and most general is progressively selected, it seems likely that the performance of the program will improve. After all it does not have far to go before it agrees with clinicians as closely as they agree with each other. They may have been hampered by being obliged to use standard information not collected in their own preferred way, but they did all have the *same* information and were usually members of the same institution.

Another type of automatic diagnostic procedure is based on Bayes' Theorem. This enables us to use diagnoses already made, to state for a fresh case the probability of various diagnoses being correct. If we have a large number of previously diagnosed cases and we know the symptoms and the diagnoses of each, and if these cases are a representative sample from the population of all possible new cases that we are likely to encounter, then we can count both how many cases of each diagnosis there are and which symptoms were most common in each diagnostic category. We can use such counts of frequency as estimates of probability. Thus for a new case we can state the probability of the various possible diagnoses before we even speak to him (this is the prior probability) and the probability of occurrence of various patterns of symptoms in the various diagnostic categories. In this context Bayes' Theorem is an expression which links the probability of a particular diagnosis, given a particular set of symptoms, with the probability of the set of symptoms, given the disease (diagnosis) and the prior probability of the disease in the population studied. Thus in formal terms:

$$(pd|s) = \frac{p(d).p(s|d)}{\sum p(d).p(s|d)}$$

Where

$p(d|s)$ is the probability of the disease given the symptoms;
$p(d)$ is the probability of the disease;
$p(s|d)$ is the probability of the symptoms given the disease.

Now in any population under study, for example a large number of patients each already diagnosed on the basis of a number of symptoms, the probability of the disease is known (it is the proportion of people in the population who have it) and the probability of a particular set of symptoms given the disease is known (the proportion of people suffering from a particular illness who have that set of symptoms). Thus in any one study the bottom line of the right-hand side of the equation is always the same. We can therefore say:

$$p(d|s) \propto p(d).p(s|d)$$

The probability of the disease given the symptoms is proportional to the product of the probability of the disease and the probability of the symptoms given the disease.

Maxwell (1961) gave a very clear and well set-out hypothetical example of the use of this principle in diagnosis. Clearly, if we have a set of patients for whom the diagnosis and the symptoms are known we can calculate in terms of frequencies in this existing group, what $p(d)$ and $p(s|d)$ are. Maxwell's hypothetical group contained 148 affective disorders, 100 anxiety states and 132 neurotic depressives, and the task he set himself was to predict the classification of individuals from symptom patterns composed of dichotomous symptom scores; the symptoms were either present (1) or absent (0). These data are much simpler than the rating scales used in discriminant methods and so if the results were comparable it is likely that a method based on Bayes' Theorem which could be used on raw 'yes/no' data would have a distinct advantage over discriminant methods which demand such considerably processed data as the CAPPS protocols.

The next step was to specify every possible answer pattern. Such patterns would be composed of sets of ones and zeros, for example 1011010110 for ten symptoms. The number of such patterns for ten symptoms is 2^{10}, a very large number. A count was then made of the number of individuals in each diagnostic category with each symptom pattern. The resulting frequencies gave a probability for the occurrence of each symptom pattern in any one diagnostic category. This is $p(s|d)$, one of the terms of our equation. The other term, the prior probability of the diagnosis $p(d)$, was available from the frequencies of the diagnoses in the population. Thus the probability of the diagnosis given the symptoms $p(d|s)$ was easily calculated.

This probability forms a decision rule. For each answer pattern (patient) $p(s|d)$ would be multiplied by $p(d)$ for each diagnostic category to give values of $p(d|s)$. The answer pattern would then be allocated to the diagnostic category for which the highest $p(d|s)$ was obtained, that is, to the most probable diagnostic category. In Maxwell's example the application of this rule led to the correct classification of 51 per cent of his hypothetical population. What of the rest? Like discriminant analysis this method gives probabilities for other diagnoses as well as the most probable one and so misclassification could be reduced by accepting as an agreement with a clinician's diagnosis any of a group of most probable categories. The rule can also be modified so that it avoids particularly undesirable specific misclassifications. For instance, in Maxwell's group it might be more serious to misclassify affective disorders than neurotic depressives and the probabilities can be adjusted so that there is a decrease in the misclassifications of the former at the expense of an increase in the misclassification of the latter.

So far we have dealt only with the performance of the technique on the sample from which the probabilities were calculated. As in the case of the discriminant technique, the crux is the application of the decision rule to entirely new data. The proportion of misclassifications will almost certainly be much greater.

Another disadvantage of this sort of approach is that the number of symptoms that can be dealt with is limited. Fifty symptoms, for example, would yield an astronomical number of symptom patterns and this would mean that a very large sample of people would be needed to establish the probabilities of the symptoms given the diagnoses, $p(s \mid d)$. One way to combat this disadvantage would be to take symptoms a few at a time and discard those that discriminated least well so that the probabilities were finally calculated from only a few very important questions. But is is doubtful whether psychiatric diagnosis could ever be made on 'yes/no' replies to as few as, say, ten questions.

Scheinok and Rinaldo (1968) reported a comparison of a discriminant technique with a modified Bayesian method. Neither of the two was clearly better; each was better for certain diagnostic categories, but the problem used was that of diagnosis of upper abdominal pain and only eleven symptoms were used. Thus one important difficulty in the Bayesian approach was avoided.

The problem of diagnostic categories

Of the two actuarial techniques discussed here the discriminant technique seems to have the wider scope and fewer disadvantages. DIAGNO II compares well with it in agreement with clinicians. The point has been emphasized before, however, that other clinicians do little better than these programs in agreeing with their colleagues. Now clearly psychological or psychiatric diagnosis has special problems of this sort that are not such an important feature of physical medicine. In the latter, the diagnosis can usually be confirmed even if it has to be at autopsy. In mental disorder such clear confirmation is rarely available.

The diagnostic techniques mentioned so far have started out with diagnoses already made by clinicians and have compared with them the diagnoses of computer programs. However, there are also methods which do not start with previously diagnosed groups but instead the categories are derived from the analysis. Systems of content analysis such as that of Iker and Harway (1969) use factor analysis on the transcripts of interviews and other material. The use by Gurney, Roth and Garside (1970) of principle component analysis is another example. They attempt to distinguish by this means between anxiety and depression. This may seem to be an easy thing to do, but what these investigators were seeking were crucial differences between the two in terms of detailed symptoms and the patients' past history. There is no room here to describe the study in detail, only to say that when the computer program is given the task of producing classifications it might produce classifications which are new to us and which could be clinically useful. For example, whereas we may have failed to find biochemical differences between two current categories of diagnosis, a rearrangement of patients on the basis of new categories might expose differences. Such new classifications could eventually become regarded as disease entities. Disagreement between clinicians may stem partly from the heterogeneity of kind and form of the information they seek from patients, but to regard current diagnostic categories as immutable would be unduly complacent.

The computer as therapist

It is only a small step in fancy to imagine the computer as therapist. It could be compared with human therapists in any way in which comparisons *between* human therapists are made. One does not need to enter into any controversy about whether the computer is acting intelligently or 'knows' what it is doing. If the therapy is effective then the program has justified its existence. In such sophisticated use of computer programs the storage capacity of the computer would need to be very large and more rules would be required than those generating output from input. For example, the system would have to be capable of bringing a particular interview to an end after an appropriate time. The main point to be made by this speculation is that the problems at this stage are problems of what *any* interview, live or automated, is achieving. If we are to judge the quality of automated interviewing against that of live interviewing conducted for the same purpose, then we need to be sure that the latter is achieving what we would like it to achieve. This is the same problem as that found in the use of computers in interpretation and diagnosis.

A simpler problem is posed by the automation of behaviour therapy.

in which the interaction between patient and therapist is less complex than in the usual interview. Particularly because of its repetitive and logical arrangement this is a likely candidate for early and widespread automation. Lang (1969) reports that desensitization therapy carried out automatically on phobic patients has achieved results comparable with those obtained with a human operator. His first system consisted of two decks of recorded material each of which could be switched in automatically in response to output from the patient. One deck contained the usual hierarchy of fear-producing scenes composed from knowledge of the patient's symptoms. The other contained relaxation instructions. During a session the patient was exposed to fear stimuli of increasing strength until he reported fear by pressing a button. This switched to the other deck which gave instructions to stop imagining the fear-producing scene and resumed relaxation instructions before switching back to the first deck for a repeat of the fear stimulus. If the patient then 'succeeded' on this item further trials were given, if he reported fear again an item was selected one step lower in the hierarchy. This is the basis of Lang's system. He reports that a new system, on-line with a LINC 8 computer, will be much more flexible in response and will deal not only with the patient's fear as expressed by his pressing the button but also with antonomic activity recorded first-hand.

The analysis of physiological responses in clinical psychology

The use of electro-physiological recording for diagnosis in neurology is well established. Such measures as the E.E.G. and various stimulus-evoked responses from the central nervous system have been made much more powerful tools by means of on-line averaging and frequency analysing techniques. Thus the E.E.G. waveform can be analysed into separate frequencies and the presence detected of unusual frequencies or unusual frequency spectra. Responses, in terms of a change in electrical potential at the scalp not visible on a single occasion, evoked from the central nervous system by a stimulus, can be made detectable by averaging techniques. When signals recorded from several occasions are averaged, the noise which hides the signal on any one occasion tends to cancel out, making the evoked response visible. Such instances, and many more, are described by Uttal (1967).

The use of these measures as instruments for the assessment of various internal states, such as anxiety, falls clearly within psychology, as does their relation to behaviour in general. Such use was mentioned at the end of the last section. One of the biggest contributions made by experimental psychology to clinical practice has been the introduction of training procedures to eliminate undesirable behaviour or emotional states. It is not unlikely that such methods, which now deal with such disorders as phobias and anxiety states, will broaden out into psycho-somatics. Indeed, the autonomic nervous system may be capable of quite detailed and effective training and retraining. Miller (1969) clearly sees this possibility. This is likely to be the chief growth point in the on-line analysis of physiological recordings in clinical psychology.

Sensory prosthesis

A very exciting recent development, of interest to psychologists because it involves sensory experience, introduces the possibility of a miniature portable computer on-line to the human brain directly, though such a computer may be an analog computer and therefore not part of the main concern of this book. A recent conference (Sterling *et al.*, 1971) explored the idea of visual prosthesis in some detail.

The method proposed makes use of 'phosphenes'. These are the visual experience which results from direct stimulation of the surface of the cerebral cortex. They take the form of a point of light occupying a spatial position. This means that stimulation of two points on the brain surface will yield an experience of two separate points of light, and indeed there is some experimental evidence favouring the possibility that if many points are stimulated, then a pattern of lights will be seen which corresponds to the spatial pattern of the points of stimulation.

It thus seems more than likely that a complex pattern of stimulation can be experienced visually without the use of the eyes. Input to a prosthesis could be in the form of a camera-like instrument which throws an image on to a sensitive screen (the eye of a guide dog has been suggested). The problem then is to convert this image into a matrix of points, each of which will drive a stimulator. It is not known how com-plex the pattern could be, that is, how large a matrix of points of stimu-lation could be used, but whatever the size of such a matrix it is very likely that its effectiveness can be increased by relatively simple pre-processing of the input after the matrix of points has been formed.

Such preprocessing would require a simple computer. The type of processing that has been suggested (Sterling and colleagues, 1971) is somewhat similar to the processing carried out by the visual system between input and the primary projection areas. Imagine a matrix of points each of which can be one of many shades of grey. A newspaper photograph is such a matrix. Various transformations can be carried out on the brightness values of these points which will have the effect of intensifying useful information in the picture at the expense, perhaps, of other (but less useful and therefore expendable) information. Such preprocessing increases the information-carrying capacity of a matrix of a given size. Since in a prosthetic device of the kind envisaged, the size of matrix is likely to be fairly limited, preprocessing will add considerably to the complexity of 'visual' input with which the device can cope.

Both during the development of these instruments and in their use there will be psychological problems, problems of what perceptual information is likely to be most useful to a newly 'sighted' patient and problems of sensory and perceptual learning involved in processing such information. Previous reports of recovery of sight suggest also that the emotional problems may be significant (Gregory and Wallace, 1963).

Conclusion

Computers have been shown to be capable of playing a useful part in several of the tasks of clinical psychology and psychiatry. In data storage and retrieval they are clearly already successful; in test administration and interpretation their usefulness has been proved; and in diagnosis they have achieved good agreement with clinicians.

A final problem that should be mentioned pervades all the uses of computers described in this chapter. It is that of confidence. Even if the computer is dedicated in the technical sense to a clinical task, safeguards must be provided to prevent confidential information from being available to those who should not have it. It should not be difficult to build into a program devices which prevent unauthorized access and this must be done. One might argue that a computer store is less accessible than a clinician's files, but unauthorized access to the latter would usually involve something akin to burglary. The stealing of information from a computer is too new a kind of misdemeanour to have, as yet, elicited from society any adequate self-protective response.

Further Reading

Kleinmuntz, B. (1969) *Clinical Information Processing by Computer.* Holt, Rinehart and Winston, New York. A full account of automatic processing of clinical data.

Maxwell, A. E. (1961) *Analysing Qualitative Data.* Methuen, London. Chapter 10 gives a simple application of Bayes' Theorem to diagnosis.

Meehl, P. E. (1954) *Clinical Versus Statistical Prediction.* University of Minesota Press, Minneapolis. A classic in the field of automatic decision-making.

CHAPTER 10

The Computer in Education and Training

Michael J. Apter and Geoffrey Barrett

Consider a schoolteacher, weary and chalk-covered, fighting to make his voice heard. Then consider a modern high-speed electronic digital computer humming away in its impeccable air-conditioned surroundings. These two images, when juxtaposed, have a certain surrealistic quality. And yet the world of the teacher and the world of the computer are already being brought closer to each other.

There are of course a number of ways in which computers may become of service to teachers and lecturers—and to training officers in industry—in the future. In particular, there are obvious administrational uses: for example, they may be used to help solve complex problems of resource allocation and time-tabling and also for record-keeping. Important as such administrational applications may turn out to be however, they are not the subject of this chapter. This chapter is concerned with the far more interesting and central topic of teaching and learning itself and with the role of the computer as instructor in schools and universities and training departments. This field is usually referred to as 'Computer-Assisted Instruction' (CAI) or, less frequently, 'Computer-Assisted Learning' (CAL). Presumably the shorter and less modest terms 'computer instruction' and 'computer learning' are not used because of possible confusion—in the former case with learning *about* computers and in the latter with learning *by* computers. Also, the longer terms are presumably less provocative to educationists.

The origin and development of CAI

Computer-assisted instruction may be said to be the child of computer technology and programmed instruction, the latter being in turn an offspring of the psychology of learning.

As computer technology developed, especially during the 1950s, it became increasingly evident that it should be possible to apply it to teaching. After all, teaching can be regarded as essentially a form of information-processing and transmission in which two kinds of information are involved: subject-matter information (history, geography, etc) and information about students. The latter is used, at least in part, to determine certain aspects of the presentation of the former—such as speed of presentation. However, it was not until the crucial development of time-sharing and multi-access computer systems (see Chapter 1) that the use of the computer for real-time teaching began to seem as if it might become an economic feasibility. 'Real-time' in this context means that the computer responds immediately to the student throughout instruction. But even with time-sharing systems, which allow a large number of students to be taught simultaneously by one computer, it has to be admitted that it may be many years before computers become economically comparable to teachers. It has been estimated, by projecting the trend for increasing teacher salaries and decreasing computer hardware costs, that it will be nearly forty years, in the United Kingdom, before the costs of large system computer-assisted instruction will become equal to the costs of conventional secondary school education for the lower forms (National Council for Educational Technology, 1969). This may seem discouraging, but it is likely that sooner or later computer-assisted instruction will become economically advantageous and that in certain areas of education (e.g. at university level) this will happen in the nearer future. If this is true it follows that it is worth developing software techniques now for the day when it might be possible to put them, or variants of them, into practice widely. It should also be added that for some purposes, like remedial teaching, cost may not be the primary consideration for a system that proves itself to be effective.

Meanwhile, too, the computer can already be used reasonably economically for off-line guidance of the instructional process, rather than for direct on-line teaching. That is, it can be used to prescribe learning materials which are already available and are not stored in the computer or its terminals (e.g. film loops, sections of books, conventional teaching machine programmes) to individual students. The decision as to which particular materials a particular student is to use at a particular time can be made by the computer on the basis of regular tests given to such students by the teacher and marked off-line by the computer. Such tests may be given daily for example, the computer marking them and prescribing on the basis of each student's results which materials he is to use the next day. This realistic approach to the immediate use of the computer in the classroom is becoming known as 'Computer-Managed Instruction' (see Brudner, 1968) and is something of a cross between using a computer for administrational and instructional purposes. In this chapter however, for reasons of space, attention will be confined to computer-assisted instruction proper.

Not only is it to be expected that computers will become cheaper over the years, but also that they will become more sophisticated in various ways that will be advantageous to CAI. A good example of this is in input-output equipment. A standard way of communicating with computers in an on-line mode has for a long time been by means of computer-controlled teletypewriters, used both for typing information into the computer and for getting information out. In the latter case, the computer types the information on to a roll of paper. Much early work on CAI used this kind of equipment as the student-computer interface. It has the advantage of being flexible, but it can be rather slow and noisy and has obvious limitations where graphic material is involved. An alternative was to store information peripherally by means of computer-controlled slide-projectors or tape-recorders and perhaps to allow the student to respond by means of a small set of buttons as in branching teaching machines (see below). Indeed, teaching machines themselves under computer control have been used as student terminals. But the use of buttons for student response is restrictive. And although the use of peripheral storage facilities can overcome the problem of the display of graphic material, there may still be problems of speed: for example it may take some time for the correct slide or section of tape to be found and moved into position. It also has the disadvantage that a great deal of material has to be pre-programmed and the computer may lose much of its flexibility in this way. Such CAI systems, where the computer controls peripherally stored information only, have been referred to scathingly, if a little unfairly, as 'degenerate computer teaching machines' (Uttal, 1967).

However, recent developments have in principle overcome these kinds of problems and considerably extended the possibilities for flexible computer-student interaction. In particular, the use of the cathode-ray tube (CRT) allows centrally stored or generated information to be displayed rapidly and quietly to the student. Such information can include graphic displays like geometric diagrams, engineering drawings, etc., as well as text. Also, parts of the display may be altered without the whole display having to be changed: for example, arrows may be introduced and removed to emphasize different parts of the diagram or words can be underlined with the same effect. A further advance has been in the development of CRT terminals which can be used in conjunction with a 'light pen' (Chapter 1, p. 22). When this touches the CRT the computer can sense the coordinates of the area touched. The student can be required to respond by touching an appropriate area of the CRT display, the computer being programmed to accept certain areas as correct and others as incorrect. In even more elaborate systems light pens can be used to draw lines and using such pens students can construct their own graphic responses. It need hardly be added that light pen systems even of the simpler kind are still prohibitively expensive except for special experimental work. But looking to the future it seems almost inevitable that they will become widely used for CAI purposes.

As already noted, CAI has emerged as a result not just of the advent of computer technology but also as part of the development of that branch of the psychology of learning which concerns programmed instruction and teaching machines. The major catalyst in bringing this area into being in the early 1950s was the work of B. F. Skinner. Although Skinner was not the first to conceive of the idea of teaching machines he gave the idea shape and direction by using such machines to present programmes constructed on the basis of principles derived from his work on operant conditioning, especially with pigeons. (N.B. To avoid confusion, from this point on in this chapter the spelling 'programme' will be used to refer to teaching programmes, and the spelling 'program' to refer to computer programs.)

The paradigm Skinner carried over into human teaching was that of 'shaping'. This is a technique which can be used to teach an animal responses of, seemingly, any degree of complexity, under the control of reinforcement. For example, a pigeon can be taught to pace out a figure eight. As soon as the animal makes a response which could be a start to this piece of behaviour, e.g. turning its head or taking a step towards the right, it is reinforced (usually with food). The reinforced response is quickly repeated (in accordance with the law of effect). Reinforcement is then withheld until the response is more marked. In this way reinforcement is progressively withheld until a complete half-turn is built up. In a similar way, the pigeon is led to produce the complete figure eight until it is finally only reinforced for producing the complete piece of behaviour.

Classroom teaching, it seemed to Skinner, could proceed on the same kind of basis. The aim of the teaching should be specified in terms of behavioural responses, the student being led to the attainment of these responses, however simple or complex, by means of a step-by-step shaping procedure. Instead of waiting for behaviour to occur spontaneously, questions could be asked (often in the form of blanks in sentences which have to be filled in) and reinforcement was said to occur whenever the student got the answer to the question right: i.e. getting the answer right was believed to be itself reinforcing in this context. And thus the so-called 'linear' method of programmed instruction was developed in which a linear sequence of 'frames' is presented to the student, each frame containing some information, asking a question and (at the beginning of the frame) giving the right answer to the question on the previous frame. The essence of the technique is that the student should be getting the answers to the questions right most of the time, and the programme is constructed to ensure this as far as possible. Such programmes can be presented in book form, or by means of special machines.

In the late 1950s a different method of programmed instruction was developed in America by Norman Crowder and others. It seemed to Crowder that the linear method of teaching was unnecessarily slow and cumbersome for teaching human beings, and that it would be possible to teach more efficiently by moving in larger steps and using questions for diagnostic purposes rather than for purposes of reinforcement. Then if the student made a mistake on any frame, he could be given information relating to this particular mistake: his error might be explained to him, the relevant concept described again in a different way, and so on. To accomplish this Crowder conceived the idea of following the question on each frame by a set of alternative answers to that question: i.e. the questions would be of the 'multiple-choice' rather than the 'constructed response' variety used in Skinnerian programmes. If the student made the right choice he would be taken automatically to the next frame in the main teaching sequence and he would be informed of his correctness at the beginning of this frame. If he made a mistake by choosing a wrong answer then he would be taken automatically to a different, remedial, frame relating to that mistake. He would then be returned to the frame on which he made the original error for another attempt at answering the question. In more complicated cases there may be a further question and alternative answers on the remedial frame itself. In this kind of way each student would have just as much information as he needed and no more: if he was making right choices he could proceed through the programme more rapidly than would be possible with a linear programme, if he made mistakes then remedial action would be taken relating to those particular mistakes. In other words, the programme would adapt to some extent to each student who took it. The structure of such a programme is a branching one with remedial frames branching away from main sequence frames. Figure 10.1 depicts a simple example of this, in which each main sequence frame is related to two different remedial frames. In more complicated cases other remedial frames may branch from first order remedial frames. Programmes of this general kind have therefore become known as 'branching programmes' as distinct from the Skinnerian 'linear programmes'.

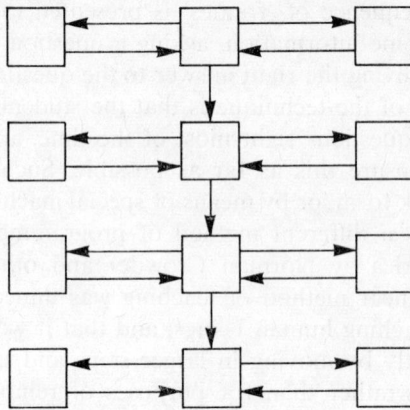

Figure 10.1—*A branching sequence of frames. The main sequence is shown in the centre row*

As with linear programmes, branching programmes can be presented in book form. In this case there is typically one frame per page and the alternative answers have page numbers against them, the student turning to the page whose number corresponds to the answer which he thinks is correct. It is, however, less time-consuming for the student, if more expensive, for the programme to be presented on a teaching machine. Here the alternative answers may have letters against them and the student simply has to press the button with the letter corresponding to the answer he has chosen; the machine does the rest.

The computer as can be seen played no direct part in the development of programmed instruction. It may, however, have played an important indirect one in the sense that the development of computers created an atmosphere in which it no longer seemed absurd to think of machines behaving intelligently and in ways that were previously assumed to be uniquely human. If machines, like computers, could play chess and write poetry and music, why should they not also be able to teach? Because of computers, therefore, many teachers and others have become less hostile to the strange idea of machine teaching than they otherwise would have been.

Once programmed instruction had developed, however, it became increasingly likely that computer technology would begin to play a direct part in it and that the computer would become used as a more sophisticated kind of teaching machine. If teaching machines of the branching type make decisions about what information and exercises to present on the basis of student responses, then in principle the more intelligent the machine the more appropriate and adaptive the decisions it can make might become. It will be clear, then, that computer-assisted instruction is an extension of the branching rather than the linear type of programmed instruction. It shares, however, with both kinds of programmed instruction an insistence on the setting of objective instructional goals.

Not everyone even in the field of programmed instruction has welcomed computer-assisted instruction. It is ironic that some of the arguments used by teachers to oppose programmed instruction are now being used by supporters of programmed instruction against CAI: for example, that it is too expensive, it is likely to replace the teacher, and so on. To adapt Shaw's famous maxim, it is almost as if there is a sequence of sneering of the following kind: 'He who can, does. He who cannot, teaches. He who cannot teach, writes teaching programmes. He who cannot write teaching programmes, gets a computer to write teaching programmes for him.'

The compelling reason why one should want to use a computer emerges if one realizes the many limitations upon the degree and precision of adaptation possible with a branching teaching programme (and, *a fortiori*, a linear teaching programme). Among them are the following:

1. A given programme is constructed and validated for a limited range of subjects, e.g. those of average intelligence. The programme may be inappropriate for subjects outside this range.

2. Teaching programmes are completely pre-programmed. Although some adaptation occurs during teaching with a branching teaching programme, the amount and kind of adaptation is limited to what has already been written in the programme. This may be far from ideal for a particular student:

   (*a*) he can make a mistake not accounted for in the multiple-choice answers provided;

   (*b*) he can choose the correct answer from a list of answers by chance;

   (*c*) if he exhausts the list of incorrect multiple-choice answers, no new ones are created to prevent him getting the right answer by a process of exclusion;

   (*d*) he can make a mistake for which there is a branch, but not have his particular reason for making the mistake explained to him;

   (*e*) he may get answers right throughout the programme but only do so after spending an inordinately long time on each question;

   (*f*) he may get all the answers right throughout the programme but

could have reached the same standard at the end of the programme
with a shorter programme;

(g) he can want information which is not in the programme.

It is probably true to say that each of these limitations has already
been at least partially overcome in one or another computer teaching
system. Some of the ways in which this has occurred will emerge in the
next section of this chapter in which different CAI techniques are looked
at and examples given.

Although CAI can be regarded as an extension of the branching
method, the latter method, as we shall see, has been developed and
extended in so many different ways in CAI that it is perhaps misleading
to think of CAI as a distinct method, like the linear or branching
methods of programmed instruction. A preliminary distinction which it
is useful to make about CAI systems is between drill-and-practice
systems, tutorial systems and Socratic systems. This distinction is not
based on hardware but on the general organization of the instruction.
Nor is the distinction a clear-cut one and there is a great deal of over-
lapping between these categories. The simplest CAI systems are the
drill-and-practice ones. These tend to deal with rather low-level skills
like spelling and elementary arithmetic skills (simple addition, subtraction, multiplication and division). The computer presents graded
exercises and problems but apart from this, little is given in the way of
information, including hints, to the student. Problem-choice and presentation variables may relate to student performance in various ways
however. *Tutorial systems* operate like branching programmes in giving
a great deal of information as well as questions which follow the information to which they are related. Instruction is computer-determined
although contingent on student performance; indeed, branching programmes have sometimes been looked on as the simplest form of tutorial
system. But CAI tutorial systems tend to be more complex than branching programmes, taking into account more information than the most
recent response in making instructional decisions. *Socratic* CAI systems
are the most elaborate and sophisticated of all in that they are more
student-determined in their instructional sequence than tutorial systems.
That is to say the student can, within limits, determine the course of
his instruction. For example, he might ask the computer questions
rather than wait to be asked questions. Unfortunately, these terms are
not yet well standardized, which can make reading CAI literature a
little confusing. For example, the term 'adaptive' is sometimes used
instead of 'tutorial'. Again the terms 'dialogue' and 'inquiry' are sometimes used instead of 'Socratic'. (Indeed, the word 'interactive' as used

in Chapter 4 of the present book, would also be suitable to describe Socratic systems in CAI; and Project Grammarama, given there as an example of an interactive study, involved a Socratic teaching technique.)

There are many other sources of confusion. For example, 'Socratic' is not to be confused with the important (but now terminated) SOCRATES CAI project at the University of Illinois which, in fact, did not use Socratic methods. SOCRATES will be described in the next section. Again, the term 'adaptive' is sometimes used more generally to mean any teaching system which adapts to the student; in this sense it would include 'Socratic' and 'drill-and-practice' as well as 'tutorial' systems. The term 'adaptive' is also used specifically to refer to teaching systems in which the value of stimulus parameters may be altered as a function of some feature of a subject's previous performance. The term used in Chapter 4 to refer to systems which function in this way was 'closed-loop'. The aim of such closed-loop systems in CAI is to optimize learning in some way and they are used especially to teach skills. The closed-loop study of Guest and Sime described in Chapter 4 (pp. 105–6) is an example of an adaptive teaching system of this kind. Another example would be the work of Kelley as it relates to training, which was referred to in Chapter 6 (pp. 170–1). The best known adaptive systems in this sense must be the special teaching machines which have been built by Gordon Pask (viz. Pask, 1965, 1966). With these, skills like punching business machine cards are taught through practice tasks in which the difficulty of the task at each stage is related to the student's measured proficiency. It should be noted that adaptive teaching of this kind often involves the construction of special-purpose computing equipment rather than the use of general-purpose digital computers. In this chapter, for simplicity, we shall keep strictly to the 'drill-and-practice'/'tutorial'/'Socratic' terminology. We shall be concentrating on the use of general-purpose computers for instructional purposes rather than specially built teaching devices.

In Chapter 2 it was noted that high-level languages have been developed for particular problem areas. Computer-assisted instruction is one such area that has seen the development of a number of problem-oriented high-level languages. These languages allow CAI programs to be written conveniently and simply. A good example of such a language is COURSEWRITER developed by Grubb and Selfridge (1963). The programmer using this language has available a number of symbols which can bring into operation complex sequences of computer instructions. For example the symbol 'qu' when attached to a unit of course material designates this material as a question and, when encountered by the computer, causes it to type out the question to the student. The computer then automatically waits for the student to respond and stores the response.

CAI techniques

The computer has the possibility, suitably programmed, of being more life-like and intelligent than a teaching machine, and of interacting with and adapting to the student in ways which might resemble much more closely the ways in which a human teacher interacts with students. It does not necessarily have limitations of the kind that, as we have seen, so restrict the conventional teaching machine. The problem in computer-assisted instruction, therefore, is generally seen as being to program the computer to perform all the instructional functions that the teacher does so well: making decisions, adapting the teaching material, generating questions, responding to questions and answers by students in natural language, and in general attempting to optimize the learning process. This being the case, it is perhaps surprising that the designers of instructional systems have started by merely postulating models for these processes instead of making a thorough investigation of the methods used by teachers for these processes or taking previous investigations into account. The latter approach has been used in the design of a man-machine counselling system. The prior investigation was an initial survey of eighty-seven counsellors and a systems analysis of the counselling operations on a field site (Cogswell *et al.*, 1968). The pilot study for this work suggested that the counsellors were merely processing and transmitting information, and that the computer could free them from this to deal with more difficult individual cases. Teachers process and transmit information perhaps in a similar way.

In this section some of the techniques used for decisions, adaptation, etc., in CAI are considered. Some techniques are simple and some complex, but this really depends on the method of instruction used; techniques used for drill-and-practice can be extremely simple while those for tutorial and Socratic systems are necessarily more complex.

First, because many CAI techniques depend on the history of responses, consideration is given to this aspect of instruction and to an example from the literature illustrating how comprehensive the history can be, and how the history is used to optimize the learning of a spelling list.

History of responses

The concept of a *sufficient* history is considered by Atkinson (1967). An instructional program can branch according to the value of the sufficient history, which is an estimate of the student's state of learning. The history is called *sufficient* because it summarizes all the information concerning the state of learning in such a way that no other history could provide additional information. The concept is similar to that of a sufficient statistic. For example, the mean summarizes all the information about the central tendency of a parametric set of data, and it is *sufficient* because no other measure can tell us more about this central tendency. However, the validity of these measures is also important— the statistician does not use variance as a measure of central tendency and, similarly, the form of the learning history depends on the variables used in the instructional model. Such variables may include counts of correct and incorrect responses and the reaction times of these responses (reaction time being used as a measure of response confidence).

Groen and Atkinson (1966) distinguish between two types of decision rule: response sensitive and response insensitive. Response sensitive strategies act on a moment-to-moment assessment of the student's history. Thus the linear programmes of Skinner, which do not use any measure of past performance, are examples of a response insensitive strategy. Branching programmes are minimally sensitive in these terms because although they are response sensitive they are only sensitive to the single, most recent, response. Computers, in contrast, may store and respond on the basis of many previous responses and therefore be highly response sensitive. Atkinson and Wilson (1968) describe how the one-element model of stimulus sampling theory has been applied at Stanford University to the learning process for a spelling task. This response sensitive procedure illustrates how the instructional technique determines the type of response history to be kept.

The task is to learn the spelling of N items on n trials where n is much greater than N. In this case a trial is the presentation of a single item. The items are presented in any order for the first N trials and the following strategy is used over the remaining $n-N$.

(i) Two counters are set up for each item in the list. The P-counter keeps track of the number of times the item has been presented, and the R-counter counts the length of the most recent run of correct responses to the item. At the end of trial N all the P-counters are set to 1 and all the R-counters to 0.

(ii) On any trial, an item is presented if its R-count is least among the R-counts for all items. When several items are eligible, the item that has the smallest P-count is presented. When several items are still eligible, the item with the slowest reaction time on its last presentation is presented.

(iii) Following a trial the P-counter for the item presented is increased by 1. The R-counter for the item is increased by 1 if the subject's response was correct and reset to 0 if the response was incorrect.

Briefly, the item with the shortest run of correct responses is presented. If more than one item has the same length run, the item that has been presented fewest times will be given. If more than one item still qualifies, that with the slowest reaction time (least confidence) is presented. The same sort of history might be kept by the teacher—i.e. number of presentations of a particular item, number of times in succession that this item is spelt correctly and confidence of response. The last measure, for the teacher, would involve more than reaction time; it would include a host of interpersonal measures.

Not all instructional models use the same type of history as that outlined, nor do they use the history in the same way, as will be indicated in the examples given later. This is just one way in which storing a history of responses may be used in CAI.

Decision structures

Decisions can be made in CAI on simple histories or on more complex histories. An example of a simple decision procedure is that which was used in the Stanford Arithmetic Program (Suppes *et al.*, 1968). The project was designed to teach addition, subtraction, multiplication and division to children from grades 3, 4, 5 and 6 of an American elementary school. The method of instruction was drill-and-practice and the material presented was graded into five levels of difficulty, where level 1 was mainly remedial in character and level 5 contained the most difficult material. Difficulty here was judged on an intuitive basis. Each student took one five-minute lesson per day during which 20 problems were presented. The level of difficulty of problems presented depended simply on the previous day's score. If the student scored between 60 per cent and 70 per cent, the level of difficulty remained the same on the next day. If the student scored less than 60 per cent, the level of difficulty dropped by one, while if the student scored 80 per cent or more, the level of difficulty went up by one. The students could not go below level 1 or above level 5 (see Figure 10.2). On the first day all students started at level 3, and the problems within each level became more difficult from day-to-day to keep pace with topics introduced by the teacher.

The history in this example is simply the student's score on the twenty problems presented during one lesson. The decision according to the student's performance is taken while the student is off-line; i.e.

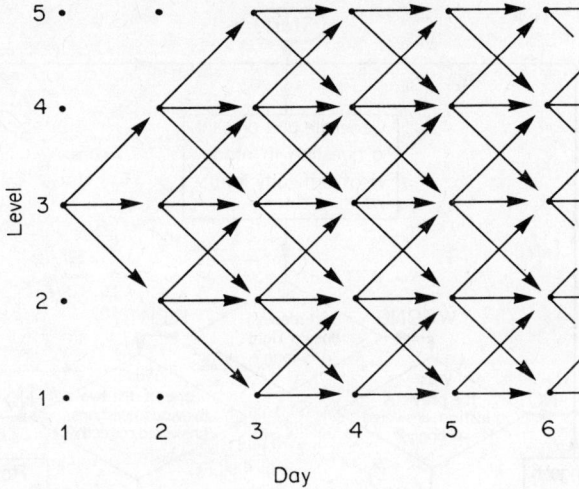

Figure 10.2—*Branching structure used in the Stanford Arithmetic Program*
(from Suppes, Jerman and Brian, 1968)

there is no decision to change a difficulty level whilst the student is working through a block of problems.

Another instructional program for arithmetic involves a much more dynamic decision-making procedure for varying the levels of problem difficulty (Wexler, 1970). The program, COACH (COnstructed Arithmetic and Controlled Help) uses eight levels of difficulty, where 'difficulty' is defined objectively in a way which will be described later in the chapter. Each difficulty level is subdivided into ten ranges which represent finer gradations of difficulty and the history of performance on problems in these ranges determines the difficulty of the problem to be presented next (see Figure 10.3). The range is raised if the student answers two out of three consecutive questions in a range correctly. A student who needs to be told the correct answer to two consecutive questions from the same range has his range lowered. Another feature of the decision structure is an acceleration factor. This allows the student with obvious ability to progress through the ranges faster than normal. The student answering each question correctly would normally be asked two questions in the first range of a level, two in the second, two in the third, etc. However, this slow rate of increase may prove boring to the student, so an acceleration factor is added to the last range to give the next range, which may yield a higher than normal range for the next question. The acceleration factor may start at one, at the beginning of a level, and be increased by one for every two consecutive ranges that

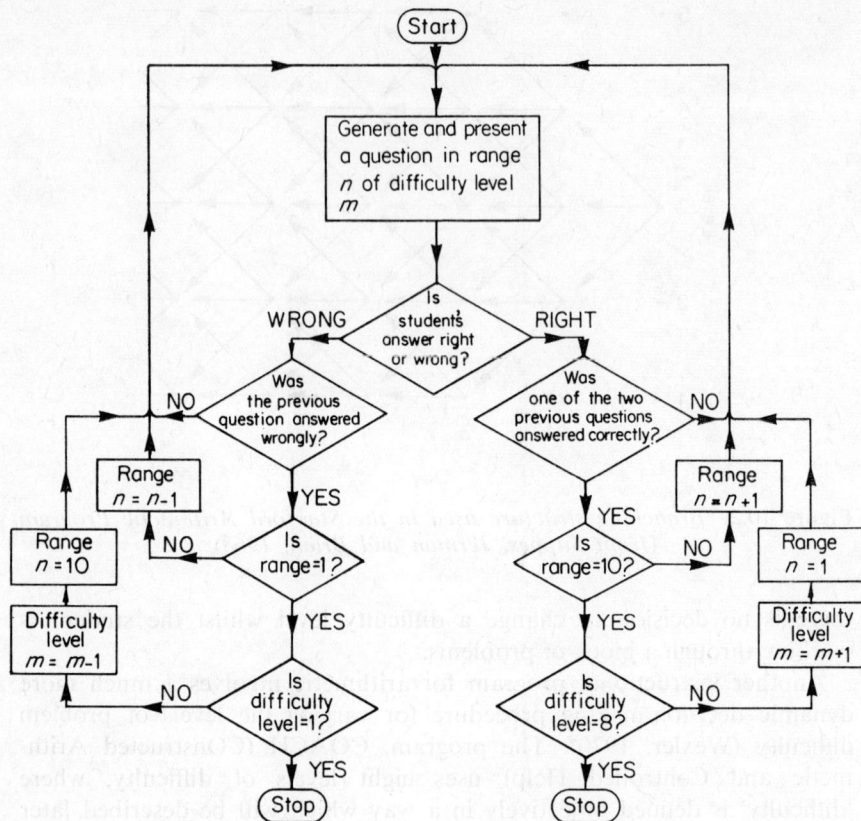

Figure 10.3—*Decision procedure in COACH (based on Wexler, 1970)*

have their questions answered correctly. For example, the following
progression of ranges can occur:

Range in level 3	1	2	3	5	7	10
Acceleration factor	1	1	2	2	3	3

Instead of returning the acceleration factor to one for the start of the
next level, the program reduces the factor by one so that the student can
continue working at his own fast rate. Thus acceleration factor 3 in
this example would be reduced to 2 and the following progression would
occur in level 4 if the student continued to answer all the questions
correctly:

Range in level 4	1	3	5	8
Acceleration factor	2	2	3	3

The acceleration factor is also used in the decision procedure for decreasing ranges, when the student has to be told the correct answer to a question.

One difference between this project and the Stanford project, is the amount of time spent at the teletypewriter terminal by the students. The Stanford students could only spend five minutes a day at the teletypewriter while Wexler quotes a run of forty minutes using his program.

The COACH program is an example of an enriched drill-and-practice instructional system because it provides hints to the student when he gives an incorrect answer. However, it does not provide new information to the student; this prevents it from being a tutorial system. The decision rules applied in COACH could easily be implemented on the Stanford system which used rather inflexible decision procedures. As can be inferred from the examples given, a student using the COACH system can advance immediately by one level of difficulty after answering twelve questions. The student using the Stanford system has to answer twenty questions of the same difficulty before a decision is made, and wait until the next day. (Note, however, that the concept of 'difficulty' differs between the two systems). In the absence of comparative data on teaching effectiveness the COACH system is probably to be preferred. This is because with the hints it provides it might well be more interesting for the student—as well as being, as we have seen, more flexible.

A more complex decision procedure is described by Smallwood (1962). This is designed so that the history of outcomes of a particular decision determines whether that decision is made again under the same circumstances. In other words, the decision procedure can be changed with experience, i.e. the computer learns about teaching a topic from students' attempts to learn that topic from it. The information to be taught is divided into 'levels' in the same way that information is divided into frames in programmed instruction. But for each level there are a number of parallel frames which cover the same information in different ways. These, Smallwood refers to as 'blocks'. The student therefore progresses by moving from level to level of the program but which block he goes to at each level is determined by the decision structure. It is rather as if the student had access to a number of parallel teaching machine programmes and can be switched between programmes as he proceeds, according to the suitability of each programme for his needs (See Figure 10.4). Students are asked a question about the material presented in a block immediately after it has been presented. If they answer incorrectly the decision structure either branches them to a different block in the same level or to a block in the previous level. The decision is based on the student's past history (in this system defined as the ratio of total number of correct responses to total number of questions presented) and on the probability of giving a particular response to the block question. The probability is estimated on the basis of the responses of a sample of students with the same history of responses as the student being instructed. Where there are no students with the same response history a decision is made on the basis of a statistical formula.

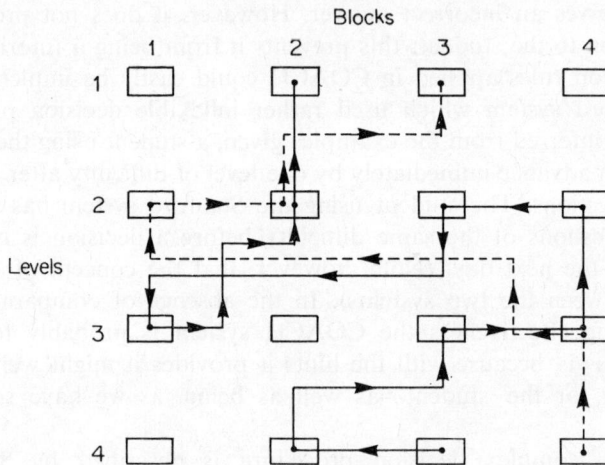

Figure 10.4—*Two possible routes through a combination of blocks and levels*

Smallwood's decision structure can also be modified by the instructor according to specific criteria such as:

(i) a maximization of the increase of a student's score on tests administered at the beginning and end of a course of instruction,
(ii) a maximization of the rate of learning,
(iii) a minimization of the time to complete the course.

Stolurow (1965) describes a system that uses extrinsic as well as intrinsic information about the student. The attempt to use extrinsic information, such as measures of aptitude and personality, in the decision structure makes this approach different from any discussed so far. Intrinsic information is Stolurow's term for the student's response history. The basic philosophy of the decision structure is very similar to that of Smallwood except that extrinsic information about the student replaces the performance estimation model used in Smallwood's system. Combinations of intrinsic and extrinsic information about the student are used, for example, in decisions about presentation of knowledge of results and any other feedback.

The system developed by Stolurow at Illinois has the acronym SOCRATES, denoting System for Organizing Content to Review and Teach Educational Subjects. Some of SOCRATES' decisions are made at a much higher level than those of systems discussed earlier. For any given subject-matter there are a number of different teaching programmes. The decision structure determines not only which programme to give the students initially, but also whether to change the programme during the course of instruction for another programme covering the same material. The extrinsic information about the student is used to determine the initial programme, and the intrinsic information added, during the course of instruction, to the extrinsic information, determines whether the programme should be exchanged. The SOCRATES model divides the teaching process into two stages. During the first stage, called the pre-tutorial stage, a decision is made about which programme to present to the student during the second, tutorial, stage. The decision is based on the student's aptitude level and his performance on a pretest. Also taken into account in the decision process are the objectives of the course of instruction. These are: the final level of performance to be achieved, and the time within which this final level must be achieved by the student.

The tutorial phase of instruction proceeds at two levels both of which have decision structures affecting the method of instruction in some way. At the lower level, referred to as the Teacher Function, decisions are made on the basis of history of responses about the content of the instruction, in other words which particular branches to take in the programme being used. At a higher level a monitor, called the Professor Function, is able to decide whether the instructional programme itself is suitable on the basis of student performance, and if not to exchange the whole programme for another. The Professor Function is an important feature because, to quote Stolurow: 'In order for a system to adapt to a wide range of individual differences in learning it is necessary for it to be capable of changing strategies as well as frames.'

An impressive system described by Grubb (1968) involves decisions made by the student rather than the computer. The system uses a cathode-ray tube display to present the student with a map of a complete course in statistics. The student can point to an area on the map with a light pen and be immediately presented with a more detailed map of this area. In this way he can choose which topic he will study at a particular time. He progresses through the course by using the maps and is therefore responsible for the route he takes.

Optimization

By optimization is meant adaptation by a system to secure the best possible performance in some specified respect, e.g. to maximize the value of some variable. Optimum performance in one respect does not necessarily mean an optimum performance in another. For a system to attempt optimization in CAI a response sensitive decision structure is, it can be argued, highly desirable. Response insensitive structures are not likely to optimize because, as their name suggests, they do not take a student's past history into account.

There are a number of variables which can be considered when choosing which ones are going to be optimized in a CAI system. For example, the designer of an instructional system may wish to optimize the amount of learning, measured as the differences between the scores on a pre-test and a post-test, or he may be concerned with optimizing the rate of learning, or with optimizing the overall cost of instruction or the cost per unit time. He might even wish to optimize variables like student attitude to the subject being taught.

Groen and Atkinson (1966) describe a decision procedure for optimizing the amount of learning at all possible decision stages. It makes use of a mathematical method of optimization based on a dynamic programming analysis as developed by Bellman (1957). This type of analysis is virtually impossible when a large number of stages occur, but Groen and Atkinson suggest that the procedure could be used to find a locally optimal decision for a small number of stages. This decision can then be used in the analysis of the next few stages and so on, until all the possible decision stages have been considered. The experimental procedure of Atkinson and Wilson (1968) which was described earlier is an outcome of this optimization process. However, an experiment reported in the paper by Groen and Atkinson suggests that the method of presentation used by Atkinson and Wilson is no better for improving post-test scores than presentation of the N items an equal number of times, in random order, for n trials. The authors suggest that an optimization theory which assumes a more complicated learning model is required.

In the examples already presented in this chapter all the decision structures are designed to optimize the amount of learning. The acceleration factor included in the COACH decision structure is designed to optimize also the rate of learning, and Smallwood's decision structure allows the instructor to define which of these two factors he wishes to optimize. SOCRATES takes decisions which optimize both the amount of learning and the time spent.

For two reasons the ability to optimize both of these aspects of learning is a desirable feature of decision structures. First the computer needs to prove that it can truly individualize instruction, by teaching people to the limits of their ability. Secondly, from an economic point of view, it is possible to teach more people when they can be taught quickly.

Question generation

Once the decision structure has determined the next question to be presented to a student, the question may be retrieved from the store of the computer and either typed on a teletypewriter or displayed on a cathode-ray tube display. As the size of the store of a computer system is limited there is a finite number of stored questions that can be presented. One method of overcoming this limitation and simultaneously decreasing the amount of money spent on backing store, is to include a procedure for generating the required question or problem. This could also considerably increase the flexibility of the instruction. It is clear, as Uttal (1967) has pointed out, that one major dimension of CAI progress will be from systems that select pre-stored information to systems which can increasingly generate questions and information in accordance with general rules.

The COACH program includes a procedure for generating arithmetic problems with the appropriate difficulty scores described below. In the acknowledged absence of guidance from the psychological literature, Wexler describes a method for calculating the difficulty score of a problem, as a combination of the difficulty scores of the operands (i.e. the numbers used in the calculation). In turn, the operand difficulty score is a combination of a digit score and a position score. In more detail each of the scores mentioned is estimated in the following way:

(i) Digit scores—Wexler considers that the fact that some digits are easier to work with than others should be taken into account, and the following digit scores are assigned to the decimal digits:

Decimal digits			
Digit score = 1	0		
Digit score = 2	1	2	5
Digit score = 3	4	6	8
Digit score = 4	3	7	9

(ii) Position scores—the digits in a number are identified by a particular position. For example, the number 3879 has the digit 9 in position 1, 7 in position 2, and so on. The position scores are:

Position	Position score
1	2
2	3
3	5
4	7
$\geqslant 5$	9

(iii) Operand difficulty scores—this score is equal to the sum of the products of the digit scores times their respective position scores for each digit in the number. Thus the number 3879 has an operand difficulty score of:

(digit score of 9) $\times$ 2 + (digit score of 7) $\times$ 3 + (digit score of 8) $\times$ 5 + (digit score of 3) $\times$ 7
= $(4 \times 2) + (4 \times 3) + (3 \times 5) + (4 \times 7)$
= 8 + 12 + 15 + 28
= 63

Similarly, 25 has an operand difficulty score = $2 \times 2 + 2 \times 3 = 10$

(iv) Problem difficulty score—for addition and subtraction this score is the sum of the operand difficulty scores. Thus 3879 + 25 and 3879 — 25 both have difficulty scores equal to 73. The multiplication metric uses the sum of the operand scores times 1.5, thus 3879 $\times$ 25 has a score of $73 \times 1.5 = 109.5$. For division the score is calculated as the sum of the operand score for the denominator and twice the numerator, all multiplied by two. Therefore, 3879/25 has the score:

$(2 \times 63 + 10) \times 2 = 136 \times 2 = 272.$

Once the decision procedure for COACH has determined a difficulty range for the next problem to be presented, a series of routines generate the numbers to be used in the problem. For example, if an addition problem with difficulty in the range 73 to 75 were required, the routines might generate the problem 3879 + 25. The problems are generated by a process of trial-and-error within the bounds of the maximum problem difficulty score and the minimum problem difficulty score, and the maximum number of digits possible in the operands.

The importance of this procedure is not the programming mechanics by which a problem is generated, but that a metric is defined as a basis for the generation to take place. It would be interesting to compare the objective difficulty of the problems generated by COACH with the subjective difficulty of problems used in the Stanford Arithmetic Program. In fact, Suppes *et al.* (1968) later describe a performance model for addition, subtraction and multiplication that fits their observed data fairly well and, assuming that performance is directly related to difficulty, could be used for generating problems with varying difficulty.

In the latter model the number of steps of transformation, operation and memory, are added together to give a value for the total number of steps expected to be taken by the student in solving a problem, called NSTEPS. Examples of the three classes of operation for addition and subtraction are given below:

(i) Transformation—this refers to the number of operations required to convert a problem into the form where the unknown stands alone on the right of the equal sign which is known as the canonical form. Thus:

$$T(m + n = \_) = 0$$
$$T(m + \_ = p) = 2$$

i.e. in the second case two stages are required, namely:

$$(a) \quad \_ = p - m$$
$$(b) \, p - m = \_ .$$

(ii) Operation—this step takes place after the problem has been transformed to canonical form. The process literally refers to the number of operations which take place in a calculation; e.g.

$$O(8 + 0) = 0$$

but

$$O(3 + 2) = 2$$

because no operation is required for handling zero.

$$O(36 + 21) = 2$$

because one operation is $6 + 1$, and the second is $3 + 2$. However, considering the form ab + cd, when b + d is greater than 9, there are three operations because a 1 has to be carried from the sum of b + d to be added to a; e.g.

$$O(35 + 28) = 3$$

(iii) Memory—this third step also occurs after the problem is in canonical form. It is a measure of the digits or sums that have to be held in memory during the calculation; e.g.

$$M (16 + 13) = 1$$

because only 9, the sum of 6 and 3, must be held in memory while the tens are added. However,

$$M (35 + 28) = 3$$

because, the 1 of 13, (the sum of 8 and 5), the 3 of 13, and the partial sum $1 + 3$, all have to be held in memory at different stages of the addition.

In evaluating the structure of a problem the total number of transformation, operation and memory steps is determined, and called NSTEPS. Thus, for example:

$$25 + 26 = 18 + \_$$

has an NSTEPS of 14, because:

$$\begin{aligned} T (25 + 26 = 18 + \_) &= 1 \\ O (25 + 26 - 18) &= 6 \\ M(25 + 26 - 18) &= 7 \\ \hline &14 \\ \hline \end{aligned}$$

Suppes *et al.* found, in the analysis of their linear regression model of performance, that NSTEPS was the most important variable in predicting both errors and response latencies for addition, subtraction and multiplication. A further analysis of the three components of NSTEPS showed that operation played no role in predicting errors and response latencies for addition. Memory played the most important role in predicting these performance measures and produced nearly as good a fit as NSTEPS when used as a single variable in the analysis.

A further performance model for addition has been suggested by Woods and Hartley (1971). Both the model and performance criteria are similar to those of Suppes *et al.* although the addition problems used by Woods and Hartley were presented in vertical rather than horizontal format. The model assumes that the child makes a mental ordering of the numbers 0 to 9 and that addition is accomplished by adding one to a partial sum the appropriate number of times. Thus, it is considered more difficult to add a large number because the probability of making an error is greater when more adding steps are required. Also, the model predicts that the time taken to add a large number to a partial sum will be longer because more steps have to be made than when adding a small number. The resultant model is called the 'moving pointer' model of addition and the three steps suggested for a single column are:

(i)   a pointer is pre-set to the number (the partial sum) held in memory;
(ii) the operation of moving the pointer is repeated a number of times which correspond to the number to be added to the partial sum;
(iii) the answer (the new partial sum) is stored in memory.

The loop is repeated for a particular problem until there are no numbers left to add (see Figure 10.5).

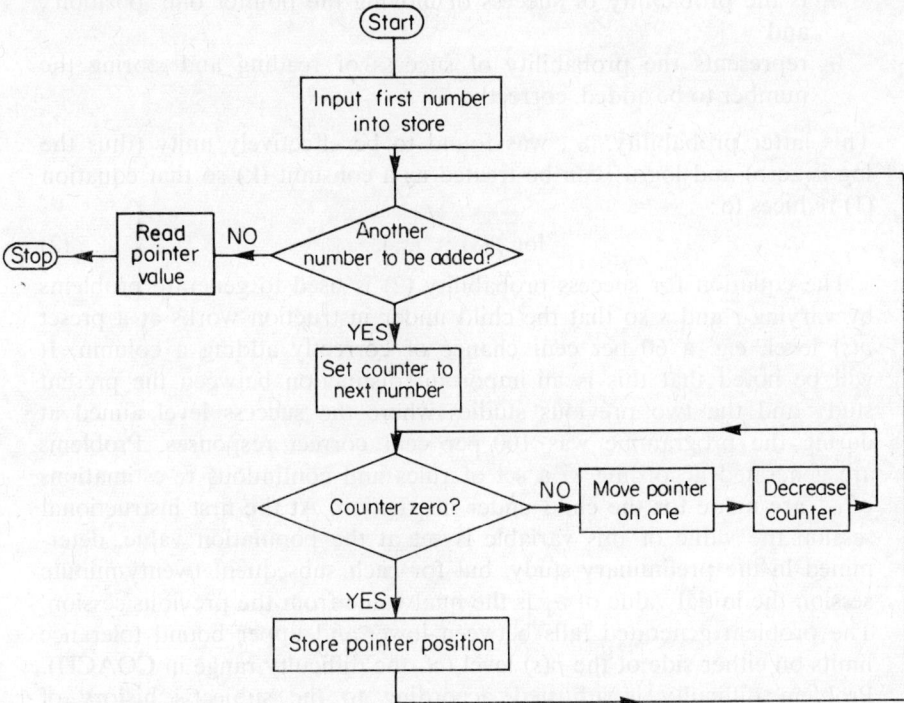

Figure 10.5—*A model for the addition task* (*from Woods and Hartley, 1971*)

An experiment was carried out on addition problems, with 7–8 year old junior-school children, in which two variables were investigated:

(*a*) The number of rows: 2, 3 or 4. (The number of columns was kept constant.)
(*b*) The average size of the digits used: $3\frac{1}{2}$ or $7\frac{1}{2}$.

Both these independent variables were found to account for a significant amount of variation in the probability of success of adding a column correctly and also in the time taken to add a column.

The significance of the two factors, rows (*r*) and number size (*s*), is used as evidence to support the 'moving pointer' model of addition and the data was used in a regression analysis showing that the probability of correctly adding a column ($p(s)$) was related to the number of rows and the number size. The relation is shown in the following equation:

$$\log p(s) = rs\log\sigma_1 + r\log\sigma_2 \qquad \ldots (1)$$

where

σ_1 is the probability of success of moving the pointer one 'position', and

σ_2 represents the probability of success of reading and storing the number to be added, correctly.

This latter probability, σ_2, was found to be effectively unity (thus the log is zero) and $\log \sigma_1$ can be treated as a constant (k) so that equation (1) reduces to:

$$\log p(s) = rs.k \qquad \ldots (2)$$

The equation for success probability (2) is used to generate problems by varying r and s so that the child under instruction works at a preset $p(s)$ level, e.g. a 60 per cent chance of correctly adding a column. It will be noted that this is an important distinction between the present study and the two previous studies where the success level aimed at during the programme was 100 per cent correct responses. Problems are generated according to a set of rules and continuous re-estimations of σ_1 are made for the child under instruction. At the first instructional session the value of this variable is set at the population value, determined in the preliminary study, but for each subsequent twenty-minute session the initial value of σ_1 is the final value from the previous session. The problem generated falls between lower and upper bound tolerance limits on either side of the $p(s)$ level (cf. the difficulty range in COACH). Problem difficulty is adjusted, according to the subject's history of responses.

Two interesting points arise from this study. First, noting that the probability σ_2 was found to be unity in this experiment using normal children, it would be interesting to evaluate the probability both for subnormal children and for younger children. If the probability were considerably less than one, it might be possible for the computer to generate problems designed to improve this probability (i.e. the ability to read and store numbers correctly) rather than the probability of success at adding these numbers.

Secondly, the probability of success for a particular child is not determined by the computer but by the teacher. The interaction of the specification of the level of success probability, and personality and motivation, is an aspect of the work which as yet has not been fully investigated. A preliminary study suggests that a success probability of 50 per cent is too low to maintain motivation amongst a group of children of mixed intelligence. The results from a comprehensive study of this interaction could be used to design tests of intelligence, personality and motivation, pertinent to the calculation of an optimum probability of success level for the individual child.

Although none of the studies of analysis of arithmetic problems described so far provides conclusive evidence for the superiority of its particular method of calculating problem 'difficulty', they do suggest that in CAI the arithmetic operations need to be split into a set of measurable processes, so that instruction can be controlled and performance evaluated. The 'moving pointer' of Woods and Hartley, 'memory' as defined by Suppes *et al.* and 'difficulty' as defined by Wexler, are of this type. It would not be difficult to generate problems with a required 'memory' score in the same way as problems with a required 'difficulty' score are generated by COACH, and problems with a specified probability of success are generated in the 'moving pointer' model.

Analysis into measurable processes, or metrics, is more easily applied to arithmetic than other topics taught by computers. It is possible to conceive measures outside the field of arithmetic, for example, complexity of sentence structure when teaching a foreign language. However, once this measure was obtained, the computer would have to generate a *meaningful* sentence and at the moment, unfortunately, this is hardly possible. It is possible to generate questions designed to teach students merely to translate words from one language to another (Uhr, 1969). But the problem of generating questions and problems of all kinds, not just those restricted to mathematics, will clearly be one of the major concerns of CAI in the future. It will certainly involve recent developments of the kind referred to in Chapter 7 on 'The Computer in the Psychology of Language'.

Student questions and answers in natural language

If the computer is to act as a teacher outside certain restricted areas, like drill-and-practice in arithmetic, it is clear that it must deal with language. In this section we shall look at how the computer can, at least in a preliminary way, deal with students' answers when these are in natural language and also reply to students' own questions posed in natural language.

Other things being equal, constructed responses have an obvious advantage over multiple-choice answers: it is probably more testing for a student to have to recall information than to recognise it when he sees it, or to have to work out an answer without the clue that one of a small number of alternative answers is the correct one. But of course with branching teaching machines it is not possible to use constructed responses because the machine is not intelligent enough to branch on the basis of such responses. With a computer, however, the possibility of being able to deal adaptively with such responses including constructed responses in natural language, does arise. This facility, where available, allows the computer in principle to overcome a good number of the limitations of programmed instruction listed earlier in this chapter.

Although the computer cannot understand the meaning of sentences, it can recognize the words and respond appropriately. Sleeman and Hartley (1969) describe a system in use at Leeds University that analyses students' responses as a set of character strings. The character strings are matched to key words in the computer to determine the nature of a student's response or request. The degree of redundancy and misspelling allowed in responses depends on the topic of instruction. The process used to compare a student's response with the stored key words is called a generalized matching algorithm, and Sleeman and Hartley consider that the following variables should be included in this algorithm:

(i) redundant words should be allowed in a student's response;
(ii) the order of words forming the response may or may not be important;
(iii) the correct spelling of words in the response may or may not be important;
(iv) the matching technique should be able to accommodate the synonyms used by students in their responses.

The degree of redundancy allowed is usually determined beforehand according to the topic of instruction and the aims of the instructional system. Correct spelling and order of words need not be important when a student is answering a question and so it is time- and space-saving for the key words to be stored as shortened, but unambiguous, character strings. For example, suppose a student were being instructed in statistics and the correct answer to a question on measures of central tendency was: 'median'. If the student typed

   MEDIAN

into the computer, this could be responded to quickly by matching it to the character string MDN. This string is distinct from both MEAN and MODE because neither of these two contain all three letters M, D and N in this order. This method also allows for mis-spellings, such as

MEEDYUN, which are prone to occur when the student is not acquainted with the method or topic of instruction.

The ability to store synonyms together, rather than store all the possible sentence combinations using these synonyms, obviously saves programming time and computer storage. For example, the correct response to the question posed by the computer 'What must you do next?' might be 'I must add the figures'. It could also be 'I should summate the numbers'. 'Quantities' could also be used here as a synonym for 'numbers' so that the total number of answers that could be accepted is twelve. However, all twelve responses could be stored for matching purposes by storing the synonyms as separate lists, using a special character, $, to indicate the synonymic relationship between members of the list; e.g.

    must $ should
    add $ summate
    figures $ numbers $ quantities

If the computer can to some extent accept and deal with constructed responses in natural language, it may also be able to respond to some extent to natural-language *questions* from the student, just as a human tutor can answer his student's questions as well as posing them himself. In fact, some CAI systems have been set up to attempt to do this and such systems are, as noted earlier, referred to as 'Socratic systems'. These allow the student to take a much more active part in determining his instruction than other kinds of machine teaching systems do.

The Leeds system has itself been programmed so that it can use the Socratic mode of instruction. But the original Socratic system, and the one which gave its name to this type of CAI, is the 'Socratic System' developed at Bolt, Beranek and Newman Inc. (Swets and Feurzeig, 1965). Here the computer sets a general problem and the student works his way towards solving this problem by being allowed to ask intermediate questions of the computer and stating attempted solutions at any stage for computer evaluation. These questions or solutions are in natural English, but the student is restricted to a list of questions and a list of statements. This is, of course, a major restriction. But within this the student can input to the computer questions and statements from the lists in any order he chooses. Clearly, he has to try to solve the problem in the shortest number of steps possible. The resulting 'conversation' with the computer may be very life-like. The computer responds to the student in natural English and may do so in a number of different ways, answering questions or perhaps giving another question in return and making comments on the student's questions and attempted answers which guide him towards a solution. In particular, errors such as the following four kinds of errors may be picked up by the computer and commented on:

(a) Consistency. An attempted answer may contradict information that has been given previously.
(b) Redundancy. A question may be asked that has been asked previously.
(c) Sufficiency. An attempted answer may have occurred too early. That is, not sufficient information has yet been given for a serious answer and so the student must be guessing.
(d) Necessity. A question may be asked that is irrelevant in that it cannot possibly help to solve the problem.

It can be seen, then, that the history of previous responses and questions is taken into account by the computer in making its comments. But the inferences from this history are essentially logical rather than quantitative as in the earlier examples in this chapter. An example is a program for teaching medical diagnosis. The student has to make a correct diagnosis and to do this is allowed to choose from a list of 40 questions like 'General appearance?', 'Blood pressure?' and 'Abdominal exam?'. There are also 35 declarative statements available to him like 'Yes', 'No', 'Acute pyelonephritis' and 'Pneumococcal pneumonia'. The following brief extract from a student(S)-Computer(C) dialogue gives something of the flavour of the system in operation (Swets and Feurzeig, p. 574).

S: Pulmonary infarction.
C: Fine. Pleural pain, dyspnœa, fever and the physical exam signs and symptoms are certainly consistent with pulmonary infarction. Do you think that shaking chills and the presence of rusty sputum further support this diagnosis?
S: No.
C: Right. Though the white count is consistent, isn't it?
S: No.
C: Wrong. The white count is consistent. This should further support your diagnosis. We've considered one possibility. Do you have another diagnosis in mind?
S: No.
C: In that case I'd like to talk about viral pneumonia. The tachycardia, high WBC, elevated respiratory rate, shaking chills, bloody sputum, and severe pleural pain all lend weight to that diagnosis—right?
S: Yes.

C: You're way off base. There's not an iota of truth to any part of what I just said; in fact, the opposite of what I said is true. You'd better review some elementary medicine, doctor.

Critique

At the present time CAI has a number of obvious general short-comings. The main one, as already noted, must be that of expense. This is something that workers in the field of CAI itself can do little about other than wait for developments in hardware technology and prepare the ground so that full advantage can be taken of such developments in the educational context when they occur. If the financial barrier is the main one which CAI must clear before it will be used to any great extent, it is not the only one. Another is that of the attitudes of educationists themselves, especially schoolteachers—who tend as a profession to be conservative and inflexible. A further barrier is likely to be that of organization, in schools if not in industrial training departments. Individualized instruction is difficult to assimilate to a system based on classes of children advancing together in a lock-step. This kind of rigid organization may have to be broken down to some extent in the future if the use of individualized machine instruction is to be optimized (viz. Apter, 1968, Chapter 7).

When we look at CAI itself in its present experimental state, a major area of weakness stands out: the inability of CAI systems to handle natural language in a flexible and creative manner. Subject-matter information presented to the student is still pre-written and presented to the student in predetermined frames (e.g. Smallwood, 1962; Stolurow, 1965). The presentation may be more flexible in CAI than in programmed instruction but the linguistic information is still selected and not generated. Again, when discussing the strategy sometimes used in CAI of having the computer generate its own problems to suit particular students it was noted that although this could be achieved in various ways with numerical information its use was very restricted with natural language. Likewise, in providing hints to students as in Swets and Feurzeig (1965) the computer selects pre-stored units of information. And yet it is clear that for the computer to be able to adapt closely to the needs of individual students, especially in teaching topics normally described in natural language, it would have to generate and not just select pre-stored linguistic information, i.e. it would have to be able to build up sentences of its own. Similarly, a great deal would be added to the potential of a computer in teaching if it were able to understand natural language as used by a student. As we have seen a start has been

10—TCIP * * ,

made on this, the example quoted being that of Sleeman and Hartley (1969). Outside the field of CAI, increasing attention is being paid to the use of natural language by computers for various purposes (see Chapter 7). If on economic grounds CAI must wait for hardware developments before it can be applied widely, it seems that it may have to wait for certain software developments before its potential as a technique can be realized to anything like the extent ultimately hoped for. For this reason those working in the field of CAI may have to pay close attention to research in artificial intelligence, especially that which relates to natural language.

From the methodological point of view one weakness is the apparent reluctance of workers in the field so far to carry out, or report on, the success or otherwise of their methods either in their own terms or in comparison with other methods. This general lack of evaluation means that the CAI literature tends to read rather like so many research proposals, admittedly exciting ones, rather than research reports. There are of course many exceptions, but without more general feedback of results between workers in the field they can only expect to progress slowly. One reason for the paucity of reference to results other than the newness of the field is perhaps the obsession with computers rather than with students which seems to afflict so many workers in CAI. Provided the machinery works, many seem to feel that the project concerned is a success, irrespective of what demonstrable educational use the machinery is put to. This is really the main criticism that can be made of the field of CAI at the present time: that *CAI is too technologically or computer-oriented rather than educationally or student-oriented.* This condition shows itself through many different symptoms, of which the relative lack of reported educational evaluations is only one.

Thus more psychological variables could be taken into account by the computer in reaching its pedagogical decisions. The only psychological variable which is generally taken into account in both programmed and computer-assisted instruction is that of intelligence. The main exception here is as we have seen that of the SOCRATES program of Stolurow in which an attempt is made to utilize measures of aptitude and person-ality. Stolurow has argued that if CAI is to be individualized, then as much information about each individual student should be utilized as possible; he suggests the name 'ideographic programming' for this approach (Stolurow, 1967). Evidence for the relationship between various aspects of personality and learning is beginning to emerge. For example, Leith (1969) has shown that introverts obtain better results from clearly structured materials, while extraverts are more successful with materials where the learner has to search for his own hypotheses.

If the computer is to adapt itself so as to optimize the learning of individual students, then use should be made of this kind of evidence. For example, on the basis of the evidence just presented the tutorial mode of CAI might be preferable for introverts and the Socratic mode for extraverts. Ideally, information about a student's personality (as well as abilities and intelligence) should be used by the computer to generate a special program which would optimize the learning of that individual student. We are obviously a long way from this point and even in the SOCRATES program the extrinsic information is used simply to choose one from a comparatively small number of equivalent programmes. The advantage of SOCRATES is that it does take some extrinsic information about personality into account in making this decision. Also, the decision made is the positive one about which programme is most suitable for the student in question rather than typical programmed instruction decision about whether the student should be accepted or *rejected* for the single programme available. The failure so far in machine teaching to use more extrinsic information means that adaptation takes place mainly in terms of intrinsic information generated by the student in the course of taking the teaching programme itself. In cybernetic terms this means that at present CAI is forced to make use to a large extent of post-error control rather than pre-error control.

There is also the question of motivation considered either as a general personality characteristic like achievement motivation and thus as a variable to be measured extrinsically or as a variable to be measured during the course of instruction itself and used for purposes of adaptation. Motivation is considered partly in decision structures such as the one used in COACH that accelerates the increase in difficulty of problems according to the progress of the student. However, this may not be enough, and procedures which outline to the student the major goals and sub-goals of the course of instruction, could help to increase motivation. A system such as Grubb's which provides the student with a map of the topics to be covered during the course, and also during a particular area of instruction, and gives him some choice in the material he will attend to at a particular time, is one step in this direction. When the student needs to spend a long time at a computer terminal it is necessary to keep his interest in the topic of instruction throughout, because unlike lessons and lectures there is little redundant information presented in a course of computer instruction. Perhaps this could be remedied by having the computer relate to the student some anecdote about a previous pupil, or fellow computer, during the monotony of instruction!

There is another general sense in which in the field of CAI insufficient attention is paid to the psychology of the student. As was stated at the beginning of the discussion of CAI techniques, the aim of CAI is widely regarded as being to make teaching machinery as intelligent and life-like as real teachers. That is, the aim is to get computers, basically, to simulate teachers. This would from the point of view of artificial intelligence be a tremendous achievement. But it is not necessarily what is most required from the point of view of the practice of teaching. Here the search should be for systems which will *improve* on the teacher, even the best teacher. It is of course true that if a computer could do those things which a teacher does, it would also almost inevitably be able to do them better. Because of its more efficient memory, the computer would be able to keep a more comprehensive record of the student's history than the teacher. The computer can store the response of every member of a class to every question set; and although the teacher can also do this by keeping paper records, storage and retrieval time is slower and the likelihood of error is greater. The teacher does keep in his memory an overall history of every student, but again this is subject to error and is kept in general terms, such as 'average', 'some difficulty with certain topics', etc. However, even here the improvement of the computer over the teacher may be limited. It is all very well for the computer to have a better memory—and this is indisputable—but it must be able to make use of it fully; and here we come up against the problem that we may not be able to find out the best ways of teaching by looking at things from the point of view of the teacher. We may need to know more about how learners learn rather than how teachers teach. If teachers are not using appropriate teaching techniques to start with there may be little point in trying to improve these techniques. Rather, the techniques should be changed. Skinner is among those who believe that traditional techniques are wrong in a number of ways (see Skinner, 1968). He has explicitly criticized CAI on the grounds that the aim of a technology of education should be to discover and to implement effective teaching procedures irrespective of how closely they resemble classroom teaching procedures; indeed too much attention to traditional practice may hinder the discovery of new and better methods (Skinner, 1963).

It can be argued that workers in CAI are attempting to do more than simulate teachers: they are attempting to develop, in effect, a theory of instruction. But if this is so it is a theory which by and large is not firmly based on a theory of learning. It will be recalled that CAI can be regarded as an extension of the branching method of programmed instruction. But the rationale for the branching method did not arise from psychological considerations and even attempts to interpret the technique subsequently in psychological terms has been sparse. This contrasts with Skinner's linear method of programmed instruction which is based closely on many years of laboratory research with animals. When it comes to writing programmes for computers to act as teaching machines the lack of rationale and a psychological underpinning for the branching method is a distinct handicap: how is one to take advantage of the comparative flexibility and information-storing capacity of the computer to do things which cannot be done in a pre-programmed way with a teaching machine? The increase in flexibility of the computer means that more decisions have to be made by the programmer and this may be embarrassing rather than helpful without guidance from psychological research. Thus programming the computer to allow it to generate exercises *ad infinitum* may simply disguise a lack of insight about how to guide the student firmly in a desired direction.

To put all this another way, computer-assisted instruction tends to use *heuristic* methods (see Chapter 5 p. 140) to achieve the goal of successful instruction. Heuristic methods have to be used in the absence of algorithms. But in the case of education it may be a better research strategy at the present stage to search for *algorithms* as Skinner and others have done rather than to assume that such algorithms are not discoverable. When found (as Skinner believes they already have been) they may not be efficient and so there may still be a need for heuristic methods; but it is defeatist, according to such an argument, to start off with heuristics. This ties in with the previous point because it is obvious that teachers, too, tend to use heuristic hit-and-miss methods rather than more deliberate algorithms in teaching.

At the same time it has to be pointed out that Skinner's supposed algorithmic techniques may in fact be no more likely to guarantee instructional success than the more heuristic methods of branching programmes. In fact it has been demonstrated pragmatically by psychologists and others that despite Skinner's criticisms of it, the simple Crowderian branching method *does* work. This has been shown for a wide variety of subject-matters and a wide variety of human subjects of different ages and degrees of intelligence. A large proportion of the whole field of research on programmed instruction attests to it, directly and indirectly; and by and large evidence does not appear to show a superiority for the linear method except in certain specific instances (e.g. see Leith and Hope, 1965). Skinner's methods may not therefore be so algorithmic and well-founded as he would like to think.

Skinner's opposition to theorizing in psychology has long been well known. This being the case it is ironic that it is Skinner who appears to be doing the theorizing in the field of programmed instruction rather than his opponents in the branching programmed instruction camp. From the outset Crowder regarded branching programming as being a control process independent of particular theories of learning (viz. Crowder, 1960) and on the whole programmers using the branching mode have been satisfied with getting the results they want without feeling a need to interpret them in terms of psychological theories. Skinner might deny that he has a theory in psychology, but his inferences from animal work to the classroom inevitably have a theoretical status, however atheoretic the animal work on which they are based. The resulting theory of programmed instruction has it that, as we have seen, operant methods of shaping animal behaviour are the appropriate methods to use to teach humans. This involves making a number of theoretical assumptions including the assumption that overt responding by the student is necessary, that getting the answer to a question right is always reinforcing to a student regardless of how easy the question is, and that the principles of operant conditioning with animals are the best ones to use with human beings even though the possession of language by humans would appear to allow various short-cuts to be taken (and indeed it is difficult to see what the status of the linguistic information on a frame is in Skinner's terms). However, without necessarily subscribing to Skinner's theory itself, it is still possible to applaud his efforts to base an educational technology on a psychological theory.

Of course new psychological theories of learning may develop eventually out of some of the work in CAI, especially where CAI systems are ones which are programmed to evaluate their own performance and adapt accordingly, e.g. the system already described of Smallwood (1962).

It is also true that some investigators *have* used psychological theories of a non-Skinnerian kind in the design of their systems, especially mathematical learning theories. Mathematical theories are obviously particularly relevant as a possible bridge between experimental psychology and computer teaching—an example is the work of Atkinson and Wilson (1968) described earlier, which is based on stimulus sampling theory. The limitation here is that mathematical theories at the present time tend to be restricted to simple learning situations like paired-associate learning. If such theories are to be of much practical use they may eventually have to be extended to cover more complex forms of learning or incorporated in more structuralist theories (see Chapter 5), perhaps in the form of computer models of the student.

Further Reading

Atkinson, R. C. and H. A. Wilson (Eds.) (1969) *Computer-Assisted Instruc-
    tion: A Book of Readings.* Academic Press, London. A good collection

of readings grouped under four headings: 'The Role of CAI', 'Educational Considerations', 'Applications' and 'Hardware, Languages and Economics'.

Bushnell, D. D. and D. W. Allen (Eds.) (1967) *The Computer in American Education.* Wiley, New York. The papers in this book were originally presented to a conference which was convened to discuss the present and future role of the computer in American education.

Gerard, R. W. (Ed.) (1967) *Computers and Education.* McGraw-Hill, New York. A set of conference papers on all aspects of the use of computers in education including their use by librarians and educational administrators.

Hickey, Albert E. (1968) *Computer-Assisted Instruction: A Survey of the Literature.* 3rd. edition. Entelek Incorporated, Massachusetts. This is a detailed survey of reported work on CAI which includes information about its application in different subject areas and about major CAI centres. An excellent reference book.

Johnson, Clemens M. (1971) *Educational Uses of the Computer: An Introduction.* Rand McNally, New York. A non-technical introduction to the computer and its varied uses in education.

Margolin, Joseph B. and Misch, M. R. (Eds.) (1970) *Computers in the Classroom: An Interdisciplinary View of Trends and Alternatives.* Macmillan, London. An examination of the potential of CAI, from various perspectives.

Programmed Learning and Educational Technology. Vol. 5, No. 1, January 1968, and vol. 9, No. 5, September 1972. These editions of this British journal are devoted to research papers on computer-assisted instruction.

Bibliography

Abelson, R. P. (1963) 'Computer simulation of "hot" cognition.' In Tomkins, S. S. and S. Messik (Eds). *Computer Simulation of Personality.* Wiley, New York.

d'Agapayeff, A. (1970) 'Software Engineering.' *Science Journal,* **6**, 10, 94–98.

Anstis, S. M., and B. P. Moulden (1970) 'After-effect of seen movement: Evidence for peripheral and central components.' *Quarterly Journal of Experimental Psychology,* **22**, 222–229.

Apostel, L. (1961) 'Towards the formal study of models in the non-formal sciences.' In H. Freudenthal (Ed) *The Concept and the Role of the Model in Mathematics and Natural and Social Sciences.* Reidel, Dordrecht-Holland.

Apter, M. J. (1966) *Cybernetics and Development.* Pergamon Press, Oxford.

Apter, M. J. (1968) *The New Technology of Education.* Macmillan, London.

Apter, M. J. (1970) *The Computer Simulation of Behaviour.* Hutchinson, London.

Atkinson, R. C. (1967) 'CAI-Learning aspects.' In Gerard, R. W. (Ed), *Computers and Education.* McGraw-Hill, New York, 11–63.

Atkinson, R. C., and H. A. Wilson (1968) 'Computer assisted instruction.' *Science,* **162**, 73–77.

Attneave, F., and M. D. Arnoult (1956) 'The quantitative study of shape and pattern perception.' *Psychological Bulletin,* **53**, 452–471.

Baddeley, A. D., R. Conrad and W. E. Thomson (1960) 'Letter structure of the English language.' *Nature,* **186**, 414–416.

Bar-Hillel, Y. (1964) *Language and Information.* Addison Wesley, Reading, U.S.A.

Barry, H., W. J. Kinnard Jr., N. Watzman and J. P. Buckley (1966) 'A computer oriented system for high-speed recording of operant behaviour.' *Journal of Experimental Analysis of Behavior,* **9**, 163–171.

Bartlett, F. C. (1932) *Remembering: A Study in Experimental and Social Psychology.* Cambridge University Press.

BCS Specialist Group: On-Line Computers and Their Languages (1967). 'A language for real-time systems.' *Computer Bulletin,* **2**, 202–212.

Bellman, R. (1957) *Dynamic Programming.* Princeton University Press.

Blakemore, C., and B. Julesz (1971) 'Stereoscopic depth after-effect produced without monocular cues.' *Science* **171**, 286–288.

Block, H. D., N. J. Nilsson and R. O. Duda (1964) 'Determination and detection of features in patterns.' In Tou, J. T. and R. H. Wilcox (Eds) *Computer and Information Sciences: Collected Papers on Learning, Adaptation and Control in Information Systems.* Spartan Books, Washington.

Blough, D. S. (1957) 'Spectral sensitivity in the pigeon.' *Journal of the Optical Society of America,* **47**, 827–833.

Bobrow, D. G. (1964) *Natural Language input for a computer problem solving system.* Massachusetts Institute of Technology Project MAC-TR-I.

281

Bobrow, D. G. (1970) 'Natural language interaction systems.' In Kaneff, S. (Ed) *Picture Language Machines*. Academic Press, New York.

Brata, S. (1970) 'Gripping thoughts of Robot Freddy.' *Engineering Now*, November 27th, 8–9.

Bratley, P., H. Dewar and J. P. Thorne (1967) 'Recognition of syntactic structure by computer.' *Nature*, **216**, 969–973.

Brown, J. (1959) 'Information, redundancy and decay of the memory trace.' *National Physical Laboratory Symposium No. 10.* HMSO London. 730–752.

Brown, R. (1964) 'The acquisition of syntax.' In Bellugi, U. and R. Brown (Eds) *Monographs of the Society for Research in Child Development*, **29**, 43–49.

Brudner, H. J. (1968) 'Computer-managed instruction.' *Science*, **162**, 970–976.

Bruner, J. S. (1957) 'On perceptual readiness.' *Psychological Review*, **64**, 123–152.

Bush, R. R., and F. Mosteller (1955) *Stochastic Models for Learning*. Wiley, New York.

Carroll, J. B. (1967) 'On sampling from a lognormal model of word frequency distribution.' In Kučera, H., and W. N. Francis, *Computational Analysis of Present-day American English*. Brown University Press, Providence Rhode Island, 406–424.

Carroll, J. B. (1968) 'Word-frequency studies and the lognormal distribution.' In Zale, E. M. (Ed) *Proceedings of the Conference on Language and Language Behavior*. Appleton-Century Crofts, New York, 213–235.

Carroll, J. B. (1969) 'A rationale for an asymptotic lognormal form of word-frequency distributions.' *Research Bulletin*, *RB-69-90*, Educational Testing Service, Princeton, New Jersey.

Carroll, J. B., P. Davies and B. Richman (1971) *American Heritage Word Frequency Book*, American Heritage Publishing Co., New York, and Houghton Mifflin, Boston.

Casey, R. G., and G. Nagy (1971) 'Advances in pattern recognition.' *Scientific American*, **224**, 4, 56–71.

Chomsky, N. (1956) 'Three models for the description of language.' *IRE Transactions on Information Theory* IT-2, 113–124.

Chomsky, N. (1957) *Syntactic Structures*. Mouton, The Hague.

Chomsky, N. (1963) 'Formal properties of grammars.' In Luce, R. D., R. Bush and E. Galanter (Eds) *Handbook of Mathematical Psychology II*, Wiley, New York.

Chomsky, N. (1964) *Current Issues in Linguistic Theory*. Mouton, The Hague.

Chomsky, N. (1965) *Aspects of the Theory of Syntax*. M.I.T. Press, Cambridge, Massachusetts.

Chomsky, N. (1968) *Language and Mind*. Harcourt, Brace and World, New York.

Chomsky, N., and G. A. Miller (1963) 'Introduction to the formal analysis of natural languages.' In Luce, R. D., R. R. Bush and E. Galanter (Eds) *Handbook of Mathematical Psychology II*, Wiley, New York.

Clark, W. A., and C. E. Molnar (1965) 'A description of the LINC.' In Stacey, R. W., and B. D. Waxman (Eds) *Computers in Biomedical Research*, **1**, Academic Press, New York.

Clarke, F. R. (1957) 'Constant-ratio rule for confusion matrices in speech communication.' *Journal of the Acoustical Society of America*, **29**, 715–720.

Clowes, M. B., D. J. Langridge and R. J. Zatorski (1970) 'Linguistic descriptions.' In Kaneff, S. (Ed) *Picture Language Machines*, Academic Press, New York.

Coe, R. M. (1964) 'Conflict, interference and aggression: computer simulation of a social process.' *Behavioral Science,* **9**, 2, 186–197.

Cogswell, J. F., C. P. Donahoe Jr., D. P. Estavan, and B. A. Rosenquist (1968) 'The design of a Man-Machine Counselling System.' *Programmed Learning and Educational Technology*, **5**, 1, 43–52.

Colby, K. M. (1963) 'Computer simulation of a neurotic process.' In Tomkins, S. S., and S. Messik (Eds) *Computer Simulation of Personality*. Wiley, New York.

Colby, K. M. (1965) 'Computer simulation of neurotic processes.' In Stacey, R. W., and B. D. Waxman (Eds) *Computers in Biomedical Research*, **1**, Academic Press, New York.

Conrad, M., and H. H. Pattee (1970) 'Evolution experiments with an artificial ecosystem.' *Journal of Theoretical Biology*, **28**, 393–409.

Conrad, R. (1964) 'Acoustic confusions in immediate memory.' *British Journal of Psychology,* **55**, 75–85.

Conrad, R. (1965) 'Order error in immediate recall of sequences.' *Journal of Verbal Learning and Verbal Behaviour*, **4**, 161–169.

Conrad, R. (1967) 'Beyond industrial psychology.' *Bulletin of the British Psychological Society*, **20**, 1–12.

Control Data Corporation (1970) 'Super scale optical character recognition.' *Data Processing*, **12**, 377–379.

Coombs, G. J., W. R. Murray and D. W. Krahn (1970) 'Automated medical histories: factors determining patient performance.' *Computers in Biomedical Research*, **3**, Academic Press, New York, 178–181.

Creelman, C. D. (1969) 'Maximising experimentation with a minimal computer and interface.' In *On-Line Computing for Psychology*, Moray, N. (Ed). Proceedings of NATO A.S.I. at Department of Psychology, University of Sheffield, England, 15–17.

Crossman, E. R. F. W. (1960) 'Information and serial order in human immediate memory.' In Cherry, C. (Ed) *Fourth London Symposium on Information Theory*, Butterworth, London, 147–161.

Crowder, N. A. (1960) 'Automatic tutoring by intrinsic programming.' In Lumsdaine, A. A., and R. Glaser (Eds) *Teaching Machines and Programed Learning: a Source Book*. Washington D.C. National Education Association, Department of Audio-Visual Aids.

Denes, P. B. (1963) 'On the statistics of spoken English.' *Journal of the Acoustical Society of America*, **35**, 892–904.

Denes, P. B. (1970) 'Some experiments with computer synthesised speech.' *Behavior Research Methods and Instrumentation*, **2**, 1–5.

Deutsch, J. A. (1960) *The Structural Basis of Behaviour*, Cambridge University Press, England.

Dewey, G. (1923) *Relative Frequency of English Speech Sounds.* Harvard University Press, Cambridge, Massachusetts.

Dimond, S. J. (1970a) *The Social Behaviour of Animals.* B. T. Batsford, London.

Dimond, S. J. (1970b) 'Visual experience and early social behaviour in chicks.' In Crook, J. H. (Ed) *Social Behaviour of Birds and Mammals.* Academic Press, London.

Dixon, W. J. (Ed) (1968) *BMD Biomedical Computer Programs.* University of California Press, Berkeley and Los Angeles.

Dunham, B. (1957) 'Computer simulation of Hull's learning theory.' *IBM Journal of Research and Development,* **1,** 341.

Eccles, J. C. (1953) *The Neurophysiological Basis of Mind.* Clarendon Press, Oxford.

Ede, D. A., and J. T. Law (1969) 'Computer simulation of vertebrate limb morphogenesis.' *Nature,* **221,** 244–248.

Eiduson, B. T., S. H. Brooks and R. C. Motto (1966) 'A generalised psychiatric information processing system.' *Behavioral Science,* **11,** 133.

Ellen, P. and A. S. Wilson (1964) 'Digital recording of simultaneous events in multiple operant chambers.' *Journal of the Experimental Analysis of Behavior,* **7,** 425–429.

Elwood, D. L. (1969) 'Automation of psychological testing.' *American Psychologist,* **24,** 287–289.

Eriksen, C. W., D. L. Schurman and O. Richter (1969) 'N-channel tachistoscopes.' *Behavior Research Methods and Instrumentation,* **1,** 119–122.

Esper, E. A. (1968) *Mentalism and Objectivism in Linguistics: the Source of Leonard Bloomsfield's Psychology of Language.* Elsevier, New York.

Evans, S. (1967) 'VARGUS 7: Computed patterns from Markov processes.' *Behavioral Science,* **12,** 323–328.

Fairbanks, H. (1944) 'The quantitative differentiation of samples of spoken language.' *Psychological Monographs,* **56,** 19–38.

Farmer, J., and W. N. Schoenfeld (1964) 'Inter-reinforcement times for the bar pressing response of white rats on two DRL schedules.' *Journal of the Experimental Analysis of Behavior,* **7,** 119–122.

Feldman, J. (1962) 'Computer simulation of cognitive processes.' In H. Borko, (Ed) *Computer Applications in the Behavioral Sciences.* Prentice-Hall, New Jersey.

Fisher, G. H. (1968) 'Ambiguity old and new.' *Perception and Psychophysics,* **4,** 189–192.

Fishman, J. A. (1968) *Readings in the Sociology of Language.* Mouton, The Hague.

Flores d'Arcais, G. B. and W. J. M. Levelt (Ed.) (1970) *Advances in Psycholinguistics.* North Holland Publishing Co., Amsterdam.

Fowler, R. D. (1969) 'The current state of computer interpretation of psychological tests.' *American Journal of Psychiatry,* **125,** Supplement January, 21–27.

Fox, R. (1970) 'The cultural animal.' *Encounter,* **35,** 1, 31–42.

Francis, J. G. F., and N. S. Sutherland (1969) 'A system for controlling animal experiments on-line.' In *On-Line Computing for Psychology,* Moray, N. (Ed). Proceedings of NATO A.S.I. at Department of Psychology, University of Sheffield, England, 43–56.

Freeman, L. (1971) 'Two problems in computer simulation in the social and behavioral sciences.' *Social Sciences Information*, **10**, 1, 103–109.

French, N. R., C. W. Carter and W. Koenig (1930) 'The words and sounds of telephone conversations.' *Bell System Technical Journal*, **9**, 290–324.

Freudenthal, H. (Ed) (1961) *The Concept and the Role of the Model in Mathematics and Natural and Social Sciences*. Reidel, Dordrecht-Holland.

Friedman, L. (1967) 'Instinctive behavior and its computer synthesis.' *Behavioral Science*, **12**, 2, 85–108.

Fromkin, V. A., and P. Ladgefoged (1966) 'Electromyography in speech research.' *Phonetica*, **15**, 219–242.

Fry, D. B. (1947) 'The frequency of occurrence of speech sounds in Southern English.' *Archives Néerlandaises de Phonétique Expérimentale*, **20**, 103–106.

Gabor, D. (1948) 'A new microscopic principle.' *Nature*, **161**, 777–778.

Gabor, D. (1968) 'Improved holographic model of temporal recall.' *Nature*, **217**, 1288–1289.

Gabor, D., W. E. Kock and G. W. Stroke (1971) 'Holography.' *Science*, **173**, 11–23.

Garrett, M. F. (1970) 'Does ambiguity complicate the perception of sentences?' In Flores d'Arcais, G. B., and W. J. M. Levelt (Eds) *Advances in Psycholinguistics*. North Holland Publishing Company, Amsterdam, 48–60.

Gelernter, H. (1963) 'Realization of a geometry-theorem proving machine.' In Feigenbaum, E. A., and J. Feldman (Ed) *Computers and Thought*. McGraw-Hill, New York.

George, F. H. (1961) *The Brain as a Computer*. Pergamon Press, Oxford.

Gibson, J. J. (1952) *The Perception of the Visual World*. Allen and Unwin, London.

Gibson, J. J. (1966) *The Senses Considered as Perceptual Systems*. Allen and Unwin, London.

Gibson, J. J., P. Olum and F. Rosenblatt (1955) 'Parallax and perspective during aircraft landings.' *American Journal of Psychology*, **68**, 372–385.

Gibson, R. (1970) *The Use of Computers for On-Line Experimentation*. Unpublished B.Sc., and dissertation, University of Hull.

Glueck, B. C., and C. F. Stroebel (1969) 'The computer and the clinical decision process; II.' *American Journal of Psychiatry*, **125**, Supplement January, 1–7.

Goldman-Eisler, F. (1960) 'Hesitation and Information in Speech'. In Cherry, C. (Ed) *Fourth London Symposium on Information Theory*. Butterworth, London.

Grason-Stadler Co. (1970) *SCAT User's Manual*. Grason-Stadler Co. Inc. Box 8, West Concord, Massachusetts 01781, U.S.A. (British outlet: General Radio (U.K.) Limited, Bourne End, Buckinghamshire).

Green, B. F. (1963) *Digital Computers in Research: An introduction for behavioral and social scientists*. McGraw-Hill, New York.

Green, B. F. (1967) 'The computer conquest of Psychology.' *Psychology Today*, **1**, 56–61.

Green, B. F., A. F. Wolf, C. Chomsky and K. Laughery (1961) 'Baseball: An automatic question answerer.' *Proceedings of the Western Joint Computer Conference*, **19**, 219–224.

Green, T. R. G. (1973) *An Aspect of the Practice of Syntax.* Unpublished Ph.D. Thesis to be deposited at the University of Sheffield.

Greenberger, F., and G. Jaffray (1965) *Problems for Computer Solution.* Wiley, New York.

Gregory, R. L., and J. G. Wallace (1963) *Recovery from early blindness; a case study.* Experimental Psychology Society Monograph No. 2, Cambridge, England.

Griffin, J. S. Jr., J. H. King Jr. and C. J. Tunis (1964) 'Pattern identification Devices using Linear Decision Functions.' In Tou, J. T. and R. H. Wilcox (Eds) *Computer and Information Sciences: Collected Papers on Learning, Adaptation and Control in Information Systems.* Spartan Books, Washington.

Groen, G. J., and R. C. Atkinson (1966) 'Models for optimising the learning process.' *Psychological Bulletin,* **66**, 4, 309–320.

Grubb, R. E. (1968) 'Learner controlled statistics.' *Programmed Learning and Educational Technology,* **5**, 1, 38–42.

Grubb, R. E. and L. D. Selfridge (1963) 'The computer tutoring of statistics.' *Computers and Automation,* **13**, 20–26.

Gullahorn, J. T. and J. E. Gullahorn (1963) 'A computer model of elementary social behavior.' In Feigenbaum, E. A., and J. Feldman (Eds) *Computers and Thought.* McGraw-Hill, New York.

Gurney, C., M. Roth and R. F. Garside (1970) 'Use of statistical techniques in classification of affective disorders.' *Proceedings of the Royal Society of Medicine,* **63**, 232–235.

Haber, R. N., S. H. Barry and T. Uhlman (1970) 'On-line FORTRAN for the PDP-8.' *Behavior Research Methods and Instrumentation,* **2**, 248–252.

Harris, Z. S. (1960) *Project Summary:* Current Research and Development in Scientific Documentation No. 6, 52–53, National Science Foundation, New York.

Harrison, G. (1967) *Recall Strategies and Short Term Retention,* unpublished Ph.D. Thesis, University of Sheffield.

Hebb, D. O. (1949) *The Organization of Behavior.* Wiley, New York.

Heider, F. (1958) *The Psychology of Interpersonal Relations.* Wiley, New York.

Herrick, R. M., and J. S. Denelsbeck (1963) 'A system for programming experiments and for recording and analysing data automatically.' *Journal of Experimental Analysis of Behavior,* **6**, 631–635.

Herriot, P. (1970) *An Introduction to the Psychology of Language.* Methuen, London.

Holder, R. L., and A. R. King (1970) 'Computer analysis of conditioned behaviour. *Physiology and Behaviour,* **5**, 7, 823–826.

Holland, H. C. (1965) *The Spiral After-Effect,* Pergamon Press, New York and London.

Holland, J. H. (1969) 'Goal-directed pattern recogition.' In Watanabe, S. (Ed) *Methodologies of Pattern Recognition.* Academic Press, London.

van Holst, E., and U. V. van Saint Paul (1963) 'On the functional organization of drives.' *Animal behaviour,* **11**, 1, 1–20.

Homans, G. C. (1961) *Social Behavior: Its Elementary Forms*. Harcourt, Brace and World, New York.

Horridge, G. A. (1968) 'The eye-movements of the crab in relation to vision.' Unpublished talk presented to the Symposium on 'The Development of Perception,' Association for the study of Animal Behaviour, London.

Horst, P. (1965) *Factor Analysis of Data Matrices*. Holt, Rinehart and Winston, New York.

Howes, D. (1966) A word count of spoken English. *Journal of Verbal Learning and Verbal Behavior*, **5**, 572–604.

Hubel, D. H. and T. N. Wiesel (1959) 'Receptive fields of single neurones in the cat's striate cortex.' *Journal of Physiology*, **148**, 574–591.

Hull, C. L. (1943) *Principles of Behavior*. Appleton-Century-Crofts, New York.

Hunt, E. (1968) 'Computer simulation: artificial intelligence studies and their relevance to psychology.' In Farnworth, P. R. (Ed) *Annual Review of Psychology*, **19**, Annual Reviews, Inc., California.

Huxley, R. (1970) 'The development of the correct use of subject personal pronouns in two children.' In Flores d'Arcais, G. B. and W. J. M. Levelt. *Advances in Psycholinguistics*. North Holland, Amsterdam.

Iker, H. P., and N. I. Harway. (1969) 'A computer approach toward the analysis of content.' In Kleinmuntz, B. *Clinical Information Processing by Computer*, Holt, Rinehart and Winston, New York.

Jordan, H. J. (1941) Die Theoretischen Grundlagen der Tierphysiologie. *Bibliotheca Biotheoretica*, **1**.

Julesz, B. (1960) 'Binocular depth perception of computer-generated patterns.' *Bell System Technical Journal*, **93**, 1125–1162.

Julesz, B. (1965) 'Texture and visual perception.' *Scientific American*, **212**, 2, 38–48.

Kappauf, W. E. (1969) 'Use of an on-line computer for psychophysical testing with the up-and-down method.' *American Psychologist*, **24**, 207–211.

Kay, H. (1953) *Experimental Studies of Adult Human Learning*, unpublished Ph.D. Thesis, Cambridge.

Kelley, C. R. (1969) 'Adaptive and automated research techniques from Engineering Psychology.' *American Psychologist*, **24**, 293–297.

Kent, G. H., and A. J. Rosanoff (1910) 'A study of association in insanity.' *American Journal of Insanity*, **67**, 37–96 and 317–390.

Kilmer, W. L., W. S. McCulloch, and J. Blum (1969) 'An embodiment of some vertebrate command and control principles.' *Journal of Basic Engineering*, **91**, 295.

Kleene, S. C. (1956) 'Representation of events in nerve nets and finite automata.' In, Shannon, C. E. and J. McCarthy (Eds) *Automata Studies*. Princeton University Press, Princeton, N.J.

Kleinmuntz, B. (1969) *Clinical Information Processing by Computer*. Holt, Rinehart and Winston, New York.

Lane, M. (Ed) (1970) *Structuralism: A Reader*. Cape, London.

Lang, P. J. (1969) 'The "on-line" computer in behaviour therapy research.' *American Journal of Psychology*, **24**, 236–239.

Lashley, K. S. (1929) *Brain Mechanisms and Intelligence*. University of Chicago Press.

Ledley, R. S. (1965) *Use of Computers in Biology and Medicine.* McGraw-Hill, New York.

Leith, G. O. M. (1969) 'Learning and personality.' In Dunn, W. R. and C. Holroyd (Eds) *Aspects of Educational Technology, II.* Methuen, London.

Leith, G. O. M. and B. Hope (1965) 'A comparison of two modes of responding to linear and branching programmes.' *Educational Review*, **17**, 3, 223–233.

Lennenberg, E. H. (1964) 'The capacity for language acquisition.' In Fodor, J. A., and J. J. Katz (Eds) *The Structure of Language.* Prentice-Hall, New Jersey, 576–603.

Levelt, W. J. M. (1969) 'The scaling of syntactic relatedness: A new method in psycholinguistics.' *Psychonomic Science*, **17**, 351–352.

Lévi-Strauss, C. (1966) *The Savage Mind.* Weidenfeld and Nicolson, London. (Original French edition, *La Pensée Sauvage*, Plon, Paris 1962).

Lieberman, P. H., D. H. Klatt and W. H. Wilson (1969). 'Vocal tract limitations on the vowel repertoires of rhesus monkey and other non-human primates.' *Science*, **164**, 1185–1187.

Liebman, L. (1971) 'Voice recognition system.' *Data Processing*, **13**, 6–7.

Lindsay, R. K. (1963) Inferential memory as the basis of machines which understand natural language. In Feigenbaum, E. A., and J. Feldman (Eds) *Computers and Thought.* McGraw-Hill, New York.

Lipkin, B. S., and A. Rosenfeld (1970) *Picture Processing and Psychopictorics.* Academic Press, New York and London.

Loehlin, J. C. (1968) *Computer Models of Personality.* Random House, New York.

Lyons, J. (1970) *Chomsky.* Fontana Modern Masters, London.

Mandelbrot, B. (1954) 'On recurrent noise limiting coding.' In Weber E. (Ed) *Symposium on Information Networks* (Proceedings 1954). Polytechnic Institute of Brooklyn, Brooklyn 205–221.

Mathews, M. V. (1963) 'The digital computer as a musical instrument.' *Science*, **142**, 533–557.

Maxwell, A. E. (1961) 'Classification procedures based on Bayes' theorem and decision theory.' *Analysing Qualitative Data.* Methuen, London.

Mays, W. (1964) 'Probability models and thought and learning processes.' In Gregg, J. R., and F. T. C. Harris (Eds) *Form and Strategy in Science,* Reidel, Dordrecht-Holland.

Mayzner, M. S., M. E. Tresselt and M. S. Helfer (1967) 'A research strategy for studying certain effects of very fast sequential input rates on the visual system.' *Psychonomic Monograph Supplements*, **2**, 73–81.

McCulloch, W. S., and W. Pitts (1943) 'A logical calculus of the ideas immanent in nervous activity.' *Bulletin of Mathematical Biophysics*, **5**, 115–133.

McLean, R. S. (1969) 'PSYCHOL: A computer language for experimentation.' *Behaviour Research Methods and Instrumentation*, **1**, 8, 323–328.

McNeil, D. (1966) 'Developmental Psycholinguistics.' In Smith, F., and G. A. Miller *The Genesis of Language.* M.I.T. Press, Cambridge, Massachusetts.

Meehl, P. E. (1967) 'Theory-testing in Psychology and Physics: A methodological paradox.' *Philosophy of Science*, **34**, 103–115.

Melrose, J. P., C. F. Stroebel and B. C. Glueck (1970) 'Diagnosis of psycho-pathology using stepwise multiple discriminant analysis.' *Comprehensive Psychiatry*, **11**, 43–50.

Metherell, A. F. (1969) 'Acoustical holography'. *Scientific American*, **221**, 4, 36–53.

Millenson, J. R. (1970) 'Language and list structure of a compiler for ex-perimental control.' *The Computer Journal*, **13**, 340–343.

Millenson, J. R., and LVE Staff (1969) *The ACT Primer: Computer Language and Hardware Interface for Controlling Psychological Experiments.* Lehigh Valley Electronics, Fogelsville, Pennsylvania. (British outlet: T.E.M. Sales Limited, Crawley, Sussex).

Miller G. A. (1967) 'Project Grammarama'. In *The Psychology of Communi-cation: Seven Essays.* Basic Books, New York, 125–187.

Miller, G. A., E. Galanter and K. H. Pribram (1960). *Plans and the Structure of Behavior.* Holt, Rinehart and Winston, New York.

Miller, G. A. and K. O. McKean (1964) 'A chronometric study of some re-lations between sentences.' *Quarterly Journal of Experimental Psycho-logy*, **16**, 297–308.

Miller, G. A., and M. Stein (1963) 'Grammarama. I. Preliminary studies and analysis of protocols,' *Science Report CS-2*, Center for Cognitive Studies, Harvard University, Cambridge, Massachusetts.

Miller, N. E. (1969) 'Learning of visceral and glandular responses.' *Science*, **163**, 434–445.

Milner, P. M. (1957) 'The cell assembly: Mark II.' *Psychological Review*, **64**, 242–252.

Moray, N. (1969) *Attention: Selective processes in Vision and Hearing*, Hutchinson Educational, London.

Moray, N. (Ed) (1969) *On-Line Computing for Psychology.* Proceedings of NATO A.S.I. at Department of Psychology, University of Sheffield, England.

Murdock, B. B. (1966) 'The criterion problem in short-term memory.' *Journal of Experimental Psychology*, **72**, 317–324.

National Council for Educational Technology. (1969) *Computers for Edu-cation.* Working Paper No. 1, National Council for Educational Tech-nology, London.

Newell, A., J. C. Shaw and H. A. Simon (1959) 'A general problem-solving program for a computer.' *Computers and Automation*, **8**, 7, 10–16.

Newell, A., J. C. Shaw and H. A. Simon (1963) 'Chess-playing programs and the problem of complexity.' In Feigenbaum, E. A. and J. Feldman (Eds) *Computers and Thought*, McGraw-Hill, New York.

Newell, A., and H. A. Simon (1956) 'The logic theory machine.' *IRE Trans-actions on Information Theory*, IT-2, 3.

Newell, A., and H. A. Simon (1963) 'GPS, a program that simulates human thought.' In Feigenbaum, E. A. and Feldman, J. (Eds) *Computers and Thought.* McGraw-Hill, New York.

Nie, N. H., D. H. Bent and C. H. Hull (1970) *Statistical Package for the Social Sciences.* McGraw-Hill, New York.

Norman, D. A. (1969) *Memory and Attention: An Introduction to Human Information Processing.* Wiley, New York.

Noton, D. and L. Stark (1971) 'Scanpaths in eye movements during pattern perception.' *Science*, **171**, 308–311.

Oettinger, A. G. (1969) *Run, Computer, Run: The Mythology of Educational Innovation*. Harvard University Press, Cambridge, Massachusetts.

Oxnard, C. E. (1969) 'Mathematics, shape and function; a study in primate anatomy.' *American Scientist*, **57**, 75–96.

Papert, S. (1964) Massachusetts Institute of Technology. Quarterly Progress Reports (15th April).

Pask, G. (1965) Teaching as a control-engineering process. *Control*, **9**, 6–11, 69–72, 153–158, 211–216.

Pask, G. (1966) 'Men, machines and the control of learning.' *Educational Technology*, **6**, 22, 1–12.

Pask, G., and G. L. Mallen (1966) 'The method of adaptively controlled psychological learning experiments.' In *Theory of Self-Adaptive Control Systems*, Hammond, P. H. (Ed), Plenum, New York.

Pelikan, P. (1964) 'Development du modèle de l'instinct de conservation.' *Information Processing Machines*, **10**, 25–36.

Pennington, K. S. (1968) 'Advances in holography.' *Scientific American*, **218**, 2, 40–57.

Pennycuick, L. (1969) 'A computer model of the Oxford great tit population.' *Journal of Theoretical Biology*, **22**, 381-400.

Penrose, L. R. and R. Penrose (1958) 'Impossible objects: A special type of illusion.' *British Journal of Psychology*, **49**, 31–33.

Piaget, J. (1971) *Structuralism*. Routledge and Kegan Paul, London. (Original French edition, *Le Structuralisme*, Presses Universitaries de France, Paris, 1968.)

Piotrowski, Z. A. (1964) 'Digital computer interpretation of ink-blot test data.' *Psychiatric Quarterly*, **38**, 1–26.

Pollock, T., L. R. Decker and H. Rubenstein (1958) 'Intelligibility of selected message sets.' *Journal of the Acoustical Society of America*, **30**, 643.

Pollen, D. A., J. R. Lee and J. H. Taylor (1971) 'How does the striate cortex begin the reconstruction of the visual world?' *Science*, **173**, 74–77.

Postal, P. (1962) *Some Syntactic Rules in Mohawk*. Ph.D. Thesis, Yale University.

Rabbit, P. (1967) 'Time to detect errors as a function of factors affecting choice-response time.' *Acta Psychologica*, **27**, 131–142.

Raichl, J. (1966) 'An attempt to simulate some simple behaviours of lowest organisms on a computer.' *Information Processing Machines*, **12**, 121–126.

Ratliff, F. (1965) *Mach Bands*. Holden-Day, San Francisco.

Reddy, D. R. (1967) 'Computer recognition of connected speech.' *Journal of the Acoustical Society of America*, **42**, 329–347.

Restle, F. (1962) 'The selection of strategies in cue learning.' *Psychological Review*, **69**, 329–343.

Restle, F., and T. V. Brown (1969) 'A computer running several psychological laboratories.' *Behavior Research Methods and Instrumentation*, **1**, 8, 312–317.

Rhodes, I. (1959) *A New Approach to the Mechanical Translation of Russian*. (American) National Bureau of Standards Report Number 6295.

Rochester, N., J. H. Holland, L. H. Haibt and W. L. Duda (1956) 'Test on a cell assembly theory of the action of the brain, using a large digital computer.' *IRE Transactions on Information Theory*, *IT-2*, 3, 80–93.

Rome, H. P., W. M. Swenson, P. Mataya, C. E. McCarthy, J. S. Pearson, F. R. Keating and S. R. Hathaway, (1962) 'Symposium on automation techniques in personality assessment.' *Proceedings of the Mayo Clinic*, **37**, 61–82.

Rosenblatt, F. (1958) 'Two theorems of statistical separability in the perceptron.' In *The Mechanization of Thought Processes*. National Physical Laboratory Symposium, HMSO London.

Rosenblatt, F. (1962) *Principles of Neurodynamics: Perceptrons and the Theory of Brain Mechanisms*. Spartan Books, Washington.

Rosenblatt, F. (1964) 'A model for experiential storage in neural networks.' In Tou, J. T., and R. H. Wilcox (Eds) *Computer and Information Sciences*. Spartan Books, Washington.

Russell, W. A., and J. J. Jenkins (1954) *The Complete Minnesota Norms for Responses to 100 Words from the Kent-Rosanoff Word Association Test*. Technical Report No. 11, Contract Number N8 onr-66216 (U.S.A.) Office of Naval Research and University of Minnesota.

Samuel, A. L. (1963) 'Some studies in machine learning using the game of checkers.' In Feigenbaum, E. A., and J. Feldman (Eds) *Computers and Thought*. McGraw-Hill, New York.

Scheinok, P. A., and J. A. Rinaldo (1968) 'Symptom diagnosis: a comparison of mathematical models related to upper abdominal pain.' *Computers and Biomedical Research*, **1**, 475–489.

Shannon, C. E. (1951) 'Presentation of a maze-solving machine.' In von Foerster, H. (Ed) *Cybernetics*. Transactions of the eighth conference of the Josiah Macy Jr. Foundation, 173–180.

Shannon, C. E., and W. Weaver (1949) *The Mathematical Theory of Communication*. University of Illinois Press, Urbana.

Shepard, R. N. (1964) 'Circularity in judgments of relative pitch.' *Journal of the Acoustical Society of America*, **36**, 2346–2353.

Shepard, R. N., and J. Metzler (1971) 'Mental rotation of three-dimensional objects.' *Science*, **171**, 701–703.

Siegel, S. (1956) *Non-parametric Statistics for the Behavioral Sciences*. McGraw-Hill, New York.

Simon, H. A., and A. Newell (1956) 'Models: their uses and limitations.' In White, L. D. (Ed) *The State of the Social Sciences*. Chicago University Press.

Singh, Gurmukh. (1968) *Multiple Variate Counter*. University of London, Atlas Computing Service.

Skinner, B. F. (1963) 'Reflections on a decade of teaching machines.' *Teachers College Record*, **65**, 168–77.

Skinner, B. F. (1968) *The Technology of Teaching*. Appleton-Century-Crofts, New York.

Slack, W. (1971) 'Computer-based interviewing system dealing with nonverbal behavior as well as keyboard responses.' *Science*, **171**, 84–87.

Slack, W., and L. J. von Cura (1968) 'Patient reaction to computer-based medical interviewing.' *Computers and Biomedical Research*, **1**, 529–531.

Sleeman, D. H., and J. R. Hartley (1969) 'Instructional models in a computer-based learning system.' *International Journal of Man-Machine Studies*, **1**, 2, 177–188.

Sluckin, W. (1954) *Minds and Machines*. Penguin Books, London.

Smallwood, R. D. (1962) *A Decision Structure for Teaching Machines*. M.I.T. Press, Cambridge, Massachusetts.

Smith, R. D. (1968) 'Heuristic simulation of psychological decision processes.' *Journal of Applied Psychology*, **52**, 4, 325–330.

Spitzer, R. L., and J. Endicott (1968) 'DIAGNO: A computer program for psychiatric diagnosis utilizing the differential diagnostic procedure.' *Archives of General Psychiatry*, **18**, 746–756.

Spitzer, R. L., and J. Endicott (1969) 'DIAGNO II: Further developments in a computer program for diagnosis.' *American Journal of Psychiatry*, **125**, Supplement January, 12–21.

Stadler, S. J. (1969) 'On the varieties of computer experience.' *Behavioral Methods and Instrumentation*, **1**, 7, 267–269.

Sterling, T. D., E. A. Bering, S. V. Pollack and H. G. Vaughan (1971) *Visual Prosthesis*, Academic Press, New York.

Stillman, R., W. T. Roth, K. M. Colby and C. P. Rosenbaum (1969) 'An outline computer system for initial psychiatric inventory.' *American Journal of Psychiatry*, **125**, Supplement January, 8–11.

Stolurow, L. M. (1965) 'A model and cybernetic system for research on the teaching-learning process.' *Programmed Learning and Educational Technology*, **2**, 3, 138–157.

Stolurow, L. M. (1967) 'A computer assisted instructional system in theory and research.' In Unwin, D. and J. Leedham (Eds) *Aspects of Educational Technology*. Methuen, London.

Suppes, P. (1961) 'A comparison of the meaning and uses of models in mathematics and the empirical sciences.' In H. Freudenthal (Ed) *The Concept and the Role of the Model in Mathematics and Natural and Social Sciences*. Reidel, Dordrecht-Holland.

Suppes, P. (1969) 'Stimulus response theory of automata and tote hierarchies. A reply to Arbib.' *Psychological Review*, **76**, 511–514.

Suppes, P., M. Jerman and D. Brian (1968) *Computer Assisted Instruction: Stanford's 1965–66 Arithmetic Program*. Academic Press, New York.

Sutherland, I. E. (1970) 'Computer displays.' *Scientific American*, **222**, 6, 56–81.

Sutherland, N. S., M. S. Halliday, J. Thomas and J. Francis (1969) 'A System for running operant experiments.' *Bulletin of the British Psychological Society*, **22**, 297–298.

Svoboda, A. (1960) 'Un modèle d'instinct.' *Proceedings of the International Conference on Cybernetics, Namur*. Gauthiers-Villars, Paris.

Swets, J. A., and W. Feurzeig (1965) Computer-aided instruction. *Science*, **150**, 572–576.

Swigert, C. J. (1967) *Computational Properties of a Nerve and Nerve Net Model*. University of California, Thesis. Available from University Microfilms, Ann Arbor, Michigan, U.S.A.

Tanner, N. (1967) 'Speech and society among the Indonesian elite: a case study of a multilinguist society.' *Anthropological Linguistics*, **9**, 3, 15–40.

Taylor, M. M., and D. M. Forsyth (1969) 'Time-shared computation for the real-time laboratory.' In *On-Line Computing for Psychology*, Moray, N. (Ed) Proceedings of NATO A.S.I. at Department of Psychology, University of Sheffield, England, 26–32.

Taylor, W. K. (1956) 'Electrical simulation of nervous system functional activities.' In Cherry, C. (Ed) *Information Theory*. Butterworth, London.

Thompson, D. (1964) 'Escape from S^D associated with fixed-ratio reinforcement.' *Journal of Experimental Analysis of Behavior*, **7**, 1–8.

Thorndike, E. L., and I. Lorge (1944) *The Teacher's Word Book of 30,000 words*. Teacher's College, Columbia University, New York.

Thorne, J. P. (1964) 'Grammars and machines' *Transactions of the Philological Society*, 30–45.

Thorne, J. P. (1968) 'A computer model for the perception of syntactic structures.' *Proceedings of the Royal Society, B. 171*, 377–386.

Thorne, J. P., H. Dewar, H. Whitfield and P. Bratley (1966) 'A model for the perception of syntactic structure.' In *Colloque International Sur L'Informatique*, Toulouse.

Tinbergen, N. (1951) *The Study of Instinct*. Clarendon Press, Oxford.

Tobach, E., T. C. Schneirla, L. R. Aronson and R. Laupheimer (1962). 'The ATSL: An observer-to-computer system for a multivariate approach to behavioural study.' *Nature*, **194**, 257–258.

Tolman, E. C. (1948) 'Cognitive maps in rats and men.' *Psychological Review*, **55**, 189–208.

Torrey, J. W. (1966) 'Some requirements of an adequate theory of grammar learning.' Abstracts of the XVIII International Congress of Psychology: *General Problems of Psychology*, Moscow, 358.

Torrey, J. W. (1969) 'The learning of grammatical patterns.' *Journal of Verbal Learning and Verbal Behavior*, **8**, 360–368.

Tou, J. T., and R. H. Wilcox (Eds) (1964) *Computer and Information Sciences: Collected Papers on Learning, Adaptation and Control in Information Systems*. Spartan Books, Washington.

Treisman, A. M. (1967) 'Selective attention: reply.' *Quarterly Journal of Experimental Psychology*, **19**, 364–367.

Turing, A. M. (1936) 'On computable numbers, with an application to the Entscheidungs-problem.' *Proceedings of the London Mathematical Society*, (Second Series) **42**, 230–265.

Turing, A. M. (1950) 'Computing machinery and intelligence.' *Mind*, **59**, 433–460.

Uber, D. C. and B. Weiss (1966) 'Computer control of operant behaviour experiments via telephone lines.' *Journal of the Experimental Analysis of Behavior*, **9**, 507–513.

Uhr, L. (1969) 'Teaching machine programs that generate problems as a function of interaction with students.' *Proceedings of the 24th National Conference of the Association for Computing Machinery*. A.C.M. Publication, P-69, New York, 125–134.

Uhr, L. and C. Vossler (1963) 'A pattern-recognition program that generates, evaluates and adjusts its own operators.' In Feigenbaum, E. A. and J. Feldman (Eds) *Computers and Thought*. McGraw-Hill, New York.

Uttal, W. R. (1967) *Real-Time Computers: Technique and Applications in the Psychological Sciences.* Harper and Row, New York.

Uttal, W. R. (1969) 'Buggywhips, whalebones and clipboards: Some notes on generating complex stimuli with small computers.' *American Psychologist,* **24**, 202–206.

Uttley, A. M. (1955) 'The conditional probability of signals in the nervous system.' *RRE Memorandum No. 1109.*

Uttley, A. M. (1956) 'Conditional probability as a principle of learning.' *Proceedings of the International Congress on Cybernetics, Namur.* Gauthiers-Villars, Paris.

Veldman, D. J. (1967) *Fortran Programming for the Behavioral Sciences.* Holt, Rinehart and Winston, New York.

Voelker, C. H. (1935) 'Technique for a phonetic frequency distribution count in formal American speech.' *Archives Néerlandaises de Phonétique Expérimentale,* **11**, 69–72.

Von Neumann, J. (1958) *The Computer and the Brain.* Yale University Press, New Haven.

Walker, E. L. (1967) *Conditioning and Instrumental Learning.* Brooks/Cole, Belmont, California.

Watt, K. E. F. (1964) 'The use of mathematics and computers to determine optimal strategy and tactics for a given insect pest control problem.' *Canadian Entomologist,* **96**, 202–220.

Weiner, H. (1963) 'Operant programming with transistorized digital elements.' *Journal of the Experimental Analysis of Behavior,* **6**, 193–195.

Weiss, B. and V. G. Laties (1965) 'Reinforcement schedule generated by an on-line digital computer.' *Science,* **148**, 658–661.

Weiss, B., V. G. Laties, L. Siegel and D. Goldenstein (1966) 'A computer analysis of serial interactions in spaced responding.' *Journal of the Experimental Analysis of Behaviour,* **9**, 619–626.

Weizenbaum, J. (1966) 'ELIZA—a computer program for the study of natural language communication between man and machine.' *Communications of the ACM,* **9**, 36–45.

Wexler, J. D. (1970) 'A teaching program that generates simple arithmetic problems.' *International Journal of Man-Machine Studies,* **2**, 1, 1–27.

Whelan, E. (1968) *Visual Perception and Cerebral Dominance.* Unpublished Ph.D. Thesis, University of Sheffield.

Widrow, B., and F. W. Smith (1964) 'Pattern-recognizing Control Systems.' In Tou and Wilcox, *Collected Papers, op. cit.*

Wiener, N. (1948) *Cybernetics.* Wiley, New York.

Wiener, N. (1950) *The Human Use of Human Beings: Cybernetics and Society.* Houghton Mifflin, Boston.

Wilson, J. A. (1962) 'An apparatus for recording figural after-effects.' *Quarterly Journal of Experimental Psychology,* **14**, 119–121.

Wolfendale, G. (1969) 'Experimentation by computer: some preliminary steps.' *The British Journal of Mathematical and Statistical Psychology,* **22**, 2, 199–215.

Woods, P., and J. R. Hartley (1971) 'Some learning models for arithmetic tasks and their use in computer based learning.' *The British Journal of Educational Psychology,* **41**, 1, 38–48.

Woods, W. A. (1967) 'Semantic interpretation of English questions on a structured data basis.' *Mathematical Linguistics and Automatic Translation*. Report NSF-17. Harvard University Computing Laboratory, Cambridge, Massachusetts.

Wright, P., and D. Kahneman (1971) 'Evidence for alternative strategies of sentence retention.' *Quarterly Journal of Experimental Psychology*, **23**, 197–213.

Yntema, D. B., and F. P. Trask (1963) 'Recall as a search process.' *Journal of Verbal Learning and Verbal Behavior*, **2**, 65–74.

Yntema, D. B., F. Wozencraft and L. Klem (1964) 'Immediate recall of digits presented at very high speeds.' Paper read to the Psychonomics Society, Niagara Falls, Ontario.

Zipf, G. K. (1935) *The Psycho-Biology of Language*. Houghton Mifflin, Boston.

Index

Page numbers in italics indicate a reference in Further Reading or the Bibliography.